of
om
of
Michi-
o the
College

cles on
to pro-
or co-
Mozart,
and the

two

TWAYNE'S WORLD AUTHORS SERIES

A Survey of the World's Literature

Sylvia E. Bowman, Indiana University

GENERAL EDITOR

SOVIET UNION

Nicholas P. Vaslef, U. S. Air Force Academy

EDITOR

Boris Pasternak

(TWAS 225)

TWAYNE'S WORLD AUTHORS SERIES (TWAS)

The purpose of TWAS is to survey the major writers —novelists, dramatists, historians, poets, philosophers, and critics—of the nations of the world. Among the national literatures covered are those of Australia, Canada, China, Eastern Europe, France, Germany, Greece, India, Italy, Japan, Latin America, the Netherlands, New Zealand, Poland, Russia, Scandinavia, Spain, and the African nations, as well as Hebrew, Yiddish, and Latin Classical literatures. This survey is complemented by Twayne's United States Authors Series and English Authors Series.

The intent of each volume in these series is to present a critical-analytical study of the works of the writer; to include biographical and historical material that may be necessary for understanding, appreciation, and critical appraisal of the writer; and to present all material in clear, concise English—but not to vitiate the scholarly content of the work by doing so.

Boris Pasternak

By J. W. DYCK

University of Waterloo

Twayne Publishers :: New York

Printed in U.S.A. by
NOBLE OFFSET PRINTERS, INC.
New York, N.Y. 10003

To Julie and Vickie

Preface

This book attempts to present an overall account of Pasternak's life and work. In discussing the individual works, we were guided by an awareness of the ever-present dualism and the dualistic nature which reveals itself not only in the original and vividly developed characters but also in the many ideas and events with which the reader is confronted, both in Pasternak's poetry and prose.

The poetry is discussed in chronological order. Nine distinct cycles demonstrate the author's own development from a poet with an early desire for originality through form, to a poet of wisdom and restraint.

The autobiographical writings, the literary appeals of various years and the essays "Chopin," "Kruchenykh," "The Black Goblet," and "Several Positions" make up the basis for the chapter entitled "Poetics in Autobiography." The notes on Shakespeare and other Western classics are milestones of Pasternak's literary theories.

Pasternak's major prose works include *Doctor Zhivago* and the short stories *Il Tratto di Apelle, Letters from Tula, The Childhood of Luvers, Aerial Ways,* and *The Last Summer.* A few short skits, such as *A District behind the Front, Aunt Olya, Without Love,* and others, are not discussed individually because their content appears in one or another form in the above works.

Out of the realization that Pasternak was not only a deep thinker but also a master of expression, and that to alter his flow of thought could mean to destroy it, frequent and direct references to his works seemed necessary. The University of Michigan's Russian Pasternak edition (eds. G. P. Struve and B. A. Filippov, cited as *Soch.*) was the major source for my readings. Direct translations from this source are punctuated with quotation marks. Various other sources, as listed in the "Acknowledgments," were very helpful.

I wish to thank the University of Waterloo and the Canada Council for generously supporting my research; Mrs. Lydia

Pasternak-Slater for her willing and sympathetic interest in this study and for the detailed biographical information on the author; the students of my Pasternak seminar for their intensive study of meaning, especially in the author's poetry; Miss Louise Bonson for typing the manuscript; and Sarah Dyck, my wife, for the many discussions, helpful comparisons with English literature, and assistance in styling this work.

J. W. D.

Waterloo

Acknowledgments

Acknowledgment is hereby made for permission to quote from the following works: *Boris Pasternak: Doctor Zhivago,* translated by Max Hayward and Manya Harari and *An Essay in Autobiography,* translated by Manya Harari (Introduction by Edward Crankshaw), Collins and Harvill Press (London, 1957 and 1959 respectively); *Pasternak: Prose and Poems,* ed. Stefan Schimanski (Introduction by J. M. Cohen), Ernest Benn Limited (London, 1959); *Boris Pasternak: Poems,* translated and introduced by Eugene M. Kayden, The Antioch Press (Yellow Springs, Ohio, 1964); *Pasternak's Fifty Poems,* translated and introduced by Lydia Pasternak-Slater, Unwin Books (London, 1963); *The Poetry of Boris Pasternak,* translated with critical biographical introduction by George Reavey, G. P. Putnam's Sons (New York, 1960); *The Three Worlds of Boris Pasternak,* by Robert Payne, David Higham Assoc., Ltd. (London, 1962).

Contents

Preface

Acknowledgments

Chronology

1. The Curse of Fame   17

2. Living Imprints   23

3. Poetics in Autobiography   35

4. Poetry   58

5. *Doctor Zhivago*   106

6. The Short Stories   161

7. The Translator   178

Epilogue   182

Notes and References   185

Bibliography   195

Index   201

Chronology

1890 Born in Moscow, February 10.

1900 Traveled in same train with Rainer Maria Rilke who was on his way to Yasnaya Polyana to visit Tolstoy.

1901 Admitted to second year of German Classical Grammar School in Moscow.

1903 Met composer Alexander Scriabin, family friend, who became great influence in his life and career.

1905 First meeting with Maxim Gorky.

1906 Visited Berlin with family.

1907 Became a member of literary circle, "Serdarda." Activities influenced by Scriabin's musical experiments. Associated with Futurists, Symbolists, and Neo-Kantians.

1908 Graduated from High School. Fell in love with daughter of a wealthy family where he was employed as tutor.

1909 Entered Moscow University to study law. Transferred to the Faculty of Arts to study philosophy. Interest began to shift from music to literature.

1910 Presented paper, now lost, entitled "Symbolism and Immortality." Witnessed Tolstoy's funeral.

1911 Joined moderate Futurist group, "Centrifuge."

1912 Studied philosophy in Marburg, Germany. Unhappy love affair. Found escape in writing poetry and in journey to Switzerland and Italy.

1913 Final examinations at University of Moscow. Tutor in home of German merchant. Wrote poetry.

1914 Met Mayakovsky. Exempted from military service because of earlier leg injury. Private tutor in home of Baltrushaitis on Oka River. Translated *Der Zerbrochene Krug* (*The Broken Jug*) by Kleist. Published collection of poems, *Bliznets v Tuchakh* (*The Twin in the Clouds*).

1915 Employed as clerk in factory in Ural Mountains.

1917 Returned to Moscow. Published volume of poems, *Poverkh Barerov* (*Above the Barriers*), and translation of *The Broken Jug* in Gorky's periodical, *Sovremennik* (*The Contemporary*).

1918 Librarian in Soviet Ministry of Education.

1920 Estrangement from Mayakovsky.

1921 Met Alexander Blok in Moscow.

1922 Married Evgenia Lourié and traveled with her to Marburg and Berlin. Published *Sestra Moya–Zhizn* (*My Sister, Life*), volume of poetry establishing him as poet.

1923 *Temy i Variatsii* (*Themes and Variations*) published. Son, Evgeny born.

1924 First fragments of *Vysokaya Bolezn* (*The High Malady*) published.

1925 Volume of short stories, *Vosdushnye Puti* (*Aerial Ways*) published: *Apellesova Cherta* (*Il Tratto di Apelle*), *Pisma iz Tuly* (*Letters from Tula*), *Detstvo Luvers* (*Childhood of Luvers*), *Vosdushnye Puti* (*Aerial Ways*).

1926- Published epic poems *Lieutenant Schmidt* and *Devyatsot*
1927 *Pyaty God* (*The Year 1905*).

1928 Published *High Malady*.

1930 April 14: Death of Mayakovsky.

1931 Published autobiographical prose, *Okhrannaya Gramota* (*Safe Conduct*) and *Spectorsky* in separate editions. Divorced. Visited with Zinaida Neuhaus, his future wife, Georgian poet Paolo Yashvili.

1932 Published *Poems for Children* and *Vtoroe Rozhdenie* (*Second Birth*), collection of poems.

1934 Various literary circles abolished. Socialist Realism formulated at newly founded Union of Soviet Writers. Translated (1934-1943) Georgian poetry, works by Goethe, Schiller, Shakespeare, and others. Moved to Peredelkino, near Moscow. Novella, *Povest* (*The Last Summer*) published.

1935 Delegate to International Writers' Congress in Paris. Collection of Georgian poetry published in Russian translation.

1936 Speech, "O Skromnosti i Smelosti" ("On Modesty and Boldness"), delivered at Writers' Plenum in Minsk.

1938 Son, Leonid, born.

1939 Mother died.

1940 *Selected Translations* published.

1941 Marina Tsvetaeva, his favorite poetess, committed suicide. Translation of *Hamlet* published.

1943 Collection of poems, *Na Rannikh Poezdakh* (*Early Trains*), published.

1945 Father, Leonid Pasternak, died. Collection of poems, *Zemnoy Prostor* (*The Spacious Earth*), published; received adverse criticism.

1946 Writings criticized by Aleksey Fadeev, First Secretary of Writers' Union. Addressed writers at literary gathering in Moscow. Zhdanov attacked "cosmopolitanism" in Soviet Literature.

1953 Goethe's *Faust I* and Shakespeare translations published.

Chronology

1954   *Znamya* printed ten poems from *Doctor Zhivago*. Adverse criticism.

1956   *Doctor Zhivago* rejected by *Novy Mir*. Italian publisher proceeds with plan to print it. Autobiography (*Avtobiografichesky Ocherk*), translated as *An Essay in Autobiography* and as *I Remember*, written, but not published in Soviet Union.

1957   Parts I and II of Goethe's *Faust* published in Russian. *Doctor Zhivago* appeared in Italian, November 15.

1958   Awarded Nobel Prize, October 23. Expelled from Writers' Union. October 29: obliged to decline Nobel Prize; October 31: Pasternak's letter sent to Khrushchev; November 5: "Confession of his errors and guilt" publicized in *Pravda*. Autobiographical sketch (*I Remember*) published outside Soviet Union.

1956-   Wrote poems of *Kogda Razgulyaetsya* (*When the Skies Clear*
1959   or *A Rift in the Clouds*), published after author's death. Working on Trilogy, *Slepaya Krasavitsa* (*The Blind Beauty*), play about liberation of Russian serfs in 19th century. Idea: "The birth of an enlightened and affluent middle class."

1960   Died, May 30.

CHAPTER 1

The Curse of Fame

I've fallen beastlike in a snare:
Light, people, freedom, somewhere bide:
But at my back I hear the chase
And there is no escape outside—
("The Nobel Prize," 1959, trans. H. Kamen)

BORIS LEONIDOVICH PASTERNAK, the most publicized
modern Russian poet, died on the night of May 30, 1960.
Death came while the poet was still in the shadow of that painful
experience which today is generally referred to as "The Pasternak
Affair." The external trappings of this "affair" were related by
newspapers, radio, and television. Indeed, immediately following
the Nobel Award, dispatches were so frequent and often reached
such proportions that Pasternak soon became a household word,
at least to readers of the Western world. However, political
journalism and sensationalism soon faded, and serious attempts
have been made to record and to understand the controversial
last years of Pasternak's life. The few of Pasternak's letters
already published, especially those to the German poetess, Renate
Schweitzer,[1] and *Letters to Georgian Friends,* contribute greatly
to this understanding.

The controversy around *Doctor Zhivago* began when early in
1954 the Russian Journal *Znamya* (No. 4) printed ten poems
which eventually were to become part of a novel. The novel
itself, the author announced,

will probably be finished in the summer. It deals with the period
from 1906 to 1929, and contains an epilogue which refers to the
great war fought for our fatherland. Its hero, Yury Andreevich
Zhivago, a meditative and ever-searching doctor, with creative and
artistic interests, dies in 1929. He leaves notes and papers, among
them verses which he wrote in his youth. These verses of which
some are printed here constitute the final chapter of the novel.[2]

The poems were harshly criticized as "unpolitical, devoid of ideas and alien to the people." Pasternak was again called a decadent individualist and for the next two years nothing of him or by him was printed in Russia. And then the times seemed to change. For a short period the Soviet literary world experienced a more liberal phase, which was to receive its name from Ilya Ehrenburg's novel, *Ottepel* (*The Thaw*). Literary works which had previously been criticized and rejected were now submitted and many of them were published. Pasternak, too, must have felt that the times had become more agreeable with the spirit of his novel. However, the editors of *Novy Mir* were of a different opinion. After a prolonged period of waiting, Pasternak's *Doctor Zhivago* was rejected for publication. Ironically, it was precisely the spirit in which *Doctor Zhivago* is written that evoked the editors' decision. Their letter of September, 1956, removes all ambiguities, as it seems, in its first paragraphs:

We have read the manuscript of your novel *Doctor Zhivago*.... We were both alarmed and distressed.... The thing that has disturbed us about your novel is something that neither the editors nor the author can change by cuts or alterations. We are referring to the spirit of the novel, its general tenor, the author's view of life, the real view, or, at any rate, the one formed by the reader. This is what we consider it our duty to discuss with you....[3]

The discussion then continues at length to a total of over twenty-five book pages. On these pages almost everything has been said that later articles and books on *Doctor Zhivago* have sought to uncover. In placing this letter against the many Western interpretations which have appeared, it becomes only too apparent—indeed, it is almost a classic example—of how contrasting ideologies can assign opposing values to one and the same descriptive fact. It should be noted that the letter to Pasternak is written throughout in a polite and congenial tone. By reasoning with the author, by using Lara's words to Zhivago that he, Yury, had changed and was now judging the Revolution too harshly and with irritation, the editors almost begged Pasternak "to think about it seriously," and hoped thus to avert a final disaster for Pasternak.

Nevertheless, between the first and last pages of warnings, the letter contains many passages of interesting observations and reveals a consummate understanding of the novel itself. Why then these details concerning a rejected manuscript? And why the many quotations from key junctures of the novel itself? One might be inclined to find the answer to these questions in the moralistic nature of the society in which Pasternak lived and wrote. It is the tradition and duty of such a society to impose didactic expostulations upon an "imperfect" individual when and wherever possible. However, Pasternak was a man of sixty-six and it was certainly too late to mold him for "more realistic" literary creations of the future. Could it be, then, that the editors, themselves men of literature, rejected the manuscript because time and circumstances required it but found Pasternak's novel too valuable for complete destruction? The choice of quotations and the deliberations on the novel note only too obviously some of Pasternak's major concepts of history, the Revolution, religion, art, and life in general. The major intention of Pasternak's novel was thus recorded for posterity.

While Pasternak awaited the decision, an Italian translation of *Doctor Zhivago* was contracted for publication. The attempt by Alexey Surkov, who at that time was First Secretary of the Soviet Writers' Association, to have the manuscript returned by the Italian publisher in Milan failed. Feltrinelli insisted on his contractual rights and became the first publisher of *Doctor Zhivago*. The publication of the novel and, even more, the subsequent award of the Nobel Prize to Pasternak, changed, almost overnight, the potentially explosive atmosphere, and tossed the controversial writer into an open "affair." When it became apparent that Pasternak was overwhelmed by the award and had sent word of his acceptance, strong ideological forces brushed aside the artist and moved against Pasternak, the man. Pasternak soon was expelled from the Union of Soviet Writers, accused of being a tool of bourgeois propaganda, and threatened with expulsion from Russia.[4] But Pasternak remained in Russia to the very hour of his death. However, to this day, Pasternak's last writings have remained unpublished in the Soviet Union. Nevertheless, the name Pasternak has become almost legendary, in Russia and abroad. His popular image is as controversial as was the publicity which he received. In one point, however, his champions and his foes agree: Pasternak always was and will remain "a poet for poets," and this in spite of the popular award-winning movie based on *Doctor Zhivago*.

Pasternak did not seek popularity. He wanted to live with his art, even if this meant a loneliness that equalled that of the "tragically lonely figure"[5]—the Russian poet of the nineteenth century. The present popularity of Pasternak may soon fade and make room for a truer image gleaned from the wealth of experience which life granted him, and from his works.

CHAPTER 2

Living Imprints

I Family Ties

BORIS LEONIDOVICH PASTERNAK was born on February 10, 1890, in Moscow. His parents were natives of Odessa, a port city on the Black Sea. Toward the end of the nineteenth century, Odessa, paronymous of Odyssey or Odysseus, was a rather cosmopolitan city, with especially large Greek, Italian, and Jewish communities. The cultural and religious diversity of this city did not fail to exert its influence upon Pasternak's parents. Later, this atmosphere was to find some expression in the breath of liberty evinced by the author himself.

Leonid Ossipovich Pasternak (1862-1945), Boris' father, was, according to Lydia Pasternak (the poet's sister), never in doubt as to his real vocation as an artist. Yet, to satisfy his parents, who insisted on a career as lawyer or physician, he went to Moscow University first. There he studied medicine, switched over to law, and graduated in his native town. Simultaneously, he studied art at the Academy in Munich, this "Athens on the Isar," which attracted distinguished painters and artists from all over the world. Pasternak's return to Moscow was marked by a spectacular success. His first big canvas, "Letter from Home," was bought from the easel by Tretyakov for his famous gallery. After his marriage in 1889, Leonid Pasternak settled down in Moscow. In order to support his growing family, he gave private lessons, then opened an art school which, with the new teaching methods acquired in Munich, became the prototype of art schools in Moscow. Through his work as an artist and teacher, contributor to art magazines, illustrator, and art editor of the magazine *The Artist*, he soon earned the favor and friendship of the Moscow cultural élite. In 1894 he accepted Prince Lvov's invitation to join the teaching staff of the Moscow School of Painting, Sculpture, and Architecture.

Boris Pasternak's mother, Rosa Kaufman-Pasternak (1867-1939), was a child prodigy. From the age of nine, she gave

21

public piano recitals in Odessa, and by the time she was thirteen, she had gained quite a reputation for herself in other Russian towns and cities. After she had completed her musical training in Vienna, a short but rich career as music teacher and concert pianist began. Anton Rubinstein recognized her skill and talent; he arranged concerts for her in numerous European music centers, from Moscow and St. Petersburg to Vienna. As a result of this glamor and fame, a successful career seemed inevitable. But fate had decreed differently. In Odessa, where Rosa Kaufman had accepted a teaching position, she met Leonid Pasternak. They were married in 1889, and thus a promising career in music gave way to a rich and rewarding family life, in which the practice of music, literature, and the fine arts was natural.

Boris Pasternak was the oldest son in a family of four children. Although he mentions, on the first page of his *Avtobiografichesky ocherk* (*An Essay in Autobiography*) (1956), some early walks with his nurse in the garden of the seminary near the Pasternak's first apartment at Arsenal Street, the poet's first conscious development seems to have begun after the family moved, in 1893, to the spacious living quarters provided by the Academy in Myasnitskaya Street. He vividly describes his impressions of the state funeral of Alexander III and of the ritual and ceremonies of the crowning of Czar Nicholas II, which he watched from the balcony of their new home. But the threshold between his childhood, free of all memories, and the beginning of his consciousness of the past occurred on that musical night on November 23, 1894, when Leo Tolstoy came to the Pasternak home to attend a concert given by Rosa Pasternak, and the professors of violin and violoncello, I. V. Grzhimali and A. A. Brandukov. "With this night," Pasternak writes, toward the end of his life, "my memory came into being and my consciousness began to work like that of an adult without further significant black-outs or failure" (*Soch.*, II, 4). In this late autobiography, Pasternak recollects almost every detail of this lasting experience: the familiar tunes of the piano, the soft timbre of the violins which the imaginative mind of a sensitive crying boy translated into voices of unhappiness and doom coming through the window from the night. He remembers the beautifully gowned ladies whose bare shoulders peered out of their dresses like flowers peeking from the frame of a flower-basket; he sees clearly before him Tolstoy and his daughters.

The family of Leonid Pasternak had moved into the center of Moscow cultural life. To the elder Pasternak's gallery of paintings, portraits of Einstein, Hauptmann, Rilke, Verhaeren, Tolstoy, and many others were added. He formed lasting friendships with Vrubel, Trubetskoy, Rilke, Scriabin, Verhaeren, and was well-acquainted with Maxim Gorky.

Much of the information on Pasternak's early life is to be found either in *Okhrannaya gramota* (*Safe Conduct*) (1931), or in the above-mentioned *An Essay in Autobiography*. The turn of the century separates his childhood from the lasting impacts which later decades made on his life. The degree of conscious memory is not the only factor which marks this cleavage. On the one hand, he remembers distinctly the early school lessons which he received at home from his mother and from a private tutor. With much appreciation he reminisces about his favorite teacher, Ekaterina Ivanovna Baratynskaya, who taught him reading, writing, arithmetic, and French and prepared him for the St. Peter and Paul Gymnasium where all subjects were taught in German. On the other hand, he sees clearly before him the suddenly changing city of Moscow at the turn of the century. This "third Rome," with its "forty times forty churches," was throbbing, almost overnight, as it seemed to the ten-year-old Boris, with construction, and a nervously hasty temper, previously unknown, filled its streets. And it was Moscow, says Pasternak, not Petersburg, that begot at this moment a new Russian concept of the Fine Arts. These were the creative arts of a young, modern, "swinging" world city.

II Scriabin

In 1901, Pasternak entered the second year of the Fifth Moscow Gymnasium to study the natural sciences, foreign languages, and Greek. He graduated from the school in 1908.

During these high school years Pasternak became well acquainted with some of the works of Andrey Bely, Knut Hamsun, Alexander Blok, and Rainer Maria Rilke. Vladimir Mayakovsky, later champion of Futurism, was enrolled in the same school, but was Pasternak's junior by two years. They did not know each other in school and only met several years later when both had become established poets.

Before relating Pasternak's years of adolescence to his early

literary interests, one experience, destined to become his first
great passion, cannot be overlooked: his admiration for Alexander
Scriabin. In *Safe Conduct* and again in *An Essay in Autobiography*, Pasternak returns to this crossroad in his life. In the
summer at Obolenskoe, where in 1903 the Scriabins and the
Pasternaks had been neighbors, Boris had become an ardent
admirer not only of Scriabin's music but of the man himself.
He tells the reader how the name Scriabin, inscribed on a poster
which accidentally fell on his school bag on the way home from
school, struck him "harder and more fantastically than fever,"[2]
and how he accompanied his father and the composer on long
walks. During these walks learned discussions took place, most
of which his twelve-year-old mind could not comprehend. Nevertheless, the boy Pasternak always quietly took Scriabin's side.
He relates how he studied music, practiced, and composed endlessly in school during Greek and Math lessons and at home,
while Scriabin spent six years away from Russia, and how, upon
Scriabin's return from Italy, the hour of decision struck. Pasternak
writes in *Safe Conduct* that he had several serious works which
he wanted to show to his idol (*SC*, 18). But Pasternak took to
Scriabin not so much his compositions as a love which was
beyond expression. Nevertheless, the aspiring composer played
several of his compositions to his "idol" and Scriabin approved
of them. Pasternak recalls: "Immediately he began assuring me
that it is foolish to speak of musical abilities when something
incomparably greater is apparent, and that it was given to me
to speak my word in music" (*Soch.*, II, 210).

But Pasternak was haunted by youthful doubts. Fate had not
bestowed on him absolute pitch which his mother had. This
deficiency, which had tormented him for many years, he also
recognized in Scriabin, when the latter repeated on the piano,
but in the wrong key, some of the phrases just played by Pasternak. Boris longed for comforting confession of equal burden:
"Borya," Scriabin should have said, "why even I have not got it"
(*SC*, 20). Instead, Scriabin talked of the harm of improvising, of
when, why, and how one should compose, of the simplicity to
which one should aspire, and advised him—by this time enrolled
in the faculty of law at Moscow University—to change over to the
study of philosophy. Pasternak transferred on the following day.
He went home with mixed feelings. He remembers that something wept in him and something exulted. "I did not know,"

Pasternak writes, "that that night I was already breaking with music" (*SC*, 22).

The influence of Scriabin did not cease with this break, nor was it confined to the musical chords in his poetry and prose. There are frequent references and allusions to Scriabin as a composer, but more often as a personality with mystical and redeeming influences. In *An Essay in Autobiography*, written late in life, Pasternak synthesizes the role of this genius as "an occasion for eternal congratulations, as a personified triumph and festivity of Russian culture" (*Soch.*, II, 13).

One more mention of Scriabin shall conclude this sphere of influence in Pasternak's life. We are thinking of Pasternak's reference to Scriabin's concept of the Superman. The following postulation taken from the autobiography may lead to a fuller understanding of the author:

Scriabin's deliberations about Superman were a peculiarly Russian expression of passion for the extraordinary. In fact, not only music must, in order to be meaningful, be super-music, but everything in the world must surpass itself, in order to fulfill itself. Man, and his activity, must embrace that element of eternity, giving each phenomenon singularity, character. (*Soch.*, II, 12)

III   *The Road to Literature*

Pasternak's formal education ended in 1913. After graduation from the gymnasium in 1908, he spent, with the exception of one semester in 1912 in Marburg, six years at the University of Moscow. During these years of study, three major experiences left their lasting marks on Pasternak, the man and the poet. These are his association with various literary groups, his encounter with Rainer Maria Rilke, and the torment of an unrequited love.

In spite of his great interest in music and philosophy, Pasternak had never neglected literature completely. As it has already been pointed out, Pasternak, between the age of twelve and fourteen, became well acquainted with the most important contemporary literary movements, with the best modern works, and with their authors. Throughout his high school and university years, he had taken an active interest in circles where literature, music, and art were loved, discussed and practiced. Furthermore, the year 1906 in Berlin, where he had gone with his parents to avoid the after-effects of the 1905 Revolution, had added vivid impressions and, at times, almost traumatic experiences to Pasternak's imaginative mind. "Everything," he writes in his autobiography, "was unusual, different from what it was at home. It was less like living than like dreaming" (*Essay*, 59). In Berlin, he absorbed to the fullest a life previously unknown to him. He spoke German, imitated the Berlin dialect, and attended performances of Wagner. In Berlin he also met Maxim Gorky.

Nevertheless, in the eyes of his associates, Pasternak was a musician. The transition to literature was gradual. In *Safe Conduct* he reminisces about how he postponed his parting with music, how music became interwoven with literature, and how the "depth and beauty of Bely and Blok could not but unfold before me" (*SC*, 25). And this in spite of the fact that for fifteen years he had sacrificed, as he says, "the word to sound."

Now, as a searching student at the University, he was an active member of the literary club, *Serdarda*. No one knew the meaning of the name, but the group consisted of young painters, poets, and musicians. Among the members, Pasternak mentions in *An Essay in Autobiography* the poet and painter Yulian Anisimov, Sergey Durylin, who, Pasternak says, helped him in his switch from music to literature and who wrote under the pseudonym of Sergey Raevsky; and Arkady Guriev who had furnished the name for the group and whom Pasternak characterizes as extremely jocular yet deeply original and with an unrestrained honesty similar to that of Mayakovsky, but with an Esenian clarity in presenting images to his readers. Other members included B. B. Krasin, a composer, Sergey Bobrov, a writer, and the publishers A. I. Kozhebatkin and Sergey Makovsky.

An even more sophisticated and influential group was the circle called *Musaget*. Many of its members have well-established names in the history of Russian music or art. The circle had assumed the role of an academy, and Pasternak's *An Essay in Autobiography* lists among its members Stepun, Rachinsky, Boris Sadovsky, Emil Metner, Shenrok, Petrovsky, Ellis and Nilender. Andrey Bely was the leader and the authority of this group. From him, says Pasternak, they all learned. His works, *Serebryany golub* (*The Silver Dove*) and *Petersburg*, determined the taste of his contemporaries, and he was to be the forerunner of early Soviet prose. The group had a wide field of interest. They studied the problems of rhythm, the histories of German Romanticism and of Russian poetry, the esthetics of Goethe, Wagner, Baudelaire, and the French Symbolists, and Greek philosophers. Bely also conducted a seminar, which was more or less a poetic laboratory. During their meetings, rhythmic figures and variations were viewed with the help of statistical analysis. Pasternak did not take part in these exercises. His refusal to participate foreshadows already in this early stage of his development his attitude toward the rejection of the use of form for the sake of form. In his *An Essay in Autobiography* he sums up his reasons as follows:

I did not participate in the work of this circle because I was then, as I am now, convinced that the music of the word is not an acoustic phenomenon, and neither is it the euphony of vowels and consonants. The music [in *Doctor Zhivago*, Pasternak speaks of the "inward music"] of the word consists of the relation between the meaning of the spoken word and its sound. (*Soch.*, II, 25)

Meaning, on the other hand, can find its most consummate expression only through the use of symbols. Pasternak therefore took a great interest in the theories of Symbolism, the movement which dominated the Russian literary scene during the first decade of this century. And when Pasternak was invited to read a paper to the *Musaget* circle, he spoke on *Symbolism and Immortality*. It is symbolic that the paper was given on the day of Leo Tolstoy's death, in 1910. Later in the evening, Pasternak, with his father, left for Astapova where Tolstoy had died, to arrange for the funeral.

Unfortunately, this first important piece of writing by Pasternak has not been preserved. Presumably it was lost in 1915, when raids on German homes in Moscow destroyed the villa of the rich merchant, Moritz Philipp. Pasternak was at that time tutor and teacher of Philipp's son, Walter. But Pasternak has given us an insight into the contents of the paper in *An Essay in Autobiography*. One of the points he makes is that sensual experience is subjective. Yet this subjectivity is not characteristic of each and everyone individually, but is superpersonal, that is, it is the subjectivity of man's world, of the human race. Pasternak also assumed that each and everyone leaves behind a fraction of this immortality, what could be called generical subjectivity, i.e., that which was in the individual during his lifetime and with which he took part in the

process of human history. The paper proclaimed that it might
well be that precisely this subjective and all-human corner, or
chamber of the soul, constitutes life's eternal cycle and must
be the main concern of art. The artist, of course, dies as everybody else dies. Nevertheless, he lives on through his work,
created out of the joy for existence which he experienced and
which others can experience generations later through his work.
The ever-present urge for joy never left Pasternak, and in
Doctor Zhivago it became one of the component elements of
life: "air, water, need for joy, earth, and sky" (*Zh,* 167).[3]

IV *Rilke*

In the formative years of Pasternak's life, his encounter with
Rilke towers far above all other experiences that contributed
so much to the making of a poet. Pasternak had seen Rainer
Marie Rilke (1875-1926) for the first time in 1900. In the first
pages of *Safe Conduct,* which is dedicated to Rilke, he tells
us about this meeting. Not that Pasternak ever tried to imitate
Rilke or borrow themes and poetic devices from him. It is much
more the poetic spirit which Pasternak found so pleasing and
to his own liking. In his article "Pasternak i Rilke,"[4] I. N. Bushman suggests that Pasternak's poetic feeling received permanent direction from the first poetic encounter with Rilke and
that Rilke influenced Pasternak's poetry for a longer period of
time and more profoundly than any Russian or other non-
Russian writer. A few fundamental features which suggest the
kinship of these two great poets may contribute toward the
understanding of Pasternak's development as a poet.

The two tangential points in the alliance of the work of two
poets are usually expressed through content and form. Pasternak, for example, uses many poetic devices which are to be
found in Rilke's poetry. Yet Pasternak was not a blind follower.
He possessed too much originality to be a mere epigone. Both
writers apply, for instance, rhyme not only to construct, but
also to decorate their verse; rhyme is not a poetic element that
must be enforced rigidly, but is flexible and variable. Both
writers often use compound rhymes, mix impure rhyme with
assonance and dissonance, and constantly search for new techniques. Having discovered a new rhyme pattern, Rilke quite
liberally repeats it in later poems. Pasternak shies away from

such a method. But then most of his early poetry was primarily an experiment with form. And this is perhaps one of the major reasons why he later rejected his own early writings. Once this search for form as the major poetic task had been satisfied, Pasternak had matured to a point where tone and subject matter or content became the concern of poetic urgency. And Rilke's influence was now not only obvious but readily admitted.

Pasternak's love for philosophy helped speed up this metamorphosis towards Rilke. German poets have always placed great emphasis on philosophical and theological themes. But Rilke exploits these themes with greater insight than other writers. He is the most profound poet-philosopher in modern literature; and Pasternak is his equal.

Philosophy and religion entered Pasternak's poetry through Rilke. *Mir zur Freude* and a second Rilke book electrified Pasternak, as he confesses in *An Essay in Autobiography*, "with their uncompromising gravity of expression, always aiming for the most essential" (*Soch.*, II, 19). In spite of this great admiration for Rilke's preoccupation with the essential, Pasternak does not merely follow or imitate his teacher; he engages in a dialogue with him, in which he answers many questions raised. I. N. Bushman[5] has demonstrated this very convincingly with the help of two stanzas from Rilke's *Die Sonette an Orpheus* and a few lines from Zhivago's poem "Christmas Star." Rilke postulates and asks: "Song is existence./ Quite easy for a god./ But when do we exist?/ And when shall he/ Turn heaven and earth/ Because of us?" And Pasternak answers:

> They stood in the shadow, in the dusk of the stall,
> And whispered their words scarcely moving a lip,
> When someone unknown from the left of the hall
> Pushed aside one of them with his hand from the crib.
> The man looked around: on the threshold ablaze,
> Like a guest, at the Maiden, Noel Star did gaze.
> (trans. J. W. Dyck)

Youth usually is inquisitive. Rilke was concerned with death, immortality, and religion very early in his life. Pasternak, on the contrary, was not interested in religion in his early years. He experienced religious consciousness much later in life than Rilke. Religion, though not the church, had its full claim on the mature Pasternak, and maturity tends to demand answers, at least to a few questions. The poetic dialogue between Rilke and Pasternak, as Bushman suggests, needs closer examination not only as to content but also as to time and chronology. The seriousness of the subject matter also determines the tone of their respective poetry. Rilke's, as well as Pasternak's, later poetry is overshadowed by this seriousness with which the problems of life and death were viewed.

Another unifying factor must still be mentioned. From his earliest poetry to the cycle *Kogda razgulyaetsya* (*When the Skies Clear*), Pasternak perceived in nature animate, often human, qualities. "Men are nature's kin, and nature is kin with men," he concludes his poem "Trava i Kamni" ("Grass and Stones"). He also expresses the relationship between organic and inorganic matter and the human spirit: "So fused are stone and plant,/ Illusion and reality/ In Poland and in Georgia/ That both are alike as twins" (trans. Kayden).

The dialogue in which Pasternak was so fully engaged, perhaps, was one-sided. Nevertheless, Rilke was well aware of the existence of Pasternak and greatly impressed by his poetry. In a letter, dated May 20, 1900, he mentions the meeting with the Pasternaks which had taken place in the train. Of greater insight, however, is a note to Pasternak. The note, which Pasternak mentions in his *Afterword* to *Safe Conduct*, reads in part:

How thankful I am to you because you have given me to see and feel what you have cultivated so wondrously within you. The fact, that you could spare me such ample harvest of your spirit, testifies to the glory of your generous heart. May the grace of God be with you in everything. I embrace you. Yours, Rainer Maria Rilke. (*Soch.*, II, 361)

A postscript, probably meant for the messenger of the above note, reads: "I am so moved by the sonority and power of his expression, that I cannot say anything more, but please send the enclosed note to my friend in Moscow."

Pasternak addresses Rilke directly only in the above-mentioned *Afterword*. Strangely enough, it is in an imaginary letter written long after Rilke's death. It seems as if the letter may have been written at various times. Pasternak tells Rilke that he has just completed *Safe Conduct* and had dedicated it to Rilke's memory. He begs forgiveness for not having answered his note, but he had wanted and hoped to meet him soon. He tells him of the experience of being torn between two women of different nature: the one is forever in need, the other is needed. And then he has the feeling that he must have been known to Rilke. Finally, he asserts what an important role Rilke had played in his life. "To tell you who you are would be the easiest task in the world. But if I began to speak of myself, that is, of our time, perhaps I would not be able to handle the immature theme." However, one summer Pasternak felt, he tells Rilke, as if he had recognized himself through revelation. He says he wrote a book about it. Perhaps, Pasternak refers to *The Last Summer.* In it, as in Rilke's *Das Stunden-Buch* or *Das Buch der Bilder,* self-recognition is the most intense and subjective theme.

V *I Beheld my Tomorrow*

Pasternak received the idea of going to Marburg from his fellow student, Dmitri Samarin, a descendant of a well-known family of Slavophile convictions, on whose former estate the present writers' colony of Peredelkino is located. Samarin, as Pasternak writes in his *Autobiography,* had "philosophy, dialectics, and the knowledge of Hegel in his blood" (*Soch.,* II, 30). He had studied in Marburg. In *Safe Conduct,* Pasternak recalls how, in the Café Grec, in February of 1912, Samarin told him and his friend, Loks, the story of Marburg. Pasternak was fascinated by the intellectual and cultural history which this comparatively small university town was breathing. Marburg was mentioned in every high school history textbook. From the discussions of a group of students that had united and called themselves "the Marburg School," he had heard about the philosophy taught in Marburg. Naturally, he articulated his dreams to his parents and, two months later, these dreams became reality when Pasternak's mother presented him with a gift of two hundred rubles, set aside from piano lessons, so that he could study abroad.

Even the journey by train had turned the fusion of past and present into an experience. "The immemorial medieval age," he records in *Safe Conduct,* "was disclosed to me for the first time. Its reality was fresh and frightening like every original" (*SC,* 36). In Poland he observed "a Romance portion of Slavism" and Berlin seemed like a city of tin soldiers who were still admiring the newness of their uniforms, bicycles, and swords.

He was not disappointed by the academic atmosphere of Marburg. A few references and chosen quotations from *Safe Conduct* may demonstrate best his discoveries. The Marburg School, i.e., its method of teaching philosophy, was refreshing compared to the many deadening "isms" and the knowledge captivated by the inertia of terminology in his home university. With remarkable insight and clarity, Pasternak satirizes the functions of the various academic disciplines as conceived at the Moscow University. At the Moscow University, Pasternak says, philosophy taught us what one or another creative writer thinks, psychology explained how the average man thinks, and logic edified how man ought to think in a baker shop to be able to figure out the change. In Marburg, Pasternak felt, philosophy was interested, without prejudice, in our historical heritage. Here one investigated how science—that is, knowledge—had thought during its two and a half thousand years of existence. At the Marburg School, Pasternak felt that history was seen through both of Hegel's eyes. Brilliant universality and at the same time rigorous judicious verisimilitude were the order of the day.

After settling down from the initial excitement produced by the external sights of Marburg, Pasternak began to prepare for the Leibniz seminar, given by Professor Nikolaus Hartmann, and he also wrote a research paper on *The Critique of Practical Reason* for Professor Hermann Cohen. Pasternak names Cohen, alongside with Plato who, he says, now took the places of Kant and Hegel, "a veritable spirit of mathematical physics." The paper, which he presented to the seminar, was received with approbation from the professor and fellow-students. It was suggested that he present his ideas in a more comprehensive paper at the end of the term. This was quite an honor and, as a rule, suggested support for and an open door to a career in philosophy.

"Surprise is the greatest gift with which life can delight us." This pithy statement was made by Pasternak in 1936 at the Writers' Plenum in Minsk. He spoke these words out of the depths of vital, personal experience. One such experience, the experience of love, constituted for Pasternak "the crossing over into a new faith." This new faith was the belief in poetry. Poetry soon replaced philosophy. However, the role of philosophy he defined much later in *Doctor Zhivago*: "I think a little philosophy should be added to life and art by way of spice, but to make it one's specialty seems to me as strange as feeding on nothing but pickles" (*Zh*, 366).

Pasternak's conversion from philosophy to poetry took place as the result of his unrequited love for the daughter of a wealthy Moscow family whom he had tutored as a high school student and had quietly loved since the age of fourteen. In *Safe Conduct* he reminisces how the two sisters stopped over to visit him on their way from Belgium to Berlin and how he experienced three days of happiness and bliss. On the third day of their visit, he tasted the bitter cup of rejection. He had asked the elder sister to decide his fate, and she did. Shocked to the degree of not being able to bid her farewell at the station, Pasternak jumped on the moving train. But the subsequent parting in Berlin only increased the painful feeling of disrupted harmony. The sisters were met by their parents and did not wish to be seen with Boris. After a sleepless night, spent in bitter tears at an open window of a cheap tavern, he returned to Marburg the next day.

This crucial night has been described in great detail in *Safe Conduct*. With special emphasis and concern he relates the inner conflict and his physical posture at various times during this fateful night. "It was the posture of a man who had fallen away from something majestic, which had long claimed and sustained him, but suddenly dropped him..."(*Soch.*, II, 237). It was his fall from Paradise, very painful and new to his experience. "The morning had recognized my face" (*Soch.*, II, 238). Similarly, he ends his poem "Marburg": "And the night vanquishes, objects leave my sight/ In the face I recognize the bright morning."

For Pasternak the Marburg experience was the morning of manhood. This recognition awakened through the encounter with love: "We all," says Pasternak at the outset of *Safe Conduct*, "have become people only to the degree in which we have loved others and had occasion to love" (*Soch.*, II, 206). However, in Marburg inner peace was not to be quickly regained. Almost day and night Pasternak poured his wounded feelings into verse. He visited his cousin in Berlin and his parents in Italy. Florence, Venice, and other places supplied later the background for *Apellesova cherta* (*Il Tratto di Apelle*) and the poem "Venetsiya" ("Venice"). His brother stopped over in Marburg. But the necessary tranquility to pursue his further studies in Marburg did not come. Poetry had chosen him and the urgency of creating poetry left no room for philosophy. Even Cohen's suggestion that he should earn his doctorate in Marburg and that a brilliant career awaited him in the universities of the West could not change the situation. His only desire was to write poetry. For the sake of a graduation certificate, he took his final examination at the University of Moscow. Thereafter, he spent the summer of 1913 with his parents in the country near the railroad station of Stolbovaya. He recalls this summer in *An Essay in Autobiography*: "I read Tyuchev and, for the first time in my life, wrote poetry not as a rare exception but regularly, every day, as people paint or compose music" (*Essay*, 80).

There are, undoubtedly, many important remaining episodes in Pasternak's life which have influenced his art. In the autobiographies there are often only hints and guesses. Nevertheless, some of these influences radiate from the pages of his works and thus complete the image of this great modern Russian poet. References to these images will be made and elaborated on throughout the discussions. For, as Pasternak put it in *Safe Conduct*, art "is not interested in man, but in his image. The image of man, it appears, is greater than man" (*Soch.*, II, 234).

CHAPTER 3

Poetics in Autobiography

"Wenn ich gestorben bin,
schreibt keine Bücher über mich. . . .
aber lasst mich vorkommen!"

(When I have died
Don't write books about me. . . .
Let me come forth!)
(Renate Schweitzer, p. 5)

I *The Poetic Climate*

IN the first two decades of this century men of letters were
deeply engrossed in replacing naturalism—which, it was
felt, had overreached itself in "objectivity" and in its all-inclusive
detail—with a more subjective artistic revelation of visions and
individual experiences. The war of 1904 and the revolution in
the following year contributed to the realization that literature
and art in the Russian cultural citadels had become stale and
that their intellectuals had grown completely provincial. Out
of this realization many young poets felt called to a new mission which did not find expression through the imitative instinct
to copy the everyday, that is, the visible realities, but rather
through the discovery and fancy of the hidden realities behind
which they suspected genuine fidelity and truth. Symbolist poets
were much concerned with the esthetic conception of art, and
the term "Symbolist" found its application only when Vyacheslav Ivanov, Bely, and Blok enriched their verses with techniques
which made poetry more musical. They also veiled it in mysticism and religion, fusing Classical, especially Greek, with Christian ideas.

Valery Bryusov, Konstantin Balmont, and a few others—that
is, the older Symbolists—although primarily concerned with
external brilliance and with the search for new word symbols,

frequently "full of the erotic, fantastic and the morbid,"[1] soon
were called "decadents." Thus, the engagement or the attitude
of the Symbolists was esthetic as well as religious.

Because they were interested in theories of art, the Symbolists
considered form not as something that stands alone and isolated
from the content of a poem but as an integral part of it, and
essential in interpreting its meaning. Although all Symbolists
agreed that realities, especially metaphysical realities, are only
recognizable behind a system or even chaos of symbols, they
disagreed over the question of whether or not it should be their
task to create new religious myths in literature or—if symbols
really denote many levels of intent—whether sense should not
be sacrificed to sound. The discord among the Symbolist theoreticians invited new considerations and with it new literary
groupings.

As a reaction against Symbolism, several movements, especially
in Russian poetry, came into being. Acmeism, founded in 1912
by Nikolay Gumilyov and Sergey Gorodetsky, and represented
by such poets as Anna Akhmatova and Osip Mandelstam, rejected the vagueness of imagery in Symbolist poetry and, as
Harkins succinctly defines it, "opposed the Symbolists' use of
images as symbols of unseen metaphysical realities."[2] The
Acmeists attempted to achieve perfection and virility with the
help of clear and concrete imagery.

The Formalist school, on the other hand, consisted of linguists,
essayists, and literary critics, who, in the words of Boris Eichenbaum—himself a member of this group—were not so much concerned with finding new methods to explore literature, but with
utilizing literature as a means of research.[3] In his essay *Die
Theorie der formalen Methode,* written in the 1920's, Eichenbaum
relates how Formalists and other literary groups had been
nurtured on the ideas of the Symbolists. But the Formalists
were determined to supplant the Symbolists' subjective and
esthetic principles with greater objectivity and scientific facts.

The task of literary criticism is the study of specific qualities
in literature, the study of what Wellek and Warren call the
"material of literature."[4] And language is the material of literature. Therefore, many Formalists took great interest in linguistics. Linguistic elements often assumed and signified autonomous
poetic values. A few of Pasternak's early poems have traces of
such linguistic exercises. But Pasternak never belonged to the

Opoyaz group. *Opoyaz*, the Society for the Study of Poetic
Language, had published, since 1916, works by such Formalist
theoreticians as Victor Shklovsky, Roman Jakobson, Yury Tynyanov, and others. And while poets in their search for form had
befriended themselves with linguistic media, linguists were
quick to stretch out their helping hands in providing what they
hoped would be permanent contours for poetry. However,
through this union the *Opoyaz* Formalists soon learned, as
Eichenbaum points out, "to distinguish between psychological
linguistics and the study of language and style."[5]

Somewhat akin to the Formalists were the Futurists. Eichenbaum calls this relationship "ein wechselseitiges geschichtliches
Einverständnis."[6] The Futurists, however, saw not only the
weaknesses of the Symbolists, but publicly rebelled against
them. Futurism was nourished and swept on to the literary stage
by young, vigorous, and determined writers who, contrary to
the essays and treatises of the Formalist theoreticians, agitated
for their theories primarily through *avant-garde* artistic writings.
The movement was founded in 1910 and counted among its
dedicated promoters talented poets and writers. First led by
Viktor Khlebnikov, soon the movement's strongest voice was
Mayakovsky. Later, when in 1923, LEF (Left Front) was
established, Pasternak sympathized with the group for a short
time. But Futurism had Messianic visions and objectives of
grandeur: "To dominate the art of the future."[7]

It is not surprising that, after having written *Sestra moya—zhizn*
(*My Sister, Life*) which had established his reputation as a
poet, Pasternak could not return to a literature in which "the
cult of technology and the machine" had taken hold of an
author's imagination and in which polemics were the supreme
order of the day. His poetry always aims to be "creative in spirit
and technique." That Pasternak rejected polemics, fanaticism,
and too loud a voice for the material world is unmistakably
suggested in the short exposition on Alexey Kruchonykh, written
in 1925. He searched for his own independent position; he
wanted his own literary Ism. However, Pasternak's dialogue
with the Futurists had begun much earlier. In 1911, he had
joined the moderate Futurist group "Centrifuge" and in 1916
he published in its symposium the short exposition *The Black
Goblet*. Pasternak, as many other young poets of those years,
had learned much from the Symbolists and from the Impres-

sionists. He recalls how the honorable nickname "Futurist" had been given to them by mutual consent.

"In the creative process of a Futurist," Pasternak writes, "exercising idle (leisured) Impressionism becomes essentially a necessity . . ."[8] (*Soch.*, III, 148). Pasternak hastens to point out the artistic differences between Impressionism and Futurism. He defines Impressionism as an art that brings into play space and time with reserved frugality. The art of the Impressionist is photographic. The artist describes reality subjectively and "at the moment of observation." Compared to the creative moment of fleeting, roadside arrangements, Futurism is above all a manifestation of real impressions in the shortest time. "A transmutation of the temporal into the eternal, this is the true meaning of Futurist abbreviation"[9] (*Soch.*, III, 148). Naturally, the subjective originality of a Futurist is, in Pasternak's opinion, not at all synonymous with the subjectivity of the individual *per se*. The Futurist's subjectivity must be interpreted as "a category of lyric poetry," and thus, it is original in an ideal sense.

All theories of art in general, and literature in particular, rise out of the propensity to reflect reality in the highest degree of veracity. And every creative mind is at some point of its career confronted with the dilemma of clarifying its own relationship to reality. Such confrontation is inevitable for two reasons: first, the artist must form and define his views and convictions on the function of his art, and secondly, he must know himself. One reason for alienating himself later from the Futurist aims is, perhaps unconsciously, voiced in Pasternak's early defense of Futurism. In spite of his confession that the Futurist is an early settler of the future, of everything new, of the unknown, Pasternak concedes that eternity could very well be "the most dangerous of the opponents" (*Soch.*, III, 149) of Futurism.

The Futuristic techniques displayed a somewhat nervous appearance, and Pasternak was already convinced, while writing his *Chyorny bokal* (*Black Goblet*) in 1916, that this nervousness was due to the way in which poetry threw itself upon reality. Much later, in his reflections in *Safe Conduct* (1931) and in *An Essay in Autobiography* (1956), Pasternak expounded and elucidated why he had withdrawn from Futurist activities. The Futurist followers were separated into two groups, the Epigones who, according to Pasternak, were "without fire or gifts," and the Novators, filled with hatred and militancy. Pasternak belonged to the Novators, but soon grew to dislike their group psychology, their outward appearance, and their pretensions to originality (cf. *SC*, 94-95).

In his entire experience with the Futurists, collective thinking was for Pasternak the most repellent. In *Safe Conduct*, Pasternak critically depicts a confrontation, which took place in 1914, between a group of Novators and Mayakovsky and his followers. However, playing at party discipline did not appeal to Pasternak. He was not willing to sacrifice his taste and his conscience. What impressed Pasternak most in Mayakovsky was the latter's consciousness of his purpose and destiny. The author himself as one of the major sources of his art had now assumed full meaning in Pasternak's thinking. It was the discovery "that a poet is not an author, but the subject of a lyric, facing the world in the first person" (*SC*, 100). He turned to Mayakovsky with admiration. He was chained to his exceptional qualities and, at the same time, terrified. In 1956, he reminisces how Mayakovsky had been proclaimed "the most gifted poet of our era" (*Essay*, 103).

The claim was marred by political insinuations. Indeed, Mayakovsky was drawn to publicity, and he admittedly chose for his poetry themes which often resembled a balance sheet of changes and events, focused on the author himself, or it was outright *Zweckliteratur*. Concluding his thoughts on Mayakovsky, Pasternak underscores in the same autobiography that nothing was further from his mind than "a life stripped of privacy and anonymity and displayed in the glass glitter of a showcase" (*Essay*, 103). But a much deeper realization was this: a poet who imagines himself the measure of life, pays for this with his life. The Symbolists had dwelled upon such a conception of life which basically is concealed in the Romantic manner. But a conception which fuses life and art invites a categorical imperative. Pasternak knew that Blok, Mayakovsky, and Sergey Esenin had been confronted by this imperative. Pasternak took the road Blok had travelled. He gave up the Romantic manner. His art was never meant to become the measure of life. Although proud and self-centered in the beginning, it was purged by joy and sufferings and over the years transformed itself into an art of humility and universality.

II *The Artist*

In *An Essay in Autobiography,* Pasternak writes:

People who died early—Andrey Bely, Victor Khlebnikov, and several others—were, in their final years, deeply concerned with finding new means of expression. In their dreams of this new language, they searched and probed its syllables, its vowels, and its consonants. I never understood these explorations. As I see it, the most striking discoveries came about when the artist was overcharged with his subject to such a degree that it did not give him time for being thoughtful, and hastily he spoke his new word in a familiar language, not worrying whether it was old or new. (*Soch,* II, 13)

Naturally, we must keep in mind that these words of eschewal were written late in the author's life. In his earlier years, Pasternak lived and labored in the midst of various literary currents where creative detail, such as style, versification, and language, was of primary concern and major importance to him. His association with the Futurists is one example of Pasternak's early involvement with literary theory and poetic technique. Even his first contribution to the theory of literature, his lost paper entitled "Symbolism and Immortality," was not limited to purely formalistic aspects of the creative endeavor, or to a mere esthetic quest. The few remarks which the author has made about this paper suggest a deep concern with clarity of content and meaning because Pasternak was convinced that poetry is a living part of history and always in collaboration with real life. When Pasternak wrote *Safe Conduct* his views on the Arts were well established, his assigned aims to a work of art had remained basically unchanged from those he had held in his earlier years.

In the same work Pasternak observes, with regard to painting, the divergent forces which, while creating a work of art, are at their best when melted into one harmonious opus. Pasternak notes:

I also found out what syncretism accompanies the blooming of craftsmanship when, with the attained homogeneity between the artist and the material of art, it becomes impossible to say which of the three and for whose benefit projects itself the more actively on the canvas—the executor, the thing executed, or the object of the execution. (*Soch.,* II, 262)

Although Pasternak makes these observations while reminiscing about his Italian experience and with regard to painting, the method may very well find its validity and application in literature. With this in mind, each work of art, it should be said, is autobiographical. This, however, does not mean that it visibly depicts images from the author's chronology. It develops rather out of his *Existenz*, it becomes part of him, and the author is in it. While young, Pasternak admits, he had loved too much the living essence of historical symbolism which, as he later saw it, did "not embrace the genius's fate and his nature" (*SC*, 87). He had not yet experienced that the inner nature of genius "reposes in the experience of real biography and not in a symbolism refracted with images" (*SC*, 87). But in his short interpretation of Chopin, published in 1945, Pasternak recognizes the composer's originality not because it is dissimilar with that of his rivals, but because it is akin to his own nature with which he wrote. Pasternak explains: "It [Chopin's work] is always biographical... because, like other great realists, Chopin looked upon his life as a means of knowing every kind of life on earth..." (*Soch.*, III, 172).

For Pasternak good artistic craftsmanship was almost identical with originality. He concluded his speech *On Modesty and Boldness*, held before the Writer's Plenum in Minsk, February, 1936, with these words:

I am deeply indifferent to the individual parts of the integral form, provided the latter is original and true, that is, I am not worried whether or not it is artistic passion... or some other passion that provides the source of an active involvement in life as long as there do not intrude between the author and his expression the intermediate links of imitation deceitful unusualness or bad taste.... (*Soch.*, III, 223)

Perhaps it is no accident that Pasternak's most articulate ideas on the creative genius are expressed in the three literary appeals of 1925, 1934, and 1936, directed at government decrees and at his fellow writers. When in 1925, he took issue with regard to the Central Committee's resolution on literature, Pasternak concluded his essay with this note: "I think that work is wiser and nobler than man, and that any artist should expect good from nowhere else but from his own imagination" (*Soch.*, III, 159).

The neo-Kantian influences from the time of his Marburg studies are still dominant in his considerations of the meaning of human existence. In another short essay on the theory of literature, entitled "Several Positions" (1925), Pasternak is even more explicit when he claims that the living and real world is the sole expression of imagination. But only two years later, in 1927, in an aphorism about the Classics, Pasternak supplements his youthful and Romantic conviction and makes room for inspiration gained from others. He associates himself strongly with Pushkin, and advises with emphasis not to part from the esthetics of this nineteenth-century poet. The esthetics of an artist depends on his concept of the nature of art, on his views of art's role in history, and on his personal responsibility to it. More than anywhere in his works, in *Doctor Zhivago,* the example of the masters receives its highest recognition: "Forward steps in art are made by attraction through the artist's admiration and desire to follow the example of the predecessors he admires most" (*Zh,* 258).

Gradually, Pasternak experienced an estrangement from the cult of genius. The Romanticizing muse loses its creative impetus, Pasternak's image of the artist and the poet becomes more realistic, and his speech at the First All-Union Congress of Writers on August 29, 1934, even didactic. He tells his fellow writers that there are norms of behavior which facilitate the artist in his work. Pasternak recommends that his fellow writers make use of them, but warns against the enormous amount of warmth with which the people and the government surround poets and writers and against the danger of becoming literary statesmen. "Stay away from this kindness for the sake of its direct sources,[10] for the sake of a great, sensible, and fruitful love for our country, and for great contemporary personalities" (*Soch.,* III, 217). This is a striking example of intermediate links of imitation which Pasternak condemned so forcefully as intruders between the author and his expression in his speech of 1936, at the Writers' Plenum in Minsk.[11]

With the appearance of *Safe Conduct,* Pasternak's image of the artist became more moderate compared to that which he held in his earlier years. Indeed, this image remained rather constant to the very end of his life. In *Safe Conduct* Pasternak is well aware of an existing psychology of the creative genius. He himself had experienced the Romantic curse of a direct conception of the muse in his early poesy. An analysis of himself and of some of his contemporaries becomes simultaneously his lasting idea of the artist *par excellence*. Pasternak tells us in *Safe Conduct* why he abandoned the Romantic manner. He rejected a conception of life completely dominated by and concealed under the Romantic manner. He now understood why Blok had turned away from it, and why Mayakovsky and Esenin paid with their lives for it (cf. *SC*, 110). Pasternak had recognized the destructive effects which a prolonged "Sturm und Drang" can have on a writer and that a poet who thinks of himself as the measure of life must pay for this with his life too soon, as this had been the case with Mayakovsky and Esenin. Pasternak writes: "I abandoned it [a conception of biography in poetry] ... before it bore any implication of heroism and before it smelt of blood" (*SC*, 111). Already then he was convinced that the Romantic scheme of the creative genius, who is absorbed only in the study of himself, is false. If the poet desires to make the contours of his art visible, he also must speak to the non-poets, a motif which, much later, in *Doctor Zhivago*, finds its expression in the communion between mortals that invites immortality.

The Romantic scheme was, however, not rejected without first replacing it with his own ideal. "Art is unthinkable without risk and the self-sacrifice of soul,"[12] Pasternak tells his fellow writers at the above-mentioned Writers' Plenum, and Zhivago, the poet, is guided by the same stoic principle of self-denial.

In Pasternak's last two major works, in *Doctor Zhivago* and in *An Essay in Autobiography*, the artist, the poet, the creative genius in general, assumes more and more a prophetic likeness. He becomes the voice of providence, of divine guidance. In "Again Varykino," Zhivago is "carried away" (*Zh*, 391) by his poetry, as Pasternak had been in Marburg. In such moments there is no struggle for expression. Language, which Pasternak calls "the home and dwelling of beauty and meaning" (*Zh*, 391) is given to the poet by an act of inspiration. Language itself thinks and speaks. When one adds to this Zhivago's exultation: "Lord! Lord! ...Why hast Thou given me so much? Why hast Thou admitted me to Thy presence?" it indeed implies a poetics which does not overemphasize the poet and his personality,[13] as Victor Erlich has suggested. However, in giving to poetry itself a beatifying splendor, Pasternak not only implies "a

mystical notion of the creative act," an interpretation rejected
by Erlich, but draws a direct parallel to the gradually fading
theological dispute over divine inspiration in Biblical writings.
To be sure, Pasternak uses more timely and scientific terms
when he refers to Mayakovsky as to "an all-devouring poetic
energy" (Zh, 162) or to "the kinship of energy to energy, of
first principle to first principle" (Zh, 163) when depicting the
encounter between Uncle Kolya and Yury. It is also interesting
to note his analogy of poets and nightingales. The nightingale
is separated from other birds just as much as poets are from
fellow men.

Pasternak's mystic notion of the creative act, at least in
Doctor Zhivago, extends beyond mere analogies: in expression
it often becomes Biblical, in meaning prophetic. The call to
Zhivago, "time to arise, time for the resurrection" (Zh, 188),
when for the first time he meets Evgraf, and again, "Wake up!
Wake up!" (Zh, 260), when he ponders the meaning of being
a poet, is in style and meaning not only mystical but Messianic.
The foreboding (Zh, 167, 387ff) mandate of Yury points clearly
to the esoteric potency with which Pasternak believed every
true poet and artist must be endowed.

In spite of this apparent belief that mind stands over matter,
Pasternak fully appreciated the realistic side of the creative act.
Although he again emphasizes in his last autobiography that
without inspiration there can be no more than pseudo-art
(Soch., II, 22), he outlines in the same essay, drawing examples
from great writers of the past, definite qualifications which the
poet-Elect must strive to acquire. In addition to the creative
moment, a maestro of poetry must have a "strong personality
and character." The creative act can obtain its impetus from
the passion of creative vision, as it was in the case of Tolstoy,
and fullness of meaning from fantasy, which nurtured Dostoevsky's novels, or from other sources. It is seldom that all qualities
are united in one person. "But Blok," says Pasternak, "had everything that makes a great poet: fire, tenderness, the power to
convince, his own concept of the world, his gift of a special
encounter that transformed everything, and finally, his reserved
private fate which found fulfillment in itself" (Soch., II, 15).
Besides Blok, Tolstoy, and Dostoevsky, Pasternak found worthy
examples in Pushkin, Lermontov, Chekhov, and a few other
Russian predecessors, to whom he refers throughout his works

and from whom he was always willing to learn. His classical translations of Kleist, Shakespeare, Goethe, and other great poets and writers helped in shaping Pasternak's idea of the artist as an individual, rich in imagination, original in thought and expression, and entitled to privacy. "A writer must be allowed to loosen up. He must be allowed to live and develop."[14] Only then, and we concur with E. M. Kayden, can a poet's claim be "a claim which proves itself only as deeper insight and perception, as a form of love, and as a commitment to freedom in the name of individual worth,"[15] only then can his message be "a special way of apprehension, an act of vision, which, like wisdom, is an act of love and compassion in human destiny,"[16] and only then can his words reveal the Eternal. In the beautiful poem, "It is not seemly to be famous," Pasternak challenges the artist, the creative mind, the poet. The following two quatrains, translated most eloquently by Lydia Pasternak-Slater, sum up best Pasternak's idea of the creative process and its poetic genius:

> To give your all—this is creation,
> And not—to deafen and eclipse.
> How shameful, when you have no meaning
> To be on everybody's lips!
>
> And never for a single moment
> Betray your *credo* or pretend,
> But be alive—this only matters—
> Alive and burning to the end.
> (trans. Lydia Pasternak-Slater)

III *Concept of Art*

When Maxim Gorky had read Pasternak's poem "1905," written in 1925-26, he observed in a letter to the author,

The book is excellent ... before this book, I always read your poems with some effort, perhaps because they are oversaturated with imagery, and the images are not always clear to me. ... In "1905" you are more scant and simple, you are more classical in this book, which has a pathos that infects me, the reader, quickly, easily, and strongly.[17]

Gorky especially emphasizes that he is looking as a reader at Pasternak's poetry and not only as another poet. It is not enough to be "a poet for poets."

Max Hayward defines the imagery of Pasternak's early poems as "that of a fleeting, momentary association of ideas which remains unimpeded by common-sense knowledge or artistic prejudice."[18] Pasternak's later poems are, indeed, more transparent. Nevertheless, a strict evaluation of his art on the basis of chronological periodization, as attempted by Reavey in his introduction to *The Poetry of Boris Pasternak,* can be misleading. And also Pasternak's own dislike of his writings before 1940 can only be applied to his style; his philosophy with regard to the meaning of a work of art, to its sources, and to its function and aims remained essentially unchanged throughout his life. Looking back to his early works while he was associating with the Futurists, Pasternak himself states in 1931 (according to Reavey, this is Pasternak's Middle Period) that not much had changed, neither were his conclusions different from what he was thinking now. A. D. Sinyavsky agrees: "Pasternak changed without infringing upon the basis of his poetry."[19] Thus, the question of what constitutes art for Pasternak must be asked.

Answers to this question we find in Pasternak's writings throughout the years. As early as 1922, in the short paper under the title "Several Positions," Pasternak stresses the timeless nature of art. Art, he says, has no beginning just as any genuine book has no first page. But art is also omnipresent, that is, it is everywhere and in everyone. Ten years later, in *Safe Conduct,* he again ponders the nature of reality of art. As before, he feels that poetry is a living part of history and always in collaboration with real life—that art in general, and as a philosophy of life, presupposes a connection which unites the anode with the cathode, the artist with life, the poet with his time (*Soch.,* II, 279). Consequently, art manifests itself as a concept of life similar to the manifestation of religion, science, Socialism, or any other conviction. Out of these considerations, Pasternak can say in 1931 that, in creating a work of art, the artist displaces reality with feeling. Briefly, art records this displacement. In his last autobiography, he describes this process as experience presented in "real images and scenes."

Pasternak abnegates the theory that only the sublime, the unique, and the unusual can find their way into art. Art is interested in life and full of generally accepted truths. Pasternak speaks of this at length in *Safe Conduct,* in *An Essay in Autobiography,* and he practices his belief convincingly in *Doctor*

Zhivago. But a universal truth can be expressed artistically only by a method of selection and by rules which are well known and properly applied. To select and to apply is, to be sure, the work of genius. Scriabin, Pasternak says, knew how to select. His music "had no false depth" (*Essay,* 43) and was full of inspiration.

The emphasis on collective thinking, the lack of individual creativity, and the mendacious pseudo-art in the pages of "Lef" (cf. *Essay,* 100) had been responsible for Pasternak's break with the Futurists. Art without inspiration was unthinkable for Pasternak. Real art must have endless animation, without which there is no originality, that infinity which opens itself from any one point of life, in any direction, without which poetry remains a mere misunderstanding, something temporarily unexplained (*Soch.,* II, 273).

What does art or poetry without inspiration and animation really mean? For Pasternak it meant that such art had lost its real source, which is life and its purpose, which is communion. Not only had some art—art primarily concerned with outer form and techniques—failed to build what the Classicists had called a *schöne Seele,* but instead it had become an unfortunate dispute. Zhivago, in *Varykino,* echoes Pasternak's views in endless discussions about art. Zhivago, as Pasternak himself, did not think of art as a category but as a principle and a force which is, above all, concerned with truth. Zhivago never sees it "as forms but rather as a hidden, secret part of content" (*Zh,* 256).

Two elements in this statement are notably emphasized: art understood as force and art as symbol. Pasternak has applied these two elements to the fullest in *Doctor Zhivago.* But long before completing this novel, Pasternak had formulated his theory on the meaning of art in *Safe Conduct.* In this *ars poetica* of 1931, he tells us that if he were to write an esthetic of creativity, he would base his argument on two conceptions, "on the conception of power and that of the symbol" (*Soch.,* II, 242). He then explains at some length how the conception of power should be viewed. He draws an interesting analogy between the natural sciences and art. As the sciences strive for a fuller comprehension of nature, art, he says, occupies itself with life. The major theme of both, however, is the conception of power, a theme almost Nietzschean in melody. But while theoretical physics is interested in the *principle* of power and force, art—according to Pasternak—seeks out the *voice* of force and power, which are confined to the self-consciousness called feeling. The one side of Pasternak's esthetic of creativity, thus, is feeling. Graphically expressed, we could say that art equals force in the framework of self-consciousness, which equals feeling. But this is admittedly only one side of his esthetics. To be appreciated as art, this force yearns for a "language of material proof" and the proofs can manifest themselves only in a language of images. The interchangeability of such images, of symbols of power, is art. Pasternak explains in a footnote: "I am not speaking of the material contents of art, nor of the variables in its realization, but of the meaning of its image, of its place in life" (*Soch.*, II, 244). In *Doctor Zhivago*, Pasternak speaks of the "relation between imagery in art and the logical structure of ideas" (*Zh*, 80). This remark and the above quoted explanatory footnote become more meaningful when we hold them against Pasternak's suggestion that one should study the paintings of Veronese and Titian in order to understand what art really means.

Among the best known pictures of the two mentioned Renaissance painters are Paolo Veronese's *Mars and Venus* (Fortezza submissive to Carità and Titian's *Sacred and Profane Love*. The theme of both pictures is love as the greatest creative impulse. In Veronese's allegory, love is pictured as more powerful than strife, and in *Sacred and Profane Love*, Pasternak must have recognized a capricious example of how conventional views can play tricks in recognition of the true meaning of love in the creative process. For the reader it is not always easy to distinguish between the profane and the sacred in *Doctor Zhivago*. But Pasternak is willing to explain. With the brush of an experienced painter, he paints a picture of Lara experiencing beside Zhivago's coffin a love which is free of passion and necessity. To Lara life and art had been fused into one, and possessed by this free love, she suddenly realized that Yury and she had lived and thought "what others sing in songs" (*Zh*, 447). Having in mind that the moving force of Pasternak's art is a love free of passion and necessity, we now shall attempt to view somewhat closer the sources and the aims of Pasternak's art, and also his style.

IV *Sources of Art*

The origin of Pasternak's art, as of art in general, can be traced to two major sources. These are the author himself and the world in which he lives. Pasternak always recognized the creative power generated by passion, conviction, and experience, steeped in the fetters of cultural traditions from which no one can free himself. He also was aware of an existing psychology of creativity, and he considered the problems inherent in this psychology paramount to those of poetic style and technique. But the creative moment is the most important factor in creating a work of art, and the world's best creations, Pasternak claims, in reality tell of their own birth (*Soch.*, II, 241). Pasternak reasons that during the creative process the creative mind ceases to recognize reality *per se* and sees it in a new form. The attempt to identify or to name the quality of this new form results in a work of art. Pasternak maintains, however, that this new form of reality is not just in the imagination of the artist, but it is also inherent in the new form itself.

The artist is able to make the new discovery, Pasternak explains later in his *An Essay in Autobiography,* "when the sense of his work so possessed the artist that it left him no time to think and he was driven by his urgency to speak new words in the old language, without stopping to know if it was old or new" (*Essay*, 50). In this declaration, Pasternak not only rejects the theory that new art can be born only with the help of new techniques, but injects into the creative process a profound force which stresses above all the importance of originality and individuality. Individuality should, however, not be confused with passion. Pasternak warns in *Safe Conduct* that the passion which assures for us the continuation of the race will never suffice for artistic creation. Creativity, in Pasternak's estimation, is concerned with the image rather than with the race itself, and images cannot be expressed by passion alone. They are expressed symbolically through a force which for Pasternak is synonymous to *Gefühlsexistenz,* i.e., conscious feeling. In art, says Pasternak in the second part of *Safe Conduct,* the image speaks while man is silent. Art is not interested in man but in the image of man. Most great literary works of the past are dominated by this concern. *Tristan* and *Romeo and Juliet*, Pasternak interprets, do not symbolize powerful passion, as usually assumed, but their theme is much wider, it is power itself. "And it is out of this theme that art is born" (*Soch.*, II, 243).

However, power is only the generic concept of the source which creates art. This concept becomes tangible through experience or even through fate. Pasternak points to several basic experiences out of which the spirit of creativity, and consequently art itself, is born. These basic experiences are love, confrontation with one's own genius, and cultural heritage.

Pasternak's most inspiring love experience was in his youth. He himself has told not only the story of this experience, but he has on various occasions interpreted its deeper meaning and its role in the development of his poetic urge.

In the first chapters of *Safe Conduct*, Pasternak reflects on the time when he associated with poets, musicians, and painters of the *Serdarda* group, when the great affection for Rilke had not yet lost its initial potency, and when his love for a girl from a wealthy family dictated his thoughts and his actions. These experiences, and many others, made up Pasternak's reality of those formative years. Looking back to that reality, Pasternak rhetorically asks what agency there was at work in that reality when poetry was born. And he remembers in all its detail that it was born from the conflicting currents in life. Love, in particular, had made its claim, and rushed on with a much stronger impulse than all else.

Pasternak is convinced that his poetic inspiration had come from "gazing back" to those inclinations which were falling behind, as he says, "on the abstruse horizon of remembrance" (*Soch.*, II, 215). Love, on the other hand, is for Pasternak not merely one of the many inclinations that, if challenged, steps aside, but it is a competing force through which, above all, art can germinate in youth. Love thus is at the same time source and function of art. Art must always have an open mind for love. "Only art," writes Pasternak, "that over the centuries speaks of love will not succumb to the dictates of instinct" (*Soch.*, II, 235).

In Mayakovsky's case it was different, Pasternak feels. Mayakovsky's most dominant experience was not that of love but a conscious confrontation with his own genius. Pasternak had always believed in genius as creative force, and he admired Mayakovsky because he recognized this force in him. But when Mayakovsky chose his own genius for his poetic theme, Pasternak's admiration faded into "astonishment beyond words." He also recalls in the third part of *Safe Conduct* that somehow it made him sad that he could not get used to him. Perhaps, already then Pasternak saw the role of genius differently. Genius in itself as creative source and theme is bound to end in self-destruction. Pasternak, therefore, rejected the Romanticism of Mayakovsky. But the commonplace, touched by the hand of genius, this, as Pasternak expresses it clearly in *Doctor Zhivago* (259), is another major source of creativity. The commonplace, as Pasternak sees it, is in modern times at its best in a large modern city, and cities, we read in *Doctor Zhivago*, "are the only source of inspiration for a truly modern contemporary art" (436). In spite of this statement, much of Pasternak's poetry is deeply steeped in the marvels of nature.

Pasternak was also convinced that no meaningful work of art can come into being without a continuous adhesion to one's own cultural heritage. Italy was for Pasternak the sum of all of our unconsciously acquired experience. In Italian art he recognized the tangible unity of Western culture, and he portrays the history of culture as "the chain of equations in images folded into the rudiments of tradition" (*SC*, 87).

Andrey D. Sinyavsky, in his introduction to Pasternak's poems, points out that Pasternak firmly believed in his cultural past, and that one reason for breaking with the Futurists is precisely their professed dislike for tradition and cultural heritage.[20] To cast away one's own cultural heritage, means also the destruction of poetic truth, gradually acquired through the work of generations. The willful destruction of poetic truth, Pasternak warns, can only result from failure to recognize the meaning of humanity. Looking back to the mid-1920's, Pasternak records in *An Essay in Autobiography* with satisfaction and relief: "It is good that neither Mayakovsky nor Esenin turned away from what they still remembered having known in childhood..." (*Essay*, 97).

V *Aim and Function*

If one were asked to sum up Pasternak's view on the aims and function of a work of art, perhaps it could best be done with the word "message." Pasternak himself uses this word in the chapter on Scriabin in his last autobiography. And while speak-

ing of his work in general and of *Doctor Zhivago* in particular,
he stresses "the sense of obligation to bear witness, to provide
a document of the age."[21] Every work of art is in essence and
above all a means to communicate this message. A message, to
be sure, does not have to be instructive or didactic. Indeed, Pasternak's poems, short stories, and also his great novel shy away
from any attempt to moralize. Every work of art, however, has
a role to play, has a function and an aim. The aims of Pasternak's art are numerous and often diverse in nature. In all his
works, from the very beginning of his career as a poet and a
writer, Pasternak wrote under the conviction that "a work of
art could not be all on one plane, it had to speak on different
levels ... the figures of truth and falsehood must have their
way."[22] It is a "setting forth of the uniqueness of being,"[23] as
Eugene M. Kayden calls it.

To appreciate this assertion, we have only to remember a few
of the deeds of Pasha Antipov (Strelnikov), Komarovsky, or of
other characters in Pasternak's works. Some of their deeds and
even thoughts are good, others are bad, some are purposely
aimed to help friends and enemies alike, others are destructive
visibly inviting ruin and doom. But this duplicity in life is
original and very real to Pasternak, and his art, indeed, bears
witness to it. In *Doctor Zhivago*, Pasternak defines it quite
strongly: "... for he [Yury] believed that originality and vigor
alone could give reality to a work of art, and that without them
art was utterly useless, superfluous and a waste of time" (*Zh*, 68).
Originality is defined by Kayden as "a cultural event having its
source in the world's absolute total reality."[24] Pasternak's absolute
and total reality dwells within man. It is, therefore, fitting for
art to reveal images of the inner world. Comparing Pushkin and
Chekhov with Gogol, Tolstoy, and Dostoevsky, Pasternak feels
that it is not the function of art to "draw up balance sheets"
(*Zh*, 259), but art must treat lives and work "as private, individual
matters, of no concern to anyone else" (*Zh*, 259). Only art which
looks upon life with an understanding of such realities can
become of concern to all, can lift, as it is stated toward the end
of *Doctor Zhivago*, "the particular to the level of the universal
and [be] accessible to all" (*Zh*, 405).

During the time when Pasternak wrote *Safe Conduct*, and
also earlier, it might appear, that he adhered to the Symbolists'
code, according to which a work of art has no other function

than to exist in its own right. But in *Doctor Zhivago,* Pasternak practices his earlier formulated conception. For him a work of art is neither the promoter of a political system nor should it act as an ethical and moral amendment to life itself. The function of art is esthetic in nature. "Art always serves beauty, and beauty is the joy of possessing form, and form is the key to organic life since no living thing can exist without it, so that every work of art, including tragedy, witnesses to the joy of existence" (*Zh,* 406).

With this statement in mind, we begin to understand Pasternak's last confession, recorded in the conclusion of his autobiography which was written only a few years before his death. He confesses that "what I have written is enough to give some idea of how, in my individual case, life became converted into art and art was born of life and of experience" (*Essay,* 119). As subjective and personal as this observation may sound, it reaches far beyond Pasternak and his work. Here too, the particular has been lifted to the level of the universal, and Pasternak's own experience has expressed poetically the experience of many.

VI *Style*

Pasternak's dislike of his early style does not at all imply that he fully rejected his early writings. It points, however, to the fact that towards the end of his life the author himself had recognized a metamorphosis in the development of his poetic style, and that he himself considers his early poetry inferior to the poetry written after 1940. Pasternak is quite explicit in analyzing his early poetry.

In *An Essay in Autobiography,* Pasternak, indeed, regrets the hasty publication of the *Twin in the Clouds* (*Bliznets v tuchakh*). Even the title of this cycle is an imitation of Symbolist decor and in the individual poems, Pasternak admits that he had not been in opposition to anything. He is even more discontent with his early unclassical choice of words. He laments his blindness towards the Classical style and language of Marina Tsvetaeva and of Nikolay Aseev. Everything normal, he recalls, bounced off, words had to be ornamented because he had lost faith and forgotten that words can have a sense and content of their own (cf. *Essay,* 105). To be sure, there was a time when Pasternak was hiding behind the excuse that formlessness, that is, lack of character, is more complex than form. Lydia Pasternak-Slater attributes Pasternak's dislike for his early poems to his forced attempts at complexity and sophistication. In the introduction to her book *Pasternak: Fifty Poems*, she writes:

Of course some of these early poems really were too complicated, too cryptic, perhaps too hastily written, and had too many easy escapes into the brilliance of sound and words. Too little care had been taken to simplify them, to introduce order and precision into what they expressed.[25]

Pasternak himself saw the flaws of his early poetry deeply rooted in himself and in the time in which he lived. In *An Essay in Autobiography,* he reminisces how, in his early poetry, he had missed depicting the real essence of reality, looking only for decorative effects and "incidental sharpness" (*Essay,* 105).

Pasternak reread the poetry of his youth with some dismay, yet he realized that it reflected, if not the realities, then at least the spirit of that boring first decade of this century. His own style, he felt, had been very well accorded with the false excitement of the time. The many adjectives without nouns, the verbs without a subject, abruptness and fragmentation were adopted. But when poetry threatened to become a mere statistical exercise, Pasternak did some basic poetic soul-searching. In looking back to those early days, he remembers Andrey Bely as a genius who wasted himself in a vacuum. This genius conducted a practical course on Russian iambic verse. With the help of statistics he explained its rhythmic figures and variations. Pasternak did not take part in these exercises, for he believed already at that time "that verbal music is not a matter of acoustics or of harmonizing vowels and consonants as such, but a relating of sound to meaning" (*Essay,* 68). Meaning, form, and language are gradually integrated into one inseparable unit in Pasternak's poetic process.

As we pointed out above, Pasternak defined a poetic work as an expression of supplanted reality. He calls characteristics of life, which are transformed into characteristics of creation, artistic techniques (cf. *SC,* 62). Pasternak takes a close look at his own literary techniques in several of his writings. Even his earliest poetry was composed with poetic techniques in mind which purposely aimed at avoiding "poetic coquetry" (as

Manya Harari translated it—*Essay*, 80), or, as Pasternak himself writes, at avoiding "all Romantic exaggerations as well as effects created through trivialities" (*Soch.*, II, 32).

Although he calls the title of *Twin in the Clouds* stupid and pretentious, he feels, as late as 1956, that his techniques had been carefully contemplated and well chosen. He also remembers how much, already then, he disliked rigid rhythm as found in dances and songs, and he rejects critical observations that his early poetry is guided by the principles of oratory and intonation. Pasternak points out: "On the contrary, my concern has always been for meaning, and my dream that every poem should have content in itself—a new thought or a new image" (*Essay*, 81). This should not be interpreted as meaning that Pasternak minimizes the role of rhythmic display in his own poetry. He humbly insists that he has "no more of this gift than anyone who uses words" (*Essay*, 81). But "what a lot depends on the choice of meter" (*Zh*, 257), Pasternak has Zhivago record in his diary. And Zhivago further explains that as long as Pushkin was writing long lines, as long as he was concerned with "mythology, bombast, worldly wisdom, Epicureanism, sophistication" or imitated Ossian and Parny, his ambitions could only remain local. But as soon as he changed to familiar themes, as soon as "real substantial things burst into his poetry . . . concrete things—things in the outside world, things in current use . . ." Pushkin's rhymed columns are dominated by the tetrameter and analogous to "units on a yardstick used to measure Russian life" (*Zh*, 258).

In Yury Zhivago's reflections, we hear the words of Pasternak himself, and he strengthens his postulate with references to Nikolay Nekrasov whose trimeters and dactyls also reveal the rhythm and intonation of his language. Ordinary speech, on the other hand, is transparent and natural, and is enriched with stylistic elements which to Pasternak seemed imperative for good and lasting poetic art.

Renate Schweitzer records Pasternak's aim for an ideal poetic style in some of the poet's letters written to her during the last year of his life, or in her own reflections which were intended as answers to these letters. Pasternak wrote these letters in German. In the letter of July 26, 1959, we read:

I must, at the risk that duty may be dangerous, be comprehensibly true . . . Art is always alive with demands for form which, however, have no justification. To the contrary, they are disturbances which must be crushed and defeated without either attacking or eliminating them . . . We live and create and ultimately would like to come to this realization: measure and rhyme, i.e., poetry, is the means which enables us to remain natural while using artistic form.[26]

Renate Schweitzer echoes Pasternak's own words in comparing the nature of his poetry with the music of Mozart.[27] Thus, Pasternak's claim for art is that of simplicity and clarity. The right choice of rhyme, rhythm, and meter, the right poetic techniques in general: all this he recognizes as of great importance. But of even greater consequences are the powers of language.

While writing *Safe Conduct*, he remembers how Mayakovsky had spoken his poetry with almost sectarian identities (cf. *SC*, 107), that is, with a language of persuasion and with emphasis on the essential. This strong emphasis on the gravity of language and its relationship to the realities, which the poet strives to express in images or generalize through symbols, is also echoed in Pasternak's last writings, in *Doctor Zhivago* and in *An Essay in Autobiography*. Rilke's and Blok's poetry took possession of Pasternak because it too spoke to him with "the same insistent, unconditional gravity, the same directness in the use of language . . ." (*Essay*, 61). Pasternak feels that of his generation only Aseev and Tsvetaeva "possessed the mastery of an accomplished and mature poetic style" (*Essay*, 58) because their search for originality was not obstructed by a language which purposely aimed at an artificially imposed sophistication, but was natural. In other words, their poetry was guided by the principles of simplicity which above all seek unity between the uttered word and its meaning. When reflecting on Akhmatova's early poems, Pasternak envies "the simplicity of the author's means and the reality which they had netted" (*Essay*, 85).

To achieve this highest degree of maturity in style, Pasternak recognized to the very end, is a most difficult task and can only be obtained if the poet succeeds in fusing the proud gifts of his poetic urge with the unobtrusive labor of stylistic details. About Yury Zhivago's poetic style Pasternak writes:

All his life, he had dreamed of a polished and serene originality, outwardly unrecognizable and disguised under the cover of a generally acceptable and customary form, all his life he had attempted to work out a style so reserved, so unpretentious that would enable both reader and listener to master the content without being aware of the means by which they comprehend.[28]

This passage doubtlessly reflects Pasternak's own poetic position which remained ambivalent to some degree to the very end of his life. But it was not overshadowed with gloom and pessimism. Pasternak was well aware that the process of transforming the poetic urge into a work of art places the onus not only and exclusively with the artist, but finds its impetus often in the language itself. The forces which control the artist cannot always be explained, and Pasternak's protagonist, Yury Zhivago, had experienced, in Varykino, that during the creative moment "the ascendancy is no longer with the artist or the state of mind which he is trying to express, but with language, his instrument of expression" (*Zh*, 391). Both the state of mind which is longing for form and the instrument of expression play an important role in Pasternak's poetic process; and in his art, in his poetry, in real art, content and form flow into one.

Perhaps it is appropriate to conclude this chapter on the nature and meaning of art with the following words, spoken by Pasternak in 1935 at the International Writers' Congress in Paris:

Poetry always remains that celebrated pinnacle, higher than any Alps, which lingers in the grass and under our feet, and all one has to do is to bow down on the ground in order to see poetry and gather it. . . . Poetry shall always remain an organic function of the happiness of a man who is blessed with the gift of prudent speech. And, therefore, as happiness increases on earth, it shall become easier to be an artist.[29]

CHAPTER 4

Poetry

IN his article on Pasternak's early poetry, I. N. Bushman declares that Pasternak would be considered a great poet even if he had written only *My Sister, Life* (1922) and *Temyi Variatsii* (*Themes and Variations*) (1923).[1] But Pasternak has written more and was well known, especially in literary circles in Russia and abroad, long before the appearance of *Doctor Zhivago*. Although, in 1907, he had joined the literary circle "Serdarda" on the reputation of being a musician, Pasternak's first attempts in poetry were known to his close friends and confidants. The earliest poetry which we find included in available Pasternak editions originated in 1912, in Marburg, and grew out of his unhappy experience of unrequited love.

His first book of poetry, *The Twin in the Clouds*, had been written in the branches of an old birch tree. Later some of the poems were revised and included under the name *Nachalnaya Pora* in his second book of poetry called *Poverkh barierov* (*Above the Barriers*), which was published in 1917. However, it was not until 1922 that Pasternak established himself as a talented lyrical poet with the book *My Sister, Life*. These poems were written in the summer of 1917, between two Revolutions. In *Safe Conduct*, Pasternak relates vividly the circumstances in which this book was written, and how he read his poems to Mayakovsky. But a year later, after Mayakovsky had presented his *150,000,000* to an intimate circle of fellow poets, Pasternak for the first time "had nothing to say to him."[2] *My Sister, Life,* Pasternak observes, "was found to contain expressions not in the least contemporary as regards poetry...."[3] But Pasternak, as we know today, had resolved to go his own way. With the publication of *My Sister, Life,* a poet, independent of literary currents and schools, had responded to a unique and difficult literary calling.

Today Pasternak's poems fill several volumes and many of

them are translated into various languages. Since not each and every poem can be discussed within the scope of this chapter, we shall focus our interests primarily on the nine major cycles of lyric poetry and on four major epic poems which interrupted Pasternak's purely lyrical interests between the years 1924 and 1930: (1) *Vysokaya bolezn (The High Malady)*, (2) *The Year 1905*, (3) *Lieutenant Schmidt*, (4) *Spectorsky*.

Lieutenant Schmidt and *Spectorsky* were an attempt, on the part of the poet, to come to grips with the political and social changes which had taken place between the Revolution of 1905 and the time of the Civil War, yet Pasternak never lost sight of the individual and his continuous longing for identity and selfhood.

Pasternak's poetic history can be divided into four major periods. Between his first book, *The Twin in the Clouds* (1914), and the fourth, *Themes and Variations* (1923), Pasternak travelled a long and difficult road on which many personal and social obstacles had to be overcome. It was a period in search of independent creativity, a quest for self-determination.

The second period is marked by times of prudent self-evaluation and reflection. In the year 1931, two great influences, his marriage to Zinaida Neuhaus and their subsequent visit to the Georgian poet, Paolo Yashvili, were dominant. Pasternak had mellowed, and, as A. D. Sinyavsky has observed, with Pasternak's poetry of this period in mind, he wanted to be "approachable."[4] The narrative poems (1924-1927), *Second Birth (Vtoroe rozhdenie)* (1932), and a few short stories (1925) were the result of these years. Although between 1932 and the appearance of ten poems from a novel in *Znamya* (1954), *Na rannikh poezdakh (Early Trains)* (1943) and *Zemnoy prostor (Spacious Earth)* (1945) were published, and many valuable translations of Western Classics were made, this was, for Pasternak, the poet, a period of poetic soul searching, out of which grew his most mature and transparent art, *The Poetry of Doctor Zhivago*, the posthumously published cycle, *When the Skies Clear*, and finally his great novel, *Doctor Zhivago*. With these works, Pasternak's poetic journey had come to an end.

Throughout the years his themes and his poetic expression, his esthetics, reflected his concerns and convictions at a certain juncture in his life. However, Sinyavsky warns that Pasternak as a lyric poet thought in terms of books and not of individual poems.[5] A short analytical insight into the various books may best reveal changes and transformations, and at the same time provide a short biography of Pasternak's poetic evolution.

I The Twin in the Clouds

The title, *The Twin in the Clouds,* Pasternak recalls, was chosen "in imitation of the cosmological obscurities of the book-titles of the Symbolists..." (*Essay,* 80). Perched in his birch tree and still haunted by his Marburg experience of personal rejection, Pasternak felt one and united with nature. His poems of that summer reflect his creative process. The title, later denounced by the poet as "stupid pretentiousness" (*Essay,* 80) expresses Pasternak's loneliness during those summer months. The last stanza of the first poem in this early book captures Pasternak's poetic mood in a striking way:

> Beneath—[sadness] the earth is black in puddles,
> The wind with croaking screeches throbs,
> And—the more randomly, the surer
> Poems are forming out of sobs.
> (trans. Lydia Pasternak-Slater)

Sadness and tears are the poet's steady companions, and in nature he finds comfort, because in nature's arbitrariness he recognizes an equal, a twin to his genius, that creates aimlessly "at random." D. L. Plank concludes similarly. Basing his observations on Pasternak's own words that in "art the man falls silent and the image begins to speak," he suggests that an early poem by Pasternak "is not premeditated but determined in its own process, which is uncontrollable and unwilled."[6] However, Plank maintains that the completed poem is meaningful and the meaning is new. Pasternak himself has rejected suggestions that his early poetry was overshadowed by "oratorical and melodic tendencies," and clearly stated that his concern had always been for meaning and content, and that every poem should have "a new thought or a new image" (*Essay,* 81). His poems, "Venice" and "Vokzal" ("The Railroad Station") do not aim at conveying special sound effects, but have only one purpose and one concern, namely, to depict a city and a railway station.

The early poems betray an especially outspoken anthropomorphic tendency. In the third poem of this early cycle, the poet refers to sadness and to himself as partners in one and the same campaign. But not only are abstractions animated, objects and things also are alive and conversant. Courtyards think, houses grow higher, and life itself is the backbone of Pasternak's early crusade.

Although Pasternak expresses dislike for many of his earliest poems in 1928, some have kept their original and personal passion. "Feeling," as Helen Muchnic has pointed out, "for Pasternak is the theme of art, not its method."[7] The final quatrain of one of the first poems in the cycle may serve as an example of the poet's personal involvement:

> I am the light. Well known and famous
> For shadows which my self can stray.
> I am the life of earth, its zenith,
> Its first and everlasting day.
>   (trans. J. W. Dyck)

By writing the poems of *The Twin in the Clouds,* Pasternak tried to free himself from the torments which time and experience had placed upon him. "To write these poems—to scribble, to scratch out and to restore the vanished lines," he recalls, "this was my need and joy" (*Essay,* 80).

II Above the Barriers

The torments of personal passion are also the major theme of the book *Above the Barriers.* In *Safe Conduct,* Pasternak tells us which forces had been active in shaping this, his second book. Time and influences, Pasternak reminisces, bound him to Mayakovsky, and although he realized that they had much in common, he could not adopt Mayakovsky's heroic style. "I abandoned the Romantic manner. And that is how the non-Romantic style of *Above the Barriers* came about" (*SC,* 110). Nevertheless, "the poet's tendency to dramatize himself in his work"[8] was by far not overcome by Pasternak when in 1914 he presented this book of poetry. But Pasternak revised many of the poems in 1928, reduced the original number of forty-nine poems and omitted the epigraph, which reads: "To the soul in my soul that rejoices/ For the song that is over my song" (Swinburne). Later on, Pasternak recorded:

In the course of time my concept of *Above the Barriers* changed.
What formerly had been thought as a name for a book had now
become the designation for a period or manner of thought, and
consequently I included under this heading later writings if they
fitted in with the character of the original book.[9]

Such widening of the cycle liberates the theme from its original
subjectivity and becomes a testimonial document which reveals
to us through the torments and passions of the poet, a poetic
history of the mind of those who experienced, felt, and therefore
lived, in the years between 1905 and 1917. In spite of this
potentially universal application, *Above the Barriers* displays
a visible thematic movement which spirals from the poetic "I"
outward into the world of experience, returning like a boomerang
—a simile Pasternak himself uses in a poem of *My Sister, Life*—
to the poet in "Marburg," the last poem of the cycle. "Marburg,"
writes Erlich, "is ostensibly about a major emotional setback,"[10]
when, to the contrary, its theme is recovery. To be sure, in
"Marburg" the poet relives, what N. Anatoleva has called, "his
first great grief."[11] But in the end the poet overcomes his agonies,
he recovers through self-analysis. The poet turns to history and
in doing so his feeling for fame and immortality awakens, and
passion, the poet now knows, "will grow grey as a witness in
the corner." The poet's final conviction is this: "And the night is
victorious, images fade/ I perceive the face of a bright morning."
Most poems of this cycle that precede "Marburg" deal with
the agonies of a tormented mind or, on an allegorical scale,
depict the heart and soul of Russia's prerevolutionary years.
Thus, the grand theme of *Above the Barriers* is that of mental
and spiritual strife. The main hero, a mental traveller, through
contemplation, willpower, and art, frees his mind and finally,
at least in his imagination, rises above all barriers. This is the
message of Pasternak's poetry between 1914 and 1917.
As we read through the individual poems of the cycle, we
find a gallery of subordinate themes. "Dvor" ("Courtyard") is
symbolic of group loyalty, often enticing: "People, there [in
the courtyard of the group] is love and work!/ People, there is
frenzy more distinguished than mine!/ There even I bend my
knees." But the author warns "be careful, you may sink" and, in
the last quatrain, advises the mind to remain free through actively participating in the creative process, through poetry.

In the poem "Durnoy Son" ("Bad Dream") the mind is on the move, but now the threat of destruction is greater than it was in the glorified cage of the "Courtyard." The optimistic note of this rather gloomy poem is in the hope that movement is possible on the part of the mental traveller. Although the future is still dark, the poetic "I," in the last line, is compared to a supernal faster who at least can "dream and dream."

As we read on in the cycle, the atmosphere gradually relaxes. In the rather personal poem "Possibility," the speaker remembers how immortality began. He is now more concerned with the role which he has to play in the surroundings so vividly depicted in "Courtyard" and in "Bad Dream."

In "Desyatiletie Presni" the poet's concern with the future grows more intense. With the fervency of Hamlet, he rhetorically asks whether this future "is to be or not to be." The allusion to the witches in *Macbeth*, alternately visible and invisible while hovering in the twilight of history, injects into the poem a prophetic tone and thus widens the vision of a mind that is in search of freedom.

The poem "Petersburg" delineates the will power of a great man. Through the poem's mood of expectation, Peter's will and the elements of nature become one:

> Clouds, like hair, stood on end
> Over the smoky, pale river Neva.
> Who are you? But whoever you are,
> This city is thy invention.
> (trans. J. W. Dyck)

It is this poem that gave the name to the cycle and later to an entire period. With the help of Peter's growing city, the author exemplifies the possibility of breaking out into freedom. In the poem "Petersburg" we read: "Just try it, to be complacent/ Under grey clouds/ Here one leaps in practice/ Over the barriers."

The other poems of the cycle speak of disharmony (in "Winter Skies"), or of fleeting time and longing for creativity as in "Soul." In "Snowstorm" (Metel) the theme is that of suppression and of a demonic world full of people who are willing to destroy souls. Only in nature can the burning mind find union with others. The poem "The Urals for the First Time" speaks of such a union. "The flames of sunrise .../ They suddenly lighted the firs with crowns,/ And roused them to enter their kingdom again." A similar hopeful tone is expressed in "Spring" (Vesna) by a reminder that sin plays havoc in the city, "But is filth all that you can see,/ Doesn't the splendor stun your eyes?" The poem "Happiness" carries the most optimistic answer to this reminder. In it happiness overcomes guilt as spring overcomes winter. Rebirth, love, and the poet's voice accompany the persona on his way to freedom, not only in his moments of happiness and harmony but also in his moments of strife and torment.

"Two Fragments from a Poem" is the prelude to "Marburg." In this poem the experienced traveller reminds us that he too has loved; he also knows that passionate love can be the greatest torment and can enslave man. The poem "Marburg" stands at the end of a long mental and spiritual journey, at the end of a search for an individual view of life in which the poetic "I" has to learn to overcome, above all, his own ego. Once freed of himself and from the tentacles of external torments, man's mind and soul shall forever stand above all barriers. Pasternak's time of poetic experimentation had come to an end. With the publication of *Above the Barriers*, he was firmly on his way to carve his own niche in the literary movements of his time. With his next book, in 1922, Pasternak took his place within the ranks of the best recognized lyric poets of the twentieth century. Whereas the years between 1912 and 1916 can be considered *Lehrjahre*, richly sprinkled with Symbolist and Futurist chatter and dark aspects of speech, the two cycles *My Sister, Life* and *Themes and Variations* established his poetics.

III   My Sister, Life *and* Themes and Variations

My Sister, Life was first published in 1922 in Moscow. One year later, during Pasternak's visit to Germany, it was reprinted in Berlin. This book is the most lyrical of Pasternak's entire poetic canon. The Soviet edition, *Stikhotvoreniya i Poemy*, refers to it as a "peculiar novel" presumably because of the arrangements of the poems and the headings of individual chapters, such as "Isn't it Time for the Birds to Start Singing," "The Book of the Steppes," "Lessons in Philosophy," "An Attempt to free the Soul," and others. Whether or not this grouping has any significance in establishing continuity of thought movement within the book is questionable, because originally most of the poems were gathered under the single title "The Book of the Steppes." The choice of title was motivated perhaps by the time and place in which the author had conceived this poetry. In 1917, in the summer between the two Revolutions, Pasternak must have felt that man and nature were no longer separated as before. "Roads, trees, and stars held meetings and orated together with people," we read in his autobiography. The oneness between nature and the poet, writes A. D. Sinyavsky, is the artistic system, the credo, in *My Sister, Life*.[12]

Pasternak dedicated *My Sister, Life* to Mikhail Lermontov. In a letter to Eugene M. Kayden he had expounded on the meaning of this dedication. He writes:

I dedicated *My Sister, Life* not to the memory of Lermontov but to the poet himself as though he were living in our midst—to his spirit still effectual in literature. What was he to me, you ask, in the summer of 1917?—the personification of creative adventure and discovery, the principle of everyday free poetical statement.[13]

Pasternak was very much concerned with both Alexander Pushkin and Mikhail Lermontov. His esthetics was primarily based on Pushkin's realism, which has universal application. In *My Sister, Life,* Pasternak had not yet matured to the level of such concreteness. In "Tema" ("The Theme") of *Themes and Variations,* he places Pushkin alongside the Greek sphinx, a symbol of the sun-god, and recognizes in him, in the poem "Derivative Variation" ("Podrazhatelnaya variyatsiya"), the prophet who "stood fierce in his revolt," who felt, as Pasternak himself had felt in the 1920's "the story of his life," because "Tomorrow lived upon his lips/ As others lived with yesterdays" (trans. Kayden). In a second poem, "Originalnaya variyatsiya" ("Original Variation"), Pasternak sees Pushkin as a unifier of "two separate worlds,"... "Free primitive passion linked with/ The freedom of passion in verse." Trebizond, the ancient Turkish seaport and a cultural and spiritual crossroad between east, west, and south, provides the setting where "Twin gods for a day embattled,/ Twin seas... / Twin dramas of two ancient acts" are transformed and united by conflict.

In Lermontov, Pasternak found the needed "independent confessional note"[14] for which he longed. Pasternak's realism of that time was subjective, a realism for himself and not for others, as Korney Chukovsky[15] has so fittingly recognized it in his introduction to the Russian poetry collection of 1966.

Lydia Pasternak-Slater remembers *My Sister, Life* as

Pasternak's most celebrated book of poems. The more sophisticated younger generation of literary Russians went wild over the book. . . . Each reader discovered individually and for himself that these poems were the spontaneous outburst of a genius, of a poet by "the grace of God."[16]

But compared to the later poetry, Mrs. Pasternak-Slater willingly acknowledges that "some of these early poems really were too complicated, too cryptic, perhaps too hastily written, and had too many easy escapes into the brilliance of sound and words."[17] D. L. Plank echoes this observation in his study of Pasternak's sound and imagery, a book which is just as intangible as the poetry which it tries to illuminate. Somewhat rhetorically, almost Biblically, Plank pronounces: "The word becomes thematic in the poetry of Pasternak."[18] But then, in his own interpretation, he veils theme and meaning of that poetry in the mystery of the same Klein bottle (according to Plank, a bottle without either inside or outside) and warns that one should "be very cautious when trying to fill such a container."[19]

There is content, even in Pasternak's early poetry. To be sure, the social and political themes are not central in these early cycles, and yet, Pasternak calls *My Sister, Life* a book of the Revolution.[20] Not a single poem of *My Sister, Life* deals directly with political events. Neither can we find described in it the individual episodes of which there are so many in *Doctor Zhivago* or even in his earlier prose. But in most of Pasternak's poems of *My Sister, Life* and *Themes and Variations* the pulsation of the Revolutionary epoch can be felt very strongly.

One might be tempted to look for the unifying or central theme of *My Sister, Life* in the third poem which bears the same title as the book. But the poem does not render such insight. We only learn that the poet is in a plight, that his mirage—his creativity—is asleep and that the sun—which stands for life—grieves with him. However, much later, in "Davay ronyat slova" ("Let's strew our Words") the poet's answer to the question "who still ordains" is this: "The Almighty God of love,/ The Almighty of details." And he concludes: "But life, like Autumn silence,/ Is rich in all details." It is this abundance of detail that the poet has tried to capture in that war-torn summer of 1917.

The image of dust, mostly representing death and destruction, is heightened in conjunction with such verbs and phrases as "grind" ("About My Verses"—Pro eti Stikhi), "choke," ("Definition of the Soul"—Opredelene dushi), or "swallowed up the pills of raindrops," in "Sultry Night," a poem full of allusions to the Revolution and bloodshed.

Pasternak is concerned with many other "details" of life in *My Sister, Life*. The poem "About My Verses" might suggest that, in a time of upheaval and civil war, the poet tries to shield himself against the pressures of the time by "smoking with Lord Byron,/ Drinking with Edgar Allan Poe," with Lermontov, in other words, with the past which is more objective than the present. However, his request to the "outsiders" for information on "what millennium have we today," sounds more like an irony directed towards those who try to change life forcefully than a display of the poet's ignorance of historical developments. Direct reference to meetings of Revolutionary councils is made in "Leto 1917 goda" ("Summer 1917").

Pasternak's early poetry also projects categories of goodness, of love, of human decency, and of loss of harmony with nature. A few quatrains from the poem "Patterns" demonstrate this best:

> O wretched homo sapiens
> Entangled in his strife!
> The few alone contrive
> To live a gallant life.
>
> The many, starved in mind,
> Turn brutish, feel undone,
> And miss the miracles
> Of trees and air and sun.
> (trans. E. M. Kayden)

The poet also tells us, as exemplified by Desdemona and Ophelia, in the poem "Uroki angliyskogo" ("English Lessons") that death, "the pool of night" removes all passion (synonymous with the "wretched homo sapiens" of the above quoted poem), but that love is everlasting and shall be "transfused in light."

In spite of this short note of optimism, we find loneliness and sadness in this cycle. The third poem of *My Sister, Life*, "Plachushchy sad" ("The Weeping Garden") speaks of a loneliness from which there is no escape without hope, "no gleam of light to be seen./ Only choking sobs and the splash of slippers/ And sighs and tears between" (trans. E. M. Kayden).

Loneliness and sadness are also the mood in the poem "Mein Liebchen..." in which life, perhaps the poet himself, is in danger of being destroyed in dust and pouring rain, while nature, in this poem identical with "Mein Liebchen," remains beautiful, eternal day. Most poems of *My Sister, Life* and of *Themes and Variations* are filled with this mood of spiritual emptiness and unfulfillment. The epigraph to *My Sister, Life* states in a nutshell the dominating atmosphere which prevails in Pasternak's early poetry. This quotation from Nikolaus Lenau's poem "Das Bild" reads as follows:

> There's murmur in the woods
> And thunderstorm glides above on wings
> Into this vehemence I draw
> Thy image, my beloved girl.

Lenau despises the threat of the elements and uses their wrath, metaphorically speaking, as a blackboard on which he draws images of his idol and his ideals. And this is precisely what Pasternak did in 1917. In order not to lose his soul, his integrity, while destruction and death swept his country, he kept his life and his strength because he kept his ideals. For his "Mädchen" is, above all, nature and it is his union with nature that enables him to remain true to himself and alive while others perish.

Pasternak's poem "Encounter," in *Themes and Variations,* testifies as to how a poet, who becomes more and more alienated in a world that surrounds him, can find new ways and new allies in expressing his independent confessions. Nature and time become the poet's only confidants:

> The March Night and the author walked
> In a hurry home [from a meeting], but spied from time
> To time a phantom flashing past them,
> Or vanishing before their eyes.
>
> (trans. E. M. Kayden)

It is the dawn, the tomorrow, which is being revealed to the pair, and Pasternak explains that houses, trees, temples, i.e., nature, as well as man's creations were just "as lost, as alien in this world" as man himself. But it was Pasternak's conviction that man in harmony with nature will always have a tomorrow. Nevertheless, a new code of behavior had to be acquired. The following quatrain of the above-mentioned poem is symptomatic of how man had to act in those days in order to survive:

> The pair soon spoke in hexameters.
> They slipped to right across the frame.
> But trimmers were dragged off for dead,
> And no one ever marked their loss.
> (trans. E. M. Kayden)

To speak in hexameters means to disguise thoughts and concerns, and if we read instead of "frame" the word "restrictions," placed upon the poet by time and events, and instead of "trimmers" the word "critics," then the stanza becomes self-explanatory, and also Pasternak's literary career, after 1923, will be understood.

The poem "Poesia" is representative of the poet's concern with life's detail, the central theme of both cycles. "Poesia" is an expression of the poet's total commitment to poetry. Poetry, as the poet sees it, is not only a reflection of the beauties of life, "a stiff-shirt, prim sweet singer" (Kayden). Poetry is all-embracing; it is the sum total of everyday life; it includes the average citizen who lives in the suburbs and commutes to and from work third class, "not gay with song but still with fear" (trans. E. M. Kayden). A sincere poet, according to Pasternak, must have only one want and pray for this:

> When undoubted truths, O Poetry,
> Are held like buckets at the taps,
> The hoarded stream will spout—for me
> In my open copy book to trap.
> (trans. E. M. Kayden)

For Pasternak, the experience of life's everyday details had become history, and he reproduced best the fusion of time and history in the above two cycles both by expressing his own feelings and emotions and through description of unnoticeable motions in nature. Life's details are for Pasternak the essence of life, and by unifying essence, the realities of the immediate with the eternal in his poetry, even Pasternak's early poetry transcends his "many and highly unorthodox attempts to define poetry and the creative process."[21] The many inexplicable images in Pasternak's early poetry become more accessible if it is realized that his entire early poetry is guided by the organizing principle of metonymy[22] in which the poet is inclined to ignore distinct dividing lines between characteristics of accepted concepts and conventional descriptions of things.

Many of Pasternak's recurring images, such as the color "lilac" (used in more than half a dozen poems of the above discussed two cycles, in his short stories, and also later in *Doctor Zhivago*), dust, rain, the seasons of the year, remain enigmatic, and shall continue to attract literary critics in spite of Fyodor Stepun's prudent suggestion that all the strange images in Pasternak's works are "justified because they do not call for clarification or interpretation."[23] Yet, Pasternak wanted to be read and understood. In *My Sister, Life* and *Themes and Variations,* the attempt was made, as V. Veydle has suggested, to reconcile thought with sound.[24] To the task of reconciliation, Pasternak devoted himself in his four major epic poems.

IV   *The Epic Poems*

The High Malady, the first of Pasternak's four epics, essentially relates how a poet observes and reflects the action of people, events, and the changing realities which took place immediately after the Revolution of 1917, even though Pasternak wrote the poem several years afterward. A true epic poem in imitation of the classical epics on Troy (we read in the beginning of *The High Malady*) can be written only after "years pass away—and all is in shadow."[25] However, the poet speaks with tongue-in-cheek when he laments his own music which is still with him "in an age that casts such shadows." Perhaps he too should have become a man of action, but instead he and his fellow poets had conceived the passion for free story telling during the years of the Revolution. Pasternak deplores the fact that the limitations on the freedom of creativity have become too apparent. The official point of view is decreed, and all trespasses will be forgiven to him who adjusts and paves his verse accordingly.

Whether or not the description of the Ninth Congress of Soviets and the poet's magnetism for Lenin constitute such poetic pavement of the "accepted point of view" must remain speculation. *The High Malady* is ambiguous not only in title, but also in content. Referring to earlier years, the poet asks: "Tell me now,/ What was I trying then to say," but a few lines later concedes "that everything is still the same." The lines about Lenin, "When suddenly he grew up on the tribune,/ And grew up there before he entered," are ironic. "He ruled the current of ideas/ And in this way the country too," sounds like an accolade to genius and wisdom, but is, in fact, what Pasternak has condemned so harshly in *Doctor Zhivago.*

And what about those final lines of the poem: "Endlessly I thought and thought/ About his authorship and rights/ To venture [or to dare] in the first person." Does the poem end with a note of skepticism toward unlimited authority, all in the name of genius? Furthermore, from what is the poet to awake, if not from being lulled into blind acceptance of endless narrations in which "truth and falsehood [are] all entangled," from lethargy, which Pasternak already in the mid-1920's must have recognized as a dangerous malady to the mind. Michel Aucouturier[26] feels that the poet's relationship to his time, i.e., art's relationship to the Revolution, was the major problem of that epoch and is also the major theme of this poem. Yet what or who is this "high" or "lofty" malady? It is quite conceivable that Pasternak could have had in mind the most sophisticated, the highest level of a power that was able to mystify the mind and emotions. If the "He" towards the end of the poem is really pointing to Lenin, as the Soviet edition of 1965[27] suggests, then the title, *The High Malady,* which is the crown of the hypnotic power to lull men "to sleep," might very well point to Lenin—and this in spite of Pasternak's seemingly favorable remarks on Lenin in various other places. Just a few lines, taken from the poem itself, may stimulate further thought on this matter:

> He might have been discussing oil,
> But his body's animated line
> Breathed the bare kernel of the thing
> Which had burst through the stupid husk.

Or toward the very end of the poem:

> When he referred to plainest facts,
> He knew that, rinsing out their mouth

With his own vocal extract, through them
In person history was bawling.
(trans. G. Reavey)

Of interest also is the attitude that this "He" has toward history. The revised poem camouflages direct mention of history, but in the earliest edition we can read this rather anti-Pasternakian couplet: "He was always ready to quarrel with history/ Only with history he was curt." Yet in the first sixteen lines, in the prologue of the poem, history is very important. Only out of history can epic be born, says Pasternak.

The style of *The High Malady* is unique because of its wealth of oxymorons, puns, crosscurrents of thought, and paradoxes. Thus, we read of "the joy of his [the intellectual-idealist's] decline," of the poet's lifelong wish "to be like all"—but ironically the current reverses itself and "this our age/ Proves stronger than my whimper/ And desires to be like me [the poet]"—or of "him" who was "with ages' envy, envious,/ And jealous with their jealousy."

Structurally the poem has, like a play, five distinct parts. The first sixteen lines, as mentioned above, represent some sort of prologue or exposition; and if the other four parts are not exactly comparable to four dramatic acts, the total of the poem resembles in its structure, at the least, a dramatic monologue.

The second part of the poem consists of a narrative about situations which narrator and fellow intellectuals alike had to endure "in those days." The third part begins with the narrator's experience at the Ninth Congress of the Soviets and ends with that rather "stupid" act, as the narrator himself has identified it, of sending to the victims of the 1924 Tokyo earthquake "routine Trade Union agit-print." It is immediately after this frustrating exercise that the fourth part begins with the appeal to the poet that he wake up. The last and fifth part is fully taken up by the enigmatic "He." *The High Malady* displays throughout its text various levels of meaning, but in the last part these levels have been applied with great skill and epic craftsmanship.

The Year 1905 is an epic reflection of events which influenced Pasternak for the rest of his life. On the genesis of this work, Pasternak himself recorded, in 1926, the following: "I have worked and I am still working on the poem about the year 1905. To be sure, this is not really a poem but simply a chronicle of the year 1905 in poetic form."[28] The poem, however, goes beyond a mere account of historical events or particular incidents which remain especially engraved in the memory of the poet. A year later the poet augmented his original statement. Now he is very much concerned with capturing the spirit of the time, and because of this, Pasternak wrote in the journal *Na literaturnom postu* (1927, No. 4): "I am changing from lyrical thinking to epic thinking, which, indeed, is very difficult."

For a historically minded chronicler, Pasternak was too selective. Although he marches from December to December with a mixture of epic and lyric, linked with each other only by *The Year 1905*, the seven independent sections that follow the introductory part deal, above all, with representative historical events and with a few personalities around whom the author builds his reflections into an epic echo.

As was the case in *The High Malady*, here too the author begins the poem with an introduction in which he defines more precisely than ever before his subject, which is the Revolution, and with its allusions to the Joan of Arc of the Siberian convicts, he suggests—without inflicting on the reader a restricted point of view—the mood and spirit of the poem. The pluralistic titles of individual chapters in the poem, such as "The Fathers," "Students," "Peasants and People in Factories," or the "Mutiny on the Sea," and "Moscow in December," are an attempt to obliterate the distinct contours of the individual, and place time itself as the central hero of the poem.

The first part of the poem under the heading "Fathers" is mostly a lament about fleeting time and traditions. In spite of his memorial to Sophie Perovskaya, who was hanged for her attempted attack on the Czar, or to the revolutionary Nechaev, the poet recognizes that the fathers are out of harmony with time.

The second part, "Childhood," is autobiographical. The poet remembers his home, events, the people he met, and his never forgotten idol, the divine Scriabin. The entire chapter consists of memories reproduced through a kaleidoscopic interchange of flashing details and into an organic unity of experienced reality.

December, in this chapter, is full of tension and anticipation. The difference becomes especially apparent when we compare this December in Petersburg with the December in the last chapter, after the Moscow demonstrations, with all its enforced order, house searches, interrogations, and arrests. "Childhood" depicts the march to the Czar's palace in Petersburg, the enthusiasm for the leader of the march, the priest Gapon, the confrontation with the police, the assassination of the Grand Duke Sergey Alexandrovich, and ends with the poet's approval of the political turmoil and dissent which Pasternak himself had observed and experienced when he was fifteen.

The other chapters of the poem, with the exception of "Moscow in December," concentrate on a single incident, and in this singularity they reflect the spirit among factory workers and their suppressors during a revolt in the Polish city of Lodz, the mutiny on the battleship "Potyomkin," and the march of students mourning their fellow student Bauman, who had been killed on October 18, 1905. All this flows into a final lyrical chapter, "Moscow in December," where the city dreams and the sun looks through binoculars and listens to the rattling of weapons, to the lost hopes for ultimate freedom, and to the confusion of people until the white flags are finally raised and the Cossacks again patrol the streets, as before.

It appears that the writing of this poem did not come easily to Pasternak. But, as we now know, Pasternak was encouraged by the knowledge that "my beloved master, Rainer Maria Rilke, knew of my existence..."[29] and by Marina Tsvetaeva's "Poema Kontsa" ("Poem of the Finale"), which Pasternak has called "a lyrical work of rare depth and power."[30] And Pasternak continues in the same paragraph: "These two facts were of such a concentrated impact that, were it not for them, I would never have brought to completion my work on *The Year 1905*."

Lieutenant Schmidt is the second ideological poem which deals with the Revolution of 1905. Contrary to *The Year 1905*, it is concerned with only one episode, the mutiny on the battleship "Potyomkin," and is generally less lyrical in style than his previous work. Nevertheless, the poem makes possible two stylistic approaches: narrative and dialogue alternate throughout the poem, and the narrations of the poem have not lost the lyric power of the early Pasternak.

Lieutenant Schmidt is a young officer who joins the mutinous sailors in the port of Sevastopol and, through bravery and courage, takes command of his own ship and later on of a fleet of eleven vessels. However, once out of harbor, the fleet is overcome by a superior force, and Schmidt is arrested. The rest of

the story is very simple: Schmidt is tried and loses his life. And
yet, as simple as the plot of this narrative may seem, the problems posed by Schmidt's willingness for self-sacrifice are more
complex than any expressed thought in the poem *The Year 1905*.
The problem of self-sacrifice also foreshadows Pasternak's greatest concern in his later poems and in *Doctor Zhivago*. Schmidt's
final defense is a masterpiece and, linked with the author's
ideology and expressed in poetic form, it is at the same time
a statement of faith and prophecy. The defendant tells his judges
that he is just as much part of the great changes as they are,
and that he accepts their sentence without hate and reproach.
They too, martyrs of the dogma, are victims of the age. He
even feels sorrow for his judges because he is convinced of the
providential wisdom of his mission. Schmidt concludes his
defense with this Messianic conviction:

> I know, the stake to which
> I'm led shall become the divider
> Of two different epochs of history.
> And I rejoice that I was chosen.
> (trans. J. W. Dyck)

Spectorsky is the last of the four epic poems. It "was planned
as 'a novel in verse,'" writes Gleb Struve, "and is closely related
to the prose work called *Povest*"[31] (*The Last Summer*). Some
characters and a few images are, indeed, the same in both works.
But *Spectorsky* remained incomplete. The fragment is highly
autobiographical and its setting is the time shortly before the
Revolution and during the Civil War in Russia. Three incidents
in Sergey Spectorsky's experience make up the structural frame
within which the author can meditate about and reflect on
history as experienced by himself and by those surrounding him.
   The poem's beginning reminds us of Goethe's "Zueignung" in
Faust. The author of *Spectorsky*, too, begins to write his poem
at a moment when leisure had returned, and, as he reminisces,
he begins to write blindly. At the same time, he cultivates
friendship with an unforgettable girl from Moscow.
   The first episode takes the reader to a "forgotten house" near
Moscow where friends often met before for other occasions, and
this time, for the Christmas festivities. Spectorsky, overwhelmed
by the beauty of life, and by the wonders of winter, suddenly
finds his love fully awakened for Olga, a married woman. Olga,

76

BORIS PASTERNAK

winter, and life itself grow hazy, melt into one another and create for Spectorsky, and we use the poet's own metaphor, a crack in the ice; and under the broken layer of ice Spectorsky finds, as before him many other poets discovered, "a cruelty of which she herself is the source."

Pasternak's main concern is not so much the relationship of two people overcome by passionate love, but the power of love itself. "We fall in love," the poem continues, "and we are done ... our work is gone ... we are condemned without a court and mute." Though it is realized that love is empty without dreams and without marvel, Spectorsky begins to crumble and he deserts his love. Six years later, Spectorsky meets Olga again. But this time she is with revolver and without smiles. Olga reminds him of that fateful Christmas party of the time before the Civil War and mercilessly announces: "I am a daughter of the Narodo-voltsy.[32] You couldn't grasp this at that time." From the dialogue between Spectorsky and Olga, Michel Aucouturier concludes: "With it she forces him to see in the new order in which he feels alien the continuation of a tradition that is admired by all Russian intellectuals."[33]

Whether or not Pasternak wanted to convince Spectorsky, or for that matter himself, that the spirit of Revolution and Civil War was the continuation of a tradition so much admired by the Russian intelligentsia, is difficult to establish. In spite of Olga's forceful confrontation, there is no reason to believe that she was able to change Spectorsky.

The second episode in *Spectorsky* speaks of the hero's quarrels with the time in which he lives. In fruitless and lengthy discussions with his sister Natasha, Spectorsky is accused of being out of tune with the time, and, therefore, cut off from his own generation. Yet, Spectorsky continues along his own path, and in his prophetic vision he sees how time will swallow everything that seems dear to him: the house, the people, and even the nights that veil his dreams.

The third incident relates how Spectorsky experiences idyllic love with Maria Ilyna, a poetess, who had much in common with him. Their meetings become more frequent, their love more passionate, and their conversation spills over into the hours of dawn. Verses, left by Maria, testify that for the two lovers thoughts about good and evil had lost their gravity. They were convinced, one of the poems says, that life has its darlings, and, "how painful! They do not count among the favorites."

Spectorsky loses Maria as he lost Olga, and there is no further mention of her in the final part of the fragment.

The above three incidents make neither a good story nor trace fully the spiritual life of either Spectorsky or, as it may be, of his creator. But it is the poet's attempt to fuse personal experience with the labyrinth of happenings and events. Experienced history reflected through the prism of a poet's life is Pasternak's major concern in this autobiographical novel in verse. The separate incidents, as chosen by the poet, exemplify that under whichever circumstances life may seem to end, in reality it only changes directions and in doing so assures itself of eternal renewal. For man, the author of *Spectorsky* has this message: "That you and life are ancient knick-knacks/ And loneliness is rococo." And further on, a few lines after this pronouncement, we read: "history is not a record of how we lived/ But an attestation of how we were left naked."

Spectorsky is, as we see it, a very modern character. Through him Pasternak posed the ever-growing problem of how an individual, initially in sympathy with a given ideology, is in danger of gradually being conditioned for spiritual submission to a reality which no longer reflects the truth as originally understood. Total spiritual submission, for Pasternak, was synonymous with total nakedness. *Spectorsky* had to remain unfinished because its creator was not ready for this nakedness.

The epic poems constitute a crossroad in Pasternak's poetic development. With *Spectorsky*, Pasternak "had found a direct poetic tone which allowed him to call things by their names."[34] Pasternak's later poetry, as we will see, displays greater simplicity and is more transparent in style and theme.

V   Second Birth

Vtoroe rozhdenie (Second Birth) is a cycle of lyric poetry which was first published in the year 1932, almost ten years after *Themes and Variations*. The poetry of this book is closely interwoven with Pasternak's personal life, and with the political and social developments of the late 1920's and the beginning of the 1930's. The capricious storms of the Revolution and the Civil War had blown over, the NEP (New Economic Policy)

seemed to have aimed in a direction of a more just redistribution
of wealth (however, in *Doctor Zhivago,* Pasternak refers to
this period as to the most treacherous in all of Soviet history),
and as far as Pasternak was concerned, Socialism, to which the
poet had always looked with hope, should have started its
voyage in full sail towards promised utopia. But nothing of the
sort happened, at least not as far as Pasternak could make out.
Instead, the political air was darkened with dangerous intrigue,
personal ambitions, and deadly quarrels. The deportation of
Leo Trotsky marked the beginning of a new political era
for Soviet Russia.

The full impact of this event revealed itself only between
1930 and the beginning of World War II, a decade during
which Joseph Stalin, self-assured by his wisdom and will, had
demanded absolute loyalty and received frustrated obedience.
Pasternak, earlier than most of his contemporaries, recognized
that political and social realities were moving away from early
ideals. Some reference to such deviations, coupled with poetic
skepticism, is already present in Pasternak's epic poems which
were published between the years 1924 and 1928.

A second major experience that dominated the author's poetic
outbursts of those years was Mayakovsky's sudden death on
April 14, 1930. The unexpected end of a poet, whom Pasternak
at the same time admired and rejected, came as a shock. He
commemorates this unique Russian phenomenon in *Safe Conduct*
which was published one year after Mayakovsky's death. Pasternak begins his fourteenth chapter in Part III of *Safe Conduct*
with this rather general opening sentence: "I shall tell of that
eternally recurring strangeness which may be called the poet's
last year" (*SC,* 115). With reflections from Pushkin's days and
with an eye on Mayakovsky, he views the time of an author's
creativity as "a kind of inhuman youth" (*SC,* 117), burdened
with loneliness and helplessness. In a moving finale he portrays
the sorrows of friends and relatives at Mayakovsky's deathbed.
Pasternak dramatizes despair by recreating that moment of
high tension when Olga, Mayakovsky's sister, recited a poem
of despair which her brother had written not too long before
his death:

> And feeling the "I" is not enough for me!
> Someone is stubbornly breaking out of me.

Hello!
Who speaks!? Mother?
Mother! Your son is exquisitely sick.
Mother! His heart is on fire.
Tell his sisters, Lyuda and Olya,
There was no place of refuge left for him.[35]

A third experience that played such a decisive role in Pasternak's poetic mood of this time was very personal. In 1931, he separated from his first wife, Evgenia, and travelled with Zinaida Neuhaus, the wife of a composer and friend, to Georgia where he was the guest of the poet Paolo Yashvili. Zinaida became Pasternak's second wife. Although Evgenia soon left temporarily for Germany, the loss of his son and the final break with a life to which he had grown so much accustomed stirred up painful memories. In spite of separation and remarriage, Pasternak could not easily free himself from his feelings for his family, and it is primarily out of this duality that Pasternak experienced another urge for lyric creativity. In his imaginary letter to Rilke, written after Rilke's death, Pasternak has described, in forceful images, what both Evgenia and Zinaida meant to him. A single smile on the shining face of Evgenia reminds the author of the Italian Renaissance. "A smile enkindled from outside, she resembles one of the females portrayed by Ghirlandaio. . . . And inasmuch as she always needed happiness to please" (*Soch.*, II, 344). But Pasternak is also captivated by another image. His love for Zinaida Neuhaus was young and, therefore, passionate, and passionate love to Pasternak was synonymous with life. "I know a face," he writes, "which equally teases and cuts in sorrow and in joy, and, the more often one surprises it, in positions where others long would have lost their charm, the more beautiful it becomes."

Perhaps Pasternak had lost his passion for his first wife, but he could not easily forget that eternal femininity that had remained in his memory even after his passion had subsided. Eternal femininity and passion rival each other in the poetry of *Second Birth*. The poet's ever-present feeling of guilt sets the mood in the very first poem of this cycle. The first quatrain of "Volny" ("Waves") reads:

> Here all things meet: The past I have
> so long endured, the truths I now

> live by, my values, aspirations,
> the whole of life that I avow.
>
> (trans. E. M. Kayden)

And then later in the poem: "When my melancholy is running at its fullest/ All my conducts stand before me."

Although the group of poems under the collective title "Waves" is concerned with each of the three major themes—love, Socialism, and nature—love, with its longings and passions as opposed to reasoning, is the strongest poetic energy and dominates almost each poem of the entire cycle.

The Caucasian Mountains and the province of Georgia are compared to the Garden of Eden, to Paradise. The poem "While we are climbing the Caucasus" alludes to the sinful act of tasting the forbidden apple: "Caucasus, Caucasus, what am I to do?" But the Caucasus also represents to the poet something similar to what Italy meant to Goethe. The Caucasus is a land "where the hinges of passion do not squeak," we read in section VIII of "Volny." Georgia itself is defined in section VI of the same group of poems as a place created after multiplying need by tenderness and hell by heaven; while the image of man, in this land of grandeur and unlimited beauty, is the reflection of success and work, duty and air, mixed with heaven and earth.

Socialism, as a philosophy on the basis of which society could be structured, can only be appreciated in terms of nature. Section VIII of "Volny" deals almost exclusively with Socialism. Pasternak, the author, is in favor of Socialism, but only in the name of life. "In the name of life, where we got together,— changeover!" But later on in this section, he warns that one should not seek revenge while exchanging one way of life for another, one should rather give everything that one possesses.

In section VII of "Volny," the poet makes reference to "our general plan" (later on in this cycle, he speaks of the Second Five-Year-Plan) and wishes that in planning a better society men would be willing to imitate nature. He ends his poem with these words:

> There'd be no time for us to wangle,
> To face suspicion, or to forgive;
> Instead of merely writing verses,
> I would my poems truly live.
>
> (trans. E. M. Kayden)

In the poems of *Second Birth,* the author's views on society are often interwoven with personal concerns, and nature is always the teacher. Forest, mountains, the sea, and the sky are major, recurring images in this cycle. In Poem V of "Volny," the forest in spring is the great example from which man and society can learn. Each year a forest renews itself without external help, without taking from others. Poetically the poet expresses it this way:

> It [the forest] took neither the fauna from the pheasant
> Nor from the stately fairy-cliffs—
> It kept itself captivated. As a recital
> It knew much and informed.
>
> (trans. J. W. Dyck)

Self-renewal is the key to continuity, and simplicity is the basic prerequisite in the process of renewal. The second to last poem of "Volny" speaks of an unheard simplicity which alone can procure the future. With this call for simplicity in expression and style, *Second Birth* becomes a crossroad in Pasternak's development as an artist, as the background of this poetry had been a crossroad in Pasternak's personal life. The two ballads of the cycle are symbolic of the two women who, the poet realizes, release energies within him which are opposed to each other. In the first ballad there are "all the temptations of youth," there is "prayer and ecstasy." In the second ballad the poet dreams that he has been taken back to hell, and the complex interrelationship of the poetic "I" to women and children is again before him. His mind keeps wandering back into the past, until, in the final stanza, the poet begs: "Sleep past. Sleep life a long, deep sleep/ You ballad fall asleep, sleep saga,/ As one sleeps only in early childhood."

In the poem "Leto" ("Summer"), the poet is overcome by a loneliness which takes him close to despair. Diotima comes to his mind, and emphatically he asks: "With what kind of boldness can one break away from this slumber?/ From the avenues of the heart, out of the darkness void of people!" One thought, however, has a ray of hope: "Immortality, perhaps, is a last pledge."

The next poem begins with laments for and memories of his lost family. He cannot forget the old home and the families that were suffering because of him. But after this initial sorrow, the poem turns to the irresistible force of his new love, and the poet finds justification in this new power, because in it he recognizes the source of his poetry, of his immortality.

The familiar "Thou" is used beginning with the poem "Lyubit' inykh tyazhely krest" ("To love others is a burdensome cross"). In this poem the narrator sees an analogy between the beauty of a woman and a key which can unlock life itself. The poem "Lyubimaya..." ("My Love...") speaks again of the poet's helplessness. But knowing that the "Thou," his love, is also his creative source, the poet is convinced that fame is the lure of the soil, and that he shall enter his native speech "not as a vagabond but as kinsman." The poem ends with the desire to eternalize his love in poetic form, and expresses hope that some day others will drink from the same cup and experience what now the poet and his love are experiencing. The poem "Krasavitsa moya..." ("My beautiful...") continues with the same theme. The poem reads: "Thy entire being pleases my heart./ It all wants to turn into music,/ And it all calls for poetry." And in the fourth stanza we read this confession: "And in poetry breathes that love,/ which here is difficult to endure."

Toward the end of the cycle, the poet's love, his poetry, and nature merge into one single "Thou" and thus they make true communication possible and meaningful. In the first poem of the group under IV, the "Thou" has become so much a part of the poet's life that he wants everything removed that is irrelevant to his personal concerns. The next poem, although still overshadowed by a feeling of "unforgiven guilt," assures the "Thou" of the future. This future we find described later on in *Doctor Zhivago*. Yury, too, has a vision of Lara, after Lara has left with Komarovsky, a vision reminiscent of this:

> You will appear there in the doorway
> In something white, in something plain,
> In something straight out of those fabrics
> From which the flakes of snow are sewn.
> (trans. J. M. Cohen)

Faith in the future is the final phase of a hopeful melody of *Second Birth*. The poet is fully aware of his inner struggle and of the uncertainties into which the Second Five-Year-Plan may take "the theses of the soul." Remorse and tears are still with the poet. Nevertheless, two women shine in the midst of his burdensome life, like lamps of Svetlan. All his life, the poet laments, he could have cried because of woman's chains, the torments which are placed upon her. But now in the poem, "Kogda ya ustayu..." ("When I grow tired...") the poet is suddenly overcome by an unrivalled hope: "We are in the future, I assure them, as everyone will be who lived in these days." Only this hope makes the present bearable, and it is out of this duplicity between hope and despair that the poet needs his verses "more than ever." His verses are his therapy. In the poem "Stikhi moi, begom, begom" ("My verses, hurry, hurry") the poet proclaims, "I send you, I send you and that means I love." Love thus becomes, at least for Pasternak, the major source of true poetry.

In the last poem of the cycle, love, nature, and *das ewig Weibliche* merge their images in an irreversible promise of a future. Nature is a purifying force. "My spring, don't grieve./ Thy hour of sadness coincides/ with the transfiguration of light." The tales of centuries, as the poem concludes, are in essence records of man's inability to cope with beauty which, like the salt of the earth, is constant in its purpose and, therefore, the crown of creativity.

For Pasternak, true lyric poetry could be nothing else but poetic expression of the most personal experience. At the Writers' Plenum in Minsk in 1936, he publicly confessed that he could not adjust to a poetry which bends primarily in the service of a social or political system. Courageously he announced: "I have no choice: I am now living all this, and I cannot do otherwise."[36]

After *Second Birth*, Pasternak grew silent and only toward the end of the Second World War when, as we read in *Doctor Zhivago*, "a freedom of spirit" seemed to fill the air, did the poet once again unveil his lyric voice. The cycle *On Early Trains* was published in 1943 and *Spacious Earth* in 1945.

VI On Early Trains

The period between the years 1934 and 1943 was one of the most difficult in Pasternak's life and career. The publication of *The Last Summer*, in 1934, marked the beginning of almost ten years of silence of a poet who had not only won acclaim in his own country but also abroad. Several events in Pasternak's private life, as well as impinging developments on the Russian literary stage, are in the background of this artificially imposed oblivion. Pasternak had married for the second time and moved to Peredelkino, near Moscow. A year later, in 1935, he attended an international writers' congress in Paris. From a report[37] by Josephine Pasternak, the author's younger sister, who at that time lived in Germany, it becomes clear that Pasternak suffered in those years not only physically, but also spiritually. His journey to Paris started in a sanatorium near Moscow. How he was put into new clothes with the help of a government official and then hurried off to an international congress already in progress, sheds some light on Pasternak's public and personal life of the mid-1930's. Although the author had seemingly withdrawn from original writing into translating Georgian poetry and some Western Classical writers, various scenes for future work must have been in Pasternak's uppermost thoughts. As early as 1935, during his meeting with his sister in Berlin, Pasternak was mostly concerned with the enigmatic force of beauty. He told his sister the following:

You know, I owe it to Zina—I must write about her. I will write a novel. . . . A novel about that girl. . . . Beautiful, misguided. A veiled beauty in the private rooms of night restaurants. . . . Her cousin, a guardsman would take her there. She, of course, could not help it. She was so young, so unspeakably attractive. . . .[38]

It was also in the year 1934, when the various literary circles in Russia were abolished, that the Union of Soviet Writers, hence the only writers' association permitted, was founded. Socialist Realism was defined and soon became the only accepted mode of Soviet writing. Pasternak was not able to limit his creativity to the prescribed rules and restrictions. He never wrote in the style of Socialist Realism, and Josephine Pasternak might very well be right when she observes: "Now, looking back, I think that the year 1935 must indeed have been a turning point in his [Pasternak's] life."

Most of the poems of *On Early Trains* were written either in the year 1936 or 1941. In most Russian editions the cycle is subdivided into four major groups: The Artist, From Summer Notes, Peredelkino, and War Months. Already this grouping is an indication that in spite of his withdrawal from the literary scene, the poet was deeply concerned with the fate of Soviet

art, with his immediate surroundings in Peredelkino and in
Moscow, and with the war. The cycle begins with a lament.
The artist is in hiding and possessed by a feeling of shame
because of his own books. But he knows that no man can
escape his own fate, and that an artist is bound more to fate
than are others, because an artist is born by the warmth of the
earth. The most probing battle in an artist's life is that with
himself (*s samin soboy*). In an elegy for the poet Nikolay
Dementev, who died prematurely, Pasternak prophetically predicts a resurrection for this artist, perhaps only after fifty years.
Therefore, escape from the self is scarcely the answer for a
frustrated artist. "Is suicide really a way out?" he asks rhetorically in the last line of the poem.

The second group of poems, also gathered under the title
"Traveller's Notes," presents reminiscences, reflections, and
verbal portraits of Russia's South. Pasternak sings a hymn of
praise to his poet friend Paolo Yashvili, not so much for his
poetry as for his great humanity. He remembers their outings
on horseback and compares the beauty of Tiflis with the
gardens of David; he remembers the wild river Tereck, and
finally captures all of Georgia through the image of a rose. This
is how he describes it: One scarcely comes in contact with it,
and it is as if one were in heaven. But the author is also aware
of the suddenness of its disintegration. In this group, as in the
Peredelkino poems and in some of the early poems, nature is in
dialogue with man. The Peredelkino poems express the poet's
intimate belonging to the people and the landscape that surrounds him. While reading these poems, the familiar country
house near Moscow rises before us, surrounded by uncounted
white birches which accompany the author during his lonely
walks like the daughters in Goethe's "Erlkönig," and behind the
forest—a view into the distance, unpredictable and full of mystery. No more do we have in these poems a confusing play of
words. Style, form, and thoughts are transparent.

Pasternak's poems are now dominated by the immediate
and the concrete. He tells us about the people with whom he
makes his short train hikes from Peredelkino to Moscow and
back. In the poem "On Early Trains," from which the entire
cycle received its name, the poet expresses it very simply. Between wars and poverty, he says, "I got to know Russia and its

inimitable face." For the people in the trains, who were women,
students, workers, he has this word of praise:

> Hardship, its signs, they don't display
> As a result of past disasters,
> New situations, new dismay
> They bear like gentlemen and masters.
> (trans. J. W. Dyck)

Pasternak's poems of the war months breathe patriotism and
are full of awe before the greatness of history and its heroes.
The enemy, in his reckless despotism, is likened to Herod in
Jerusalem, men and women of besieged cities are proclaimed as
heroes, and the nation's will, not that of the state, is transformed into an ever-growing force and final victory.

"The Old Park," writes Reavey, "provides him [Pasternak]
with an opportunity for an historical confrontation of the Russian past and present."[39] But past and present do not really
confront each other. The image of Napoleon suggests rather
that history is about to repeat itself, whereas the mentioning
of Samarin and the challenge to the descendant of the Decem-
brist suggest that Russia has a rich past and, "if only there will
be enough strength," so thinks the wounded soldier, "He himself will write a play, inspired by the war," and thus secure the
future.

In 1943, Russia had suddenly changed. Before the Second
World War it had been the official Soviet opinion that any war
was in its intent either imperialistic or revolutionary, but never
patriotic. By the year 1943, everything seemed different. Famous
military leaders of Czarist Russia were celebrated in poems
and songs, great Czars and statesmen of the past were linked to
a country which now ceased to be only a union of republics,
politically neatly knit together, and again, as in the past, Russia
was proclaimed as consecrated and holy.

The one poem that thematically does not fit into the cycle is
the very personal poem "In Memory of Marina Tsvetaeva."
Tsvetaeva's sudden death in 1941 again reminded the poet
of time and place within the limitations of which half-truth
and self-deceit reigned. The only hope that was now left he
saw in the belief of resurrection, a theme that overshadows all
others in *Doctor Zhivago*. The poet wants to do something
that would have pleased his favorite poetess, but he becomes

aware that death does not reveal its contours and that his attempt will remain without results. However, the poet is certain that while Marina is turning her face from this earth toward God, the last word on her work has not yet been spoken.

VII   Spacious Earth

All poems of *Spacious Earth* were written in the years 1943 and 1944. They are even more topical than the poems of *On Early Trains*. All of the poems deal with the war, yet human events and acts of nature are closely interwoven with one another. So alternate the ugly and the beautiful in masterfully sculptured images and fill the lines of every single poem with promises of new hope and peace. In the poem "Vesna, 1944" ("Spring 1944"), everything is different than in previous springs. "Light and peace," writes the poet, fill the hearts. And as the fresh grass in spring heralds a general awakening, so will all Slavic races awaken.

> Morave and Czech and Yugoslavian
> Folk-lores in spring will rise and blossom,
> Tearing away the sheet of lawlessness
> That winters past had laid across them.
> (trans. Lydia Pasternak-Slater)

The poem "Smert sapera" ("Death of a Sapper") reads like a ballad in which the poet makes an inquiry into the half-conscious mind of a dying soldier. The soldier's thoughts go to his wife and to his children, and his love for them, says the poet, "cannot be destroyed, it shall remain forever."

The battle of Stalingrad is commemorated in the poem "Ozhivshaya freska" ("A Fresco Come To Life"). It is also in this poem where the image of a shrill voice of a nightingale and the image of Saint George are mixed into a soldier's memory of childhood years.

One of the weakest poems of this cycle is "Razvedchiki" ("Spearhead"). Its content with its superhuman heroism, patched together by chance and poor military knowledge, is artificial and unreal. Nevertheless, in spite of the intent to arouse hatred toward the enemy (a very non-Pasternakian trait) in several of the poems, *Spacious Earth* proclaims freedom and hope which, according to the author, will not only come as a result

of victorious military operations, but expand far beyond into a
new national consciousness and pride.

After this cycle, Pasternak relished a short interval of popu-
larity. But the desire for dialogue and free expression among
Soviet writers was not tolerated for too long a period. *Spacious
Earth* was Pasternak's last cycle of lyric poems published in the
Soviet Union during his lifetime. The lyric poems of *When the
Skies Clear,* the last and final cycle of Pasternak's poetry, was
only published after his death.

VIII   When the Skies Clear

Kogda razgulyaetsya (*When the Skies Clear*), also translated
as *When It Clears Up* or *A Rift in the Clouds,* is a collection of
more than fifty poems which are both personal and universal
in theme and, although less religious than the poems of Doctor
Zhivago, they express the author's deepest concern for the
individual and his relationship to fellow-men and to God. Among
the most frequently recurring themes of this cycle are the poet
himself, an artist friend (usually perished), the poet's concept
of woman, and, as in all previous poetry, nature. This last group
of Pasternak's poems becomes even more meaningful if one keeps
in mind the author's chosen motto. The epigraph, taken from
Marcel Proust, reads: "A book is a large cemetery where, on
most tombstones, the washed-out names can no longer be read."

The first two poems of the cycle permit us to look behind the
façade of a completed work of art. A lasting poem, as Pasternak
tells us in the poem "Vo vsyom mne khochetsya doyt'..." ("In
Everything I Strive...") comes into being after thought, experience, and poetic meditation are fused into one harmonious unity.
Yet he is fully aware that of all the poems which an author
writes, many will remain—for various reasons—illegible, like the
illegible names of the tombstones in a cemetery. The first poem
of *When the Skies Clear* is in itself an *ars poetica.* The poet
gives us all the ingredients which a poem with a claim for
immortality must have. First, the poet must always strive, perhaps like Faust strove, to penetrate to the heart of the matter
and try, as Reavey has translated it, "to live, think, feel and
love, and make discoveries." Yet the greatest challenge to the
poet is the mystery of passion. However, the very nature of
passion is unutterable, the poet has realized that. Nevertheless,

poetic creativity is longing for highest fulfillment. The poet is therefore willing to sacrifice much in exchange for eight successful lines in a similar way as Turgenev, a century earlier, was willing to give up all of his novels, if he could only have written one poem the way Pushkin wrote.

Pasternak's master-poem is brought to mind through the image of the garden with all its beauty and fragrance, but also its raving thunderstorms. Such perfection in artistic creation Pasternak could find only in the *Etudes* of Chopin.

The second poem rejects a poet's desire for fame. The real aim of creativity is not to be sought in pomp and immediate success, but, as translated into English: "To give your all—this is creation." Pasternak had modified his early view on the position of the artist. Victor Erlich has observed it very succinctly: "In the end," he writes, "Pasternak makes no special claims for the poet as a human being. . . . He simply urges him to be himself, to be and remain fully, richly, and if need be, defiantly human— in a word, 'alive.' "[40]

The poem "Dusha" ("The Soul") is a hymn in memory of those unfortunate ones who for almost forty years lived and died in agony. But even this poem, full of gloom and doom, transmits a ray of hope. The poet's soul, embracing "everything that is experienced here," shall continue to observe and grind it into lasting poetry.

The "Chetyre otryvke o Bloke" ("Four Fragments on Blok") echo the celestial wounds to which there seem to be no limit and which "turn fair hopes to dust." Blok was a prophet. He "saw the portents written in the sky." Nevertheless, he kept his purity of soul alive. "Veter" ("Wind") is the overall title of the four fragments, an image of Blok himself who expresses freedom and, as Pasternak puts it, is illustrious and eternal in nature, not belonging to any literary school or program, not molded by someone's hand, and this in spite of all the powerful sycophants who think they determine "who should remain alive and praised,/ Who should stay dead without renown."[41]

Once more, in the last lyric poetry cycle, Pasternak glorifies the existence of woman. The author always had a feeling of pity for women, perhaps because woman was his greatest inspiration for creativity. In the last poem of *Second Birth*, the poet had realized that "From my very childhood/ I was hurt by a woman's lot/ And a poet's vestige is no more/ Than the trail of a woman's way." Several of the poems in *When the Skies Clear* celebrate woman as the eternal source for continuous creation. In the poem "Posle pereryva" ("After the Interval") femininity appears through the image of winter, whispering to the poet, who seems to have been lost in idle trifle, to hurry with his poetry. "Zhenshchiny v detstve" ("Women in Childhood") ends with a gratitude to all women who had some, even the most minute, impact on the poet's life. "I will eternally remain in debt to them," reads the last line of the poem. In one of the very late poems, in "Bozhiy mir" ("God's World") one cannot help but think of Pasternak's exchange of correspondence with the German poetess, Renate Schweitzer. "Precious letters of women! I too have fallen from the sky./ I swear before you now and forever/ Yours I shall remain in all eternity."

"Vakkhanaliya" ("Bacchanalia") is indeed a festival in recognition of feminine beauty, which is freedom with unique immunity. According to Lydia Pasternak, it was a famous actress who provided the inspiration for this poem. The section on Mary Stuart suggests that charm and beauty can be a crime. "Borne as if a dragon-fly/ By her mother's will/ To wound and charm man's daring heart/ With female flattering chill." "And, perhaps, because of this," the author continues, "the daughter's head shall fall/ By the hand of the executioner." But the poet also knows from experience that "darkest prison vaults" weigh in vain on a person in whom "everything is freedom, life." Therefore, the poet predicts: "However, her heroic death/ In time so immemorial/ Henceforth will be surrounded/ By fame and lasting glory."

The latter part of the poem ignores the art of concealing the poet's own experience. The "someone" who drinks his cognac like a "strange maniac" silently and until dawn is no one else but the poet himself. He admits that he is imaginative in the company of women, but rather unsociable with men. The poet does not deny that in the past he may have been the cause for women's tears; nevertheless, for him, women always were the major source of creativity. "From women friends his gift/ He put in circulation/ Returning thus to them/ His world as his donation."

The cycle received its title from one of the poems which, writes George Katkov, "like all the rest in the series, was born of the atmosphere of relaxation and elated happiness which the poet enjoyed in his late sixties after his friend, Olga Ivinskaya, had been released in 1953 from her first spell in a concentration camp."[42] A very stimulating discussion of these late poems can be found in Angela Livingstone's article "Pasternak's Last Poetry." The critic sees an entirely "different relation to reality"[43] as the basis for Pasternak's late poems compared to his early works. Pasternak, writes Miss Livingstone, "no longer feels that, as poet, he will transform the given world into something new and intense and extraordinary. Instead, he will go along with it, letting its whole presence work on him, until it yields its own splendid moment, its promise, its own transformation."[44]

Oddly enough, after the article has shown how the poet has transgressed to a level of firmness, clarity, and purpose, after it becomes obvious that the rift in the sky or the thaw do not necessarily refer only to changes in the political atmosphere or in the life that surrounds the poet, but attend just as much to the poet's own inner transformation, the critic concludes that "the poems are often unsatisfying because the determination seems to exceed the force of his [Pasternak's] feeling about these things."[45] The above observation is in itself correct. With the years and with experience, the poet, indeed, had matured. He still realizes that passion is a fundamental force, an *Urkraft*, in the process of creativity—why else would he have wanted to write an eight-line poem about passion. Nevertheless, in his mature wisdom he has also recognized that passion, i.e., over-abundance of feeling, can also be defined as lack of freedom, especially inner freedom. And it is this inner freedom which a person must possess in order "not to have a tragic view of life," which, Miss Livingstone rightly observes, Pasternak cherished. His "insistence on simplicity" was, indeed, "the insistence on optimism."[46]

Pasternak is, we think, unjustly accused of standing at a greater distance from the world in his late poetry.[47] If spontaneous reaction to a given phenomenon or situation, if prudent self-control means that a person is less involved with the world, then Pasternak's relation to the world could be interpreted as complacent resignation. But such logic speaks against the facts of human maturation and, therefore, it seems to be too easy a way out if we interpret Pasternak's relationship to the world as this: "He adds it up, recognizes its sum as right and good, and then leaves it: it is not any more his world."[48] In any case, the last quatrain of the poem "When It Clears Up" testifies to the contrary:

> World, Nature, Universe's Essence,
> With secret trembling, to the end,
> I will thy long and moving service
> In tears of happiness attend.
>   (trans. Lydia Pasternak-Slater)

In evaluating this last cycle of Pasternak's poetry, various critics have stressed different aspects of its content and, therefore, often differ in their conclusions. Kayden maintains that in *When the Skies Clear,* Pasternak "stands closest to the main traditions of Russian Realism by addressing himself to his readers with the quiet passion and detachment characteristic of Pushkin."[49] Robert Payne expresses his thoughts somewhat similarly to Miss Livingstone, when he writes that Pasternak "in the quietness of resignation, writing poems which are almost bare of emotion, yet colored by religious feeling ... waited for the coming storm."[50] And George Reavey feels that the mood of these late poems "is devotional and, in the end, ecstatic."[51]

Yet, Pasternak's late poems are less passionate than some of those in the early cycles. They are devotional, but never completely detached from the poet's reality, never bare of emotion, and hardly ecstatic. In Pasternak's late poems one senses an ever-present current of cautious optimism, which, as Reavey has recognized, "ultimately is both holy and happy."[52]

IX   *The Poetry of* Doctor Zhivago

It has been said on various occasions that without the poems of Doctor Zhivago, Pasternak's novel would remain incomplete, and his major character meaningless and an inexcusable non-entity. To a certain extent, and especially from the artistic point of view, this might be true. But even without these poems, the novel renders a wealth of spiritual and factual history to the memory of those who experienced directly or indirectly events and times which are so vividly pictured by Pasternak. At the same time, *Doctor Zhivago* bears witness, as the author himself saw it, for the uninformed and for future generations. Furthermore, if the argument is valid that the novel is meaningless without the support of the twenty-five poems, then it is just as questionable whether or not the poems without the novel can claim artistic independence and exclusiveness in purpose. Yet it is commonly agreed that the poems of Doctor Zhivago are among the best of Pasternak's entire poetry. They not only constitute a commentary on the novel, but can speak to us apart from the novel. They form a poetic cycle, similar to the author's other poetry, with a principal theme—life in its entirety—and they are rich in imagery drawn not only from Yury Zhivago's life, but universal in their source and application. In short, the poems of Doctor Zhivago can be read as an independent artistic structure.

That the twenty-five poems have their primary source in the novel itself has been suggested by Donald Davie[53] and other critics. Davie's reading of the novel with a particular eye on the relationship between the prose chapters and the poetry has linked each poem to one or more episodes in the novel and thus provided many answers to some of Doctor Zhivago's poetic parables which, without such mutual enrichment, could be dismissed as mere mystifying rhetoric. Davie is especially concerned with the religious poems of this group. But also poems such as "Belaya noch" ("White Night"), "Vesennyaya rasputitsa" ("Spring Floods") or "Svad'ba" ("The Wedding Party") are skillfully wrested from the prosaic part of Doctor Zhivago's odyssey. Future discussions of Doctor Zhivago's poetry cannot bypass this source. Nevertheless, this cycle, as any of Pasternak's earlier poetry, can claim poetic independence without severing its undeniable affinity with its source.[54]

Among the especially informative critical contributions on this poetry cycle are articles by Rosette C. Lamont,[55] Dimitri Obolensky, F. D. Reeve, and Ludolf Möller. R. C. Lamont has pointed out that "the order of the poems of the Appendix is not chronological, but harmonic."[56] Both Lamont and Reeve assign to the various poetic measures certain musical qualities and suggest that the poems are "Musically efficient compositions,"[57] and arranged not according to themes, meaning, or the messages which each of the poems conveys, but that solemnity of the poetic rhythm is the guiding principle in this literary orchestration. Lamont observes: "Pasternak builds tonal architecture by the use of irregular alternations of rhythmic patterns, starting with the trochaic meter of popular verse, going on to iambic verse, which is classical in Russian, and to a stately anapestic meter."[58] The suggestion that the order of the poems of Doctor Zhivago "unfolds through the succession of the four seasons,"[59] at least in tone, is well observed. This arrangement, however, is more symbolic of the wholeness of life, for which novel and poetry stand, than of the understanding that it contributes to the rather formal and tightly structured poetic comments on the prose part of the novel.

The "artistic self-sufficiency"[60] of which Reeve speaks is no doubt justified by structural perfection which is transparent—and this only in Russian—in all of Doctor Zhivago's poems. Furthermore, the degree of this self-sufficiency is heightened when we discover that the same level of perfection is achieved by the author in developing his themes through images which are all-inclusive and predisposed to the sacred as well as to the profane.

In reality, all of Doctor Zhivago's poems are religious, if we interpret "religious" in the most liberal sense of its meaning. Even the short, erotic poem, "Intoxication," is, above all, about man's dependence on the elements of nature, and nature is, as the author observed it, divine. That two loving people become intoxicated with each other while seeking shelter from nature, which threatens them, is in essence a third form of nature's claim, and the poem's allusions to sex are only incidental. In his study of the Zhivago poems, Dimitri Obolensky emphasizes "nature, love, and the author's views on the meaning and purpose of life" as the "three basic themes."[61] But life itself includes nature, love, and all other themes with which the Zhivago cycle is particularly concerned. As in the novel, so in this poetry and in most of Pasternak's other creations, the theme is singularly that of life, death, and immortality (resurrection). The motifs, i.e., scenery, settings, situations, and all other poetic inventions are manifold and mostly dualistic, often paradoxical, in aim and purpose. For the convenience of our discussion, we shall observe Obolensky's grouping and at the same time suggest a further fragmentation of the major theme. The meaning and purpose of life are fragmented into human emotions such as joy and sorrow, the poet's relationship to his work, to fellow man, to Christ and God; the fusion of time and memory in the creative act caused by the gift of the poet or, as in "Ob'yasnenie" ("Explanation") and in "Magdalena, I" ("Mary Magdalene, I") the polarity and the mystic unity between basic impulses such as joy and suffering or lust and pain.

The nature poems "Mart" ("March"), "Zemlya" ("Earth"), "Vesennyaya rasputitsa" ("Spring Flood"), and "Bab'e leto" ("Indian Summer") or even such multiplex poems as "Osen'" ("Autumn"), "Na Strastnoy" ("In Holy Week"), "Belaya noch" ("White Night") and "Avgust" ("August") speak of creation and destruction, of the joy of being, and of disappointments; they are statements of protest and affirmation, they juxtapose human happenings and the mysteries of nature, and make an attempt to sort out the relationship between life in the country and in town.

Zhivago's concern with nature finds expression in various ways. Spring, the giver of new life, provides the background in "March," "In Holy Week," "White Night," "Spring Floods," and "Explanation." In the poem "March," spring's unrestrained energy is compared to the work of a dairy maid, perhaps the least concerned with right or wrong or with beauty, but full of self-confidence and natural creativity. In the poem "In Holy Week," spring does not only smell of charcoal, a sign that man's confinement to his winter dwelling has ended, but also, "As soon as the weather breaks up," man can "Hear the spring rumor/ Death can be overcome/ Through the power of the Resurrection." The structure of the poem can be described as obvious allegorization. For nature's eternal urges and premeditated religious rituals both communicate in a poetic inter-flow, namely that death must be overcome and that the resurrection of man is the highest degree, the spiritual side, of the process of life's renewal in nature. The prerequisite for renewal is a free acceptance of change.

The inherent paradoxes of the renewal of life are captured in the image of dung. Pasternak uses this image twice, and each time, in "March" and in "Earth," in connection with spring. In the poem "March," dung is both "the culprit and the life-giver," whereas in "Earth" the bitter smell of dung, although in itself symbolic of decay, signifies the poet's calling, and perhaps even duty, to see to it "That the distances should not be lonely,/ That beyond the limits of the city/ Earth should not feel alone."

He who experiences this calling is awakening as nature rises in spring. And man's task must go far beyond the urge of self-renewal. In times when "everywhere the air is out of tune with itself," the poet must summon his equals in order to "warm the cold of life" with a secret stream of suffering placed upon the poet by his "testaments," and he must communicate, if need be, through "farewells," i.e., through premature departure. This poem may very well have had its source in Zhivago's experience at Melyuzeevo (Chapter V) but, taken in conjunction with "Holy Week" and the later religious Magdalene poems, it also points to the end of the sixth chapter and to section eight of Chapter IX where the words "time to wake up," "wake up" become "an appeal or a warning" to the poet.

Zhivago's poetic destiny is echoed in "White Night" and in "Spring Floods" by the spirit of the woods, nature's best singer, the nightingale. The poet's voice, just as "the voice of the small insignificant bird" must rouse "a bustle of delight in the depth of the spell-bound forest," which is life.

In the short poem "Veter" ("The Wind") man's creative potency is compared to the powers of the elements in nature. The poet is like the wind. With his "crying and complaining," he can rock not only individuals but the whole of mankind, "not each pinetree separately/ But all the trees together." However, Pasternak, like Heinrich Heine[62] a century before him, sees in a poet's wailing therapeutic powers, because the poet, like the wind in the poem "shakes them not out of mischief,/ Or in aimless fury,/ but finds out of his grief,/ The words of a lullaby" for fellow man.

In other nature poems of this sequence, nature is personified in various ways. Fall, in "Indian Summer," is called an "old rag-and-bone merchant" who "sweeps everything into the ravine"; and in "Spring Floods" the busy spring waters carry laughter and tears alongside uprooted trees, and earth, sky, forest, and field do not only echo the rare sound of a nightingale, but also absorb "madness, pain, happiness, torment."

Some of the most enjoyable features in Doctor Zhivago's poems are his poetic paintings. Pasternak conditions a poem's theme by creating an easily comprehensible visual setting. A couplet, a full stanza, and in rare cases the greater part of the poem, draw vivid contours of landscape, situations, or even human action, which either complement or disparage motif and theme. In the poem "March," the poet creates a mood of joy and hope by setting side by side winter's departure—helplessly sick and wasting away—with the natural rhythm of life

and the new energies that the month of March brings to man and
to the eternal process of renewal. "Spring Floods," "Leto v
Gorode" ("Summer in Town"), "Indian Summer," and "The
Earth," as observed in the poem "March," robe their messages in
visual images, and in doing so they grant to each and every
reader what Donald Davie, in connection with the poem "White
Night," has described as "the human capacity for transforming
experience into poetry."[63] To explain his conception of life, the
poet not only creates in "The Wedding Party" a chain of images
drawn from nature, but depicts in some fifty-two lines what at
first sight appears as an average Russian wedding with all its
gaiety and proximity to Mother Nature. And yet, the poem is a
parable, and all its lines are there only to help understand these
last eight lines:

> Life too is only a wink
> Only a dissolving
> Of ourselves into all others
> As if in gift to them.
> > Only a wedding, in the depth of windows
> > Bursting from below
> > Only a song, only a dream
> > Only a grey-blue pigeon.
> > > > (trans. J. W. Dyck)

"White Night" has been scanned by Rosette C. Lamont as
"the first love poem of the Appendix."[64] But there are several
others that can be placed into this group, not so much because
of their Romantic tone and diction, but because, as Obolensky
has phrased it, "of the most moving and profound accounts of
the mutual love of man and woman ... remarkable for its com-
bination of passion and restraint...."[65] The love poems are more
personal than the above discussed nature poems. This high
degree of individuality is achieved through the poetic presenta-
tion of such dualistic themes as union and separation, passion
and restraint, or love as the motor of creativity, "like a river in
flood" (*Zh,* 404) and, at the same time, love as a destructive
force.

The following poems can be placed into the category of love
poems: "White Night," "Explanation," "Autumn," "Skazka"
("A Fairy Tale"), "August," "Zemnyaya noch" ("Winter Night"),
"Razluka" ("Parting"), "Svidanie" ("Meeting"), and perhaps

"Rassvet" ("Daybreak"). In most of these poems the recognizable source is the great love between Lara and Yury.

This, however, is not the case in "White Night," nor does "Explanation" lend itself to neat background studies. With its sources scattered all over the novel, as "discovered" by Davie, it is one of the most confusing poems of the entire Zhivago cycle. The few seemingly amorous words, such as those referring to the beautiful daughter from Kursk whom, in "White Night," young men loved, or the protagonist's lifelong devotion to the miracle of women's hands, back, and shoulders, and neck, in "Explanation" do not yet make a poem into a love poem. "White Night" offers no convincing evidence that the "poet talks with his love beside him,"[66] as F. D. Reeve has concluded, assumingly based on the window-sill scene of the poem. But strangely enough, the poet has no words of affection or passion, but explains: "What I am quietly telling you/ Has such likeness to sleeping distances." The following lines, then, suggest that there is common interest, that the poet is speaking to his double, perhaps to his muse or even to Russia, rather than to a particular second person. He explains: "We are bonded to mystery/ By the same shy truth/ As wide open Petersburg [is bonded]/ By the beautiful panorama beyond the Neva." It is this imperative of the spirit in the creative genius and in nature which guides the eternal process of transformation and which suggests optimism and hope for the future.

The complexity of the poem "Explanation" has been well discussed by Donald Davie. His suggestion that in the first part of the poem, Zhivago at last "does justice to the third woman in his life,"[67] that Lara "is present most insistently,"[68] and that even Tonya is not forgotten is supported by parallels from various parts of the novel. In spite of some striking similarities between suspected sources and certain parts of the poem, the essence of this poem remains further unintelligible. Thus it appears as if, in the first five stanzas, the poet tries to create a picture which would prove that the flow of time and events is caught in a never-changing cosmic rhythm. And just as time and events can hardly alter "the fire of sunset," so can they little change habits, worries, and desires of man. To the poet, however, this routine offers no challenge. "Again I fabricate my excuses/ And again is everything indifferent to me." Since the speaker's thoughts are addressed to women, it is conceivable that the poet has

Tonya in mind, especially before life had been "so strangely interrupted," and Marina, after life had again returned. The woman in the second part could be Lara. And yet, even such lines as "We are cables charged highly charged" or "We may again be thrown together" only anticipate the poet's struggle between the forces of lust, of a lifelong devotion to Eros, to sensuality (we think of "a woman's hands, back," etc.), and the calling of his poetic destiny, as we saw it in "White Night."

In the last four lines, the poet recognizes that as strong as the ring of anguish fettered by the night (of lust?) might be, a sway away from it is stronger and the desire to change the course, to break away from it, is enticing. While considering the last four lines of this poem, we cannot but think of Goethe's "break" with Frau von Stein in 1786. And Pasternak's Zhivago, too, must have experienced how intense passion and love for a woman can lead to estrangement from the world that surrounds him and finally how it could lead to self-destruction. In the poem "Autumn," after such exclamatory outbursts as "Devotion, desire, delight!/ Let us forget ourselves in the uproar of September!" i.e., in the autumn of life, the poet at the same time knows that boldness which, he says, is the root of beauty and which drew Yury and Lara together, and finally Lara herself, "are blessings on the road to destruction."

If "Autumn" can be called a love poem of passion, sensuousness, and even guilt ("I allowed my family to scatter"), then "Daybreak" is an attempt, by the poet, to reassert his poetic genius. To be sure, he does this again through love. However, love is no longer self-centered, as it was the case in "Autumn," but has transgressed the limits of self-indulgence and opened his heart to a greater humanity. "I am drawn to people, to the crowd," or toward the end of the poem, "I feel for them, for all/ . . . With me are people without names/ . . . I am conquered by them all/ And only this is my victory." The "You" to whom the poet directs his monologue is at the same time Lara, his creative genius, or even Christ or God. To guess which lines of the poem belong to whom will remain an idle exercise because the poet, as we know it from the novel (Zh, 405), purposely aimed in his poetry for a veiled and abstruse subjectivity. One thing seems certain in this poem. The poet's victory is an allusion to Christ's victory which, too, was obtained by being conquered. By saying, "in me are people without names," the poet points to the future and to his own immortality which he has secured through them. The "You," thus, can be identified with Lara—whom Zhivago has called his life source, his source of creativity, his memory—and with his creative genius, who is essentially sustained by the same energy, or, as Rosette C. Lamont maintains, "it can only be God."[69]

Love for God, perhaps, is the purest form of love, yet one cannot help agreeing with Donald Davie who points to our literary tradition of regarding love for a woman "as a paradigm"[70] of love for God. Goethe's final words of *Faust II* are emblematic in this tradition.

"Winter Night" is in tone similar to that of "Daybreak" and "Autumn." The ever-burning candle is interpreted by R. C. Lamont as "a symbol of the poetic accidents which bring people together at troubled times."[71] And it is more than this. The candle is symbolic of Lara, and with the help of this symbol, the poem fuses time and memory, the unconscious and the conscious, temptation and restraint, ecstasy and grief. Lara was fully aware of the existence of this poem and reflects on it at Yury's deathbed.

"Fairy-tale," "Meeting," and "Parting" are love poems which suggest a Romantic vein with all its melancholy and *Weltschmerz*. From the novel we know the exact circumstances, time, and experience which prompted Doctor Zhivago to write the "Fairy-tale." It is, indeed, "a highly personal poem." Lara, who for Zhivago has become the symbol of beauty and freedom, is at the same time an invitation to endanger or even sacrifice his life. The loss of Lara to Komarovsky, which first appears as Zhivago's greatest and final defeat, is transformed in the last stanzas of the poem to the joy of victory, namely his lasting unification—perhaps possible only in death—with a being who, he knew, had been his life's energy, yet who had remained a mystery to the very end: "Who is she? A queen?/ A daughter of the soil? A princess?"

Saint George, Yury Zhivago, has scored a victory in defeat through "centuries and years" to come because the lover's heart will remain beating as the spirit of true love shall remain alive in the poetry of "Parting" and "Meeting" which Zhivago was able to write only after he lost Lara. A poet's greatest sacrifice becomes his gift of creation. "Fairy-tale," "Parting," and especially "Meeting," in which Lara remains present in spite of her loss and in which "the loved one can be recalled and recreated at will,"[72] reveal the role and purpose of the appendix of poetry to a novel in prose in an unusual, but unfailing way. Ludolf Möller[73] suggests that a poem penetrates more deeply than prose into the miracles of the world, it teaches us to be affirmative where total negation seemed the only way out, and it explains to us Pasternak's belief "that every work of art, including tragedy, witnesses to the joy of existence" (*Zh*, 407).

Seven poems of this cycle make direct use of Biblical language and imagery. And it is no coincidence that Pasternak placed one of the seven, "Gamlet" ("Hamlet"), at the very beginning and "Gefsimansky sad" ("Gethsemane") at the end. This arrangement gives to the entire cycle the mien of a religious hymn. "Hamlet" and "Gethsemane" share the spirit and logos of Christ's prayer, "If it is only possible, Abba, Father,/ Let this cup pass from me." However, in both poems the speaker tames his agony. In "Hamlet," he realizes that to live a life of duty and self-abnegation "is not just crossing a field," yet he accepts the burden of the cross, "the order of the acts." He alone, he knows, is the chosen one, and "the end of his road is inescapable."

In "Gethsemane" we find the same theme as in "Hamlet." "Now the word must be fulfilled," and a tragic hero, Hamlet, the obedient son, the poet, all are Christ-figures, and they shall become the judges of centuries because of their willingness to "go freely, through suffering, down to the grave." The poet has no obligation to struggle against falsehood and hypocrisy. His judgment will find expression in his only task, which is life itself.

In the preface to her book, *Pasternak,* Jacqueline de Proyart quotes from one of Pasternak's letters that "the list of acting persons"[74] in a man's life is rather limited. It includes God, woman, nature, a man's calling, death. In "Hamlet" and in "Gethsemane," the poet has assessed his calling in the light of death. If the poet remains true to his calling, death will ultimately be overcome, and the assurance of resurrection is man's final victory. Rosette C. Lamont refers to the last four poems of the Appendix as "highly autobiographical"[75] and to the poet's identification of himself with Christ. But only the last poem uses, and even that only toward the end, the first person. The poem "Durnye dni" ("Evil Days") juxtaposes the pre-Easter week and Yury Zhivago's return to Moscow. Nothing has been changed by time and history. The Pharisees, or in modern time, the function-aries, delivered him for judgment, while the crowd—the silent majority—remained uninvolved.

The two Magdalene poems represent woman in the list of Pasternak's "acting persons." It is no poetic accident that the poems are placed immediately before "Gethsemane." In Mary Magdalene, the poet commemorates eternal womanhood. She is at the same time sinner and saint, filled with lust, "a slave to men's whims," but, in the knowledge of her debauchery, ready to embrace the cross and to grow one with Christ in his suffer-ing and sorrow. Both Mary Magdalene poems are deeply rooted in the novel itself and always stand in some proximity to Lara. And, indeed, Lara and Mary have much in common. However, the most striking similarity becomes obvious when we compare Lara's relationship to Zhivago with Mary's total absorption in Christ. Obolensky has pointed out that such a comparison "may well appear absurd and even blasphemous"[76] if we assess Zhivago's life which was overshadowed by moral and social degradations. Obolensky, on the other hand, justifies a com-parison "on the symbolical plane," especially if we direct our attention toward the human story of Yury Zhivago and recog-nize in this story affinities to the themes of Calvary and the Resurrection. The Mary Magdalene poems leave no doubt about such kinship. Mary Magdalene as a person and the poems as a poetic creation are affirmations of the mysterious, perhaps even esoteric, oneness of the sacred and the profane, just as much as Mary Magdalene (Lara) is simultaneously symbolic of the saint and the sinner so is Zhivago very modern: he is both savior and sinner. He had to be both, because today it is in-conceivable how the perfect savior could understand the sinner. Only with this understanding could Mary Magdalene (Lara), possessed by lust, which R. C. Lamont[77] sees as an act of love, transcend to the love for God which is the highest form of love. It is because of Mary Magdalene's willingness to grow one with Jesus in her "boundless sorrow" that she can conclude her pledges to her savior with this Christ-like conviction: "I shall grow up to the Resurrection."

Lara's experience at Yury's deathbed is similar to that of Mary Magdalene. She too is convinced that weeping can turn into "Alleluias" and that Yury's breath of freedom and unconcern, which had taken hold of her, is analogous to Mary's joy in anticipation of resurrection.

The group of poems that alludes to Christ's Passion is introduced, as it has been recognized before, by the poem "Chudo" ("Miracle"). This is befitting because it is a poem of grace and doom. The road, created by this polarity, on which every man must travel, is described in the poems that follow.

The discussion of the poems of Doctor Zhivago would remain incomplete without at least a few words on the poem "Razhdestvenskaya zvezda" ("Christmas Star"). This poem occupies a special position and is placed, perhaps purposely, between the poems that are above all personal love poems and the later religious group. The poem itself suggests that "the frosty night was like a fairy-tale" with all its magic, as young Zhivago had imagined a Christmas painting, "a Russian version of a Dutch 'Adoration of the Magi.'" The poem "celebrates the simplicity and beauty of life,"[78] as R. C. Lamont has suggested, but the "Christmas Star," although compared to a guest in the last line of the poem, represents, beyond warmth and hope, Christ, "on its [his] way to Bethlehem" or, if we go one step further, the poet in his role as prophet and judge. The Christmas Star, the poet tells us, brought not only peace and good will, but it "glowed like a farm on fire," it "startled the universe," it gave "unprecedented light," and suddenly in a strange vision laid open the entire past, thoughts, and dreams of centuries; and man—as the wise men in the poem—was willing to "bow to the miracle."

The poems of Doctor Zhivago have a mysterious, realistic message. They remind us of the necessity for humility and awe before that which man cannot comprehend, that is, before the miracle of God. On the other hand, they are filled with man's desire to transcend. And it is in this desire that man is in danger of digression and arrogance, a vice from which not even the creative mind, the poetic genius, is excluded.

Perhaps it is through his poetry that we can best follow Pasternak's development as a writer. Reavey's grouping of Pasternak's poetry into an early (1914-1923), a middle (1923-1936), and a later period (1940-1960)[79] is established along recognizable organizing principles. The epic poems stand between Pasternak's early and later periods, with *Second Birth* as the turning point in Pasternak's lyric development.

All of Pasternak's lyric poetry is rich in melody, rhyme, and

assonance, and "without exception strictly rhythmical."[80] All
nature poems, early and late, are not as much portrayals of
nature's physical beauty as revelations of its claim on man.
Korney Chukovsky,[81] a Russian critic, sees humbly expressed
gratitude in all nature poems, and especially in those of *When
the Skies Clear*. The many images taken from nature support
such observation. Rain or water, for instance, wash clean from
sorrow, misfortune, and sin. They also renew life. Snow, which
seems to spread the death blanket over living nature, is not at
all a reminder of life's decay, but rather a protector and pre-
server in anticipation of new life. The forest, wind, cloud movements, thunder, the sun, and many other images are borrowings
from nature out of which Pasternak builds, as Joseph Barnes
expresses it, "the counterpoint of some exceedingly difficult
ideas."[82] The above statement is especially true with regard to
Pasternak's early poetry which is still close to the Futuristic
manner or to some other literary movement of that time. In his
late poetry, not only his relationship to reality has changed,
but his realism is no longer the product of a certain school;
everything he now writes is poetic observation and expression
to the highest degree.

In his early poetry, Pasternak tried to conceal his subjectivity
behind forced associations and vague allusions, behind a style
in which, as V. Veydle phrases it, "one word crowds the other"[83]
and behind surprisingly strange word formations which obscure
the clarity of meaning. His late poetry—and this becomes pro-
gressively apparent beginning with *Second Birth*—reads almost
like a poetic confession in a Rilkean manner. There is no more
hesitation to make thoughts of deeply spiritual and personal
inclination transparent. The spirit triumphs over space and time,
and it is for this reason that man can feel one with nature. Pasternak's later poems are mostly written in a Classical style: they
are approachable because of their almost Biblical simplicity;
they are more transparent because the author's heart has become
more transparent. Leitmotif and themes turn away from the
concreteness and absoluteness of the moment and enter into the
world of ideas and faith. The call for high morality, for self-
sacrifice, and, above all, for love speaks on every page of Pasternak's mature poetry.

The Russian author Sinyavsky thinks that nature, i.e., "astonishment before the miracle of being"[84] in Kantian terms was the

foundation of Pasternak's moral philosophy. If in Pasternak's early poetry metaphors were the predominant mediators between things, in his later poems this unity between various elements is achieved by being in constant contact with the cultural heritage, which the poet knew and cherished, and through the poet's clear concept of the world. Perhaps what always remained unchanged in Pasternak's development as a poet is the author's view of the purpose of art. For Pasternak, poetry must always testify to the importance of existence, to the value of man, and to the greatness of life—because life itself is the only true source of Pasternak's poetry.

CHAPTER 5

Doctor Zhivago

I *Genesis*

MOST critical readers of *Doctor Zhivago*, soon after its appearance, recognized in the novel deposits of Pasternak's early prose writing. Nonetheless, it was generally assumed that *Doctor Zhivago* was the sole literary product of the author's later years, and that the novel matured as a result of external changes which had taken place in Russia during those years. The many interviews with the author, some letters, and a few references made by Pasternak himself show, however, that the novel can be considered as Pasternak's *Lebenswerk*.

As early as 1927, after having completed *Lieutenant Schmidt*, Pasternak recorded: "In the future, I shall occupy myself with prose. The short story *Childhood of Luvers*, which last year was published by the publishing house Krug in a collection entitled *Tales*, is one of the chapters of a large novel on which I am planning to work" (*Soch.*, III, 216).

That Pasternak quite early pondered the idea of writing a novel finds some support in the novel itself. Yury, says the narrator in *Doctor Zhivago*, has dreamed of writing prose instead of poetry ever since his schooldays. Some time in the future, he would write a book which would contain allusions to the impressions of life which had stirred his imagination and about which he had thought much (cf. 69).[1]

This and similar references suggest that some ideas—perhaps even the major theme of the novel—had been with the author, although formless, for many years. Mrs. Lydia Pasternak-Slater suspects that her brother "had started work on his big novel as early as 1934."[2] But the actual date when work on the novel began could be set even before this year. In a letter to his parents in 1937, Pasternak writes:

I am now in the possession of the nucleus, the blinding nucleus of what one could call happiness. It is in the terribly slowly growing

106

manuscript, which again, after an interval of years, is facing me
as something substantial, lawfully increasing and spreading. . . . Do
you remember my "Povest?" That was by comparison a decadent
work. This new work is growing into something big. . . .[3]

The above passage can only refer to *Doctor Zhivago*, since
all other prose writing of Pasternak had been published by
this time. Further in the letter, Pasternak characterizes his growing work as a work of "plastic authenticity," and in form "simple,
more transparent." Allusions are made to Chekhov and Tolstoy,
and what points directly to his great novel is his lament: "But
I do not know when I shall publish it and I am not worrying
about it. (And when will I have finished it?!)." Of interest for
our purpose is also the remark, in the above quotation, that he
is again working on his big work "after an interval of years."
It could suggest that the beginning or at least the inception[4]
of this novel, if not work itself on it, can be placed far before
the year 1934. Indeed, in the introduction to her 1960 edition
of *The Last Summer*, Lydia Pasternak-Slater suspects that
"Pasternak carried the unwritten book within him for many,
many years, and its ideas and the characters in it grew and
matured and changed, until some of them became very different
from their prototypes—less tangible and more universal."[5]

George Reavey tells in his introduction to *The Poetry of
Boris Pasternak*[6] of the Russian dramatist Afinogenov who, in
his diary of 1937, reminisces about Pasternak for whom art
was a main preoccupation and poetry equal to life's content.
Reavey also cites a reference that Afinogenov made to a novel
on which Pasternak had begun working at that time and speaks
of his discovery of "four fragments of this novel, which seems
to have its roots in the beginning of the century, like *Zhivago*."

Gerd Ruge, after his interview with the author, has little to
say on the genesis of *Doctor Zhivago*. "He had worked on the
novel," Ruge writes, "before Stalin's death, and he had finished
it at the end of 1955."[7] But Pasternak himself has given us
important insight into the development of the novel on at least
two occasions. To Renate Schweitzer he writes on June 18,
1958: "I translated the first part of the tragedy during the fall
and winter months, in 1949. After a three year interruption,
during which I wrote the beginning of my novel in prose, *Dr.
Zhivago*, I continued my work on the *Faust* translation."[8]

From this letter it becomes quite clear that he wrote the beginning of the novel between 1949 and 1952, which, on the other hand, does not mean at all that he began working on his novel at that time. However, another letter to the same German poetess reveals that he began writing *Doctor Zhivago* at a time when Olga Ivinskaya was under arrest. He admits quite freely to Renate Schweitzer that "she [Olga] is the Lara of this work which I had begun to write at this time."[9]

There is no confusion as to the time of completion of this work. Pasternak does not only tell us in the conclusion of his last work, in *An Essay in Autobiography* (1957), when approximately he finished the greatest of his works, but he leaves no doubt as to how he would like to see *Doctor Zhivago* remembered by readers and, perhaps, also in the histories of literature. He is willing to let more than a quarter of his writings lapse into oblivion. But of *Doctor Zhivago* he is not ashamed, and for this work he is prepared to assume full responsibility.

II *Personae, Plot, and Problems*

In the first two chapters of *Doctor Zhivago*, Pasternak introduces us to most of the important characters. With the opening scene of the funeral of Zhivago's mother, we meet Yury, the ten-year-old orphan who has been left in the care of his bachelor Uncle Kolya. It must be observed that it is Uncle Kolya, the unfrocked priest, who first voices some of the most central problems which, throughout the novel, confront Zhivago. Here in the first pages of the novel, the reader is introduced by way of characterization to those aspects of life which Pasternak considered supreme and more urgent than any social changes which are usually imposed from without. The stage is being set. The problems are not being solved, but posed. Individualism is offset by collectivism. Immortality, life, and Christ are viewed as in constant interrelation, indeed, as one. Loyalty to immortality, to Christ is synonymous to life itself and man's Dionysian "state of nature" is pronounced as having been replaced by history, "history as we know it now began with Christ." And above all, Pasternak places some of his characters into relationship with the controversial teachings of the Gospels, proclaiming that the Gospels have provided for modern man all that is necessary. Three concepts are especially singled out: Christ's command to love one's neighbor, the ideas of free personality, and of life regarded as sacrifice.

In the second chapter, "A Girl from a Different World," Pasternak, similar to the exposition in a drama, enlarges and deepens the problems. The same Nikolay (Uncle Kolya) argues that the parables of Christ in the Gospels are more significant for him than the ethical teachings and the commandments. These parables, which have their source in the realities of daily life, illustrate the idea that "communion between mortals is immortal." Because life has meaning, its essence is captured best in symbols. For centuries, man has been inspired to reach for a level beyond that of the animals by an inward music rather than by a cudgel (cf. 47). From the time of Christ, says Pasternak, there was only man; gods and peoples were obliterated. And man must know how to communicate with his fellow man without the whip, without being a lion-tamer in the circus. Only prehistoric men, says Pasternak, did not realize that any man who enslaves others is second-rate.

Into the warp of the philosophical, theological, and psychological problems, which are stated in general terms with events of far-reaching socio-political transformation, Pasternak weaves the woof of human characters, human relations, and myth. After being introduced to Yury and his background, we meet his two lasting friends, Misha Gordon and Nicky Dudorov, both so representative of the sufferings of the time. These two outlive Yury, and it is through their reminiscences in the "Epilogue" that the many threads of the plot, often lost in the novel, are tied together.

By presenting one character after another, Pasternak also introduces problems of a personal nature. He moves from the general to the particular. Individual characters are not only pondering speculative theories, as in the case of Nikolay Nikolaevich, but they are actually confronted with daily realities. The demarcation line between freedom to choose and being chosen is often unclear and problematic. The introduction of characters in the second chapter is, in this respect, one of the major artistic devices used, and opens the door into the labyrinth of problems and conflicts in the novel.

The "Girl from a Different World," Larissa Guishar, is, at this early juncture of the novel, the centripetal force that impels the individual characters into relationship with herself and

each other. From her radiate foreboding allusions to plot development and anticipations. When we first meet Larissa, the sixteen-
year-old daughter of the widowed Amalia Karlovna, we find
her described as the purest being in the world, fitting and
harmonious in everything about her, and blessed with silent
grace. Does she really ever lose this purity? Her early relationship
with "the cold-blooded business man," the lawyer Komarovsky,
was not exactly what standards of Puritan ethics prescribe,
especially since Komarovsky is also an intimate visitor to Larissa's
mother. But Lara is also human, and the human, all-too-human
temptations which lure this symbol of purity begin with very
ordinary, everyday events: she is flattered that a man of position
should spend his time and money on her; she is showing off
and demonstrates how grown-up she is, not recognizing the
borderline. And then come the torments of self-accusation, cul-
minating in the realization that she had become a fallen woman.

At the same time, a similar problem is disturbing Yury,
Gordon, and Tonya Gromeko, who is the daughter of a chemistry
professor and, later, Yury's first wife. They, too, were obsessed
by sex, says Pasternak, but they preached chastity and soaked
themselves in *The Meaning of Love* and *The Kreutzer Sonata*.
They considered the whole physical world as "vulgar," in contrast to Larissa who was part of it. They were struggling, but
only in noble literature, against the danger of basic instincts.
Yet, when Yury sees Lara and Komarovsky for the first time,
when he experiences the relationship "between the captive girl
and her master" as incommunicably mysterious and frank, something new and conflicting enters painfully into Yury's heart. And
again Pasternak masterfully demonstrates how problems become
real and personal. Between Komarovsky and this girl "from a
different world," Yury suddenly realized that he was directly
witnessing that frightening yet attractive force which Tonya,
Misha, and he had so often talked about as "vulgar" and rejected
from the safe distance of their childish philosophy (cf. 64). But
with this experience, Yury's childish philosophy was gone, and
what was he to do now?

Pasternak does not conclude these first two chapters of character introductions with this question. He gives us hints, he
foreshadows new constellations between the existing characters
or places, and thus he keeps the reader in suspense or anticipation
of that which is to develop in the novel. While watching Lara,

Yury has suddenly matured. It was instant maturing. He did
not hear what Gordon said, for his thoughts dwelt on the girl
and the future.

But the circle had to be closed by the entry of a third man
into Lara's life. It is Pasha Antipov. Lara recognizes in him a
good-natured and childishly simple character who loves her
as if she were some sort of a birch forest with clean grass and
clouds. Pasha loved Lara madly, Pasternak says, and was committed to her for life (*Zh-M*, 50). The fierce and feared Strelnikov
(Antipov)—later in the novel a harsh and merciless revolutionary
—was once a boy with a soft heart and gentle characteristics,
predominantly motivated by feelings.

One of the most distinctive features of the novel is the mastery
of depicting the gradual transformation of the inner man, of
inner harmony to disharmony, or vice versa. To find an acceptable relationship to a world of duplicity of either internal or
external nature, this might well be considered as one of the
paramount features in the writing of this novel. What makes
man the way he is? "Cares and anxieties," Pasternak says, are
the springs of action, the prime movers of life. Life, thus, is
pulsated by a struggle for survival and against fear, by existen-
tialistic fear, which is overcome by Zhivago's very nature and
by his inherent feeling of profound unconcern. And is everyone
really a true human being, worthy to be true to himself or, as
Pasternak suggests, to Christ? When Komarovsky's conscience
begins to torment him after he has seduced Lara, he, too, uses
the same argument of being true to himself. He is afraid to be
parted from his habits because his habits are his refuge. And
is not Misha Gordon's Jobian "Why?," in essence, posing the
same problem? He wonders why he cannot replace his anxieties
with unconcern, why love cannot conquer hate, or what it
really means to be a Jew.

Almost every character in the novel, major or minor, poses
problems, asks questions. The intellectuals are accused of thinking that they are a special creation, not by the author, by one
or the other character, or by the narrator, but by the ladies
of society, the mythmakers. Lara recognizes quite early in her
life that unlike Yury and Tonya, she had never had the time and
the leisure for premature theorizing about love and chastity.

In presenting characters and problems, Pasternak also con-
trasts characteristics, inner values, and actions, especially of

opponents, who may appear as different as day and night, and yet cling mysteriously to one another. Lara and Komarovsky are a striking illustration of such conflicting attraction. Lara realizes the difference between them. Quite early in her relationship with Komarovsky, it is said that she lacked his treachery, and the narrator delineates an even gloomier picture of Komarovsky when he tells us that Komarovsky's dog was jealous of Lara, as if she were afraid that he might become infected with something human (*Zh-M*, 47). Lara realizes all this: she is horrified, yet she cannot free herself from him. Realizing this weakness within man, she comes, all too early, to the pessimistic conclusion: "Life is all treachery and ambiguity." Nevertheless, it is this woman, haunted at the outset of the novel with gloom and doom, more so because of her own character than of the threatening exterior forces, who later becomes the major inspiration, the creative force, which propels the novel's protagonist. Thus, she helps to shape the professed nonentity from whom much hope and good will radiate precisely because of his unconcern.

The first two chapters of *Doctor Zhivago* are, however, not only concerned with the introduction of characters and problems. Pasternak also sounds the first notes of a symphony which had been dear to his heart and which gradually reached its highest maturity and realization in this *Lebenswerk*. It is the author's concept of art, of literature, of the muses in general. Throughout the novel, in the words of major and minor characters, or simply the narrator, Pasternak looks at, or rather, examines, the presence of art from various points of view. The motivating forces, the esthetic appeal, art's mediating role in man's relationship to life, death, and eternity, are not as much an *ars poetica* as a philosophy of art. Again it is Uncle Kolya who states, in these beginning chapters, in general terms that which throughout the novel is dissected, explained, and always placed in relation either to a personal experience or event. When Nikolay Nikolaevich expresses his distaste for a certain Symbolistic libretto, he finds that the entire thing is an affectation, that it really cannot interest anyone because it is artificial and, therefore, deadly. However, Nikolay Nikolaevich does not think that only the form is an anachronism. He had found it before, in *Faust*. The entire *genre*, he says, is out of harmony with the motivating forces of present-day art.

With *Doctor Zhivago,* Pasternak has fulfilled this precept. Ardent formalists, who have suggested failure[10] of novelistic architecture in *Doctor Zhivago,* may at times succeed in proving their points by isolating individual passages from the plot. But *Doctor Zhivago* is neither artificial nor is it an affectation. The novel is, indeed, in keeping with the very essence, the motivating force of present-day art.

From the point of view of novelistic structure, Chapter Three still belongs to the exposition. It deepens the psychic process of the novel by interjecting complexity into characters and events. Events move faster than in the first two chapters. Through strength of character, Lara frees herself, at least temporarily, from Komarovsky. After graduation from high school, she lives for several years as a governess in the home of her classmate and friend, Nadya. These are happy years with some sense of purpose. Lara is led to womanhood, but not yet to maturity. This is the time when she makes the acquaintance of Pasha Antipov, but before she marries him, she once more is driven to utmost confusion. Wounded pride and irrevocable humiliation make her lose her nerves, her presence of mind. At the Christmas party at the Sventitskys she shoots at Komarovsky, her tormentor. Komarovsky suppresses all charges against her, because he fears a social scandal.

Yury and Tonya Gromeko, with hopes of a harmonious future, are at the same party. Before they leave for the party, Tonya's mother, who dies during the same night, joins their hands in betrothal. For the first time Evgraf, Yury's half-brother and later benefactor, is mentioned.

The remaining twelve chapters of the novel are a twentieth-century Odyssey of Zhivago, of Lara, of other characters, of generations, and of a nation. But Yury Zhivago and Lara are the two major streams which flow and merge through the pages of the novel as symbols for idea and reality, for joy and suffering, for life and immortality.

Yury marries Tonya and remains in Moscow. Lara and Pasha Antipov accept teaching positions in Yuryatin in the Urals and share several years of what seems a normal and happy family life. A daughter, Katya, is born.

Meanwhile the First World War has started and Yury has to leave Tonya in order to go as a medical doctor to the Western Front. Soon after his departure their son, Sasha, is born. While external events separate Yury and Tonya, Lara and Pasha are separated by an agonizing inner suspicion which drives Antipov away from his wife and child to enlist for service at the front. The growing germ of Pasha's agony was seeded in their wedding night when "his guesses of suspicion alternated with Lara's confession" (Zh-M, 98).

Pasternak is a master in developing character. Of Pasha he says: "In all of Antipov's life, there had been no change in him more decisive and abrupt than during this night. He got up a different man, almost surprised that he was called by his old name" (Zh-M, 98). And yet Pasha's life, away from his family, was far from being without challenge. His activities, however, all remain on the surface. He was captured by the Germans, but escaped; he became one of the ablest organizers and most feared Red Army leaders around Yuryatin and in Eastern Siberia; he was hunted by those he served, because he had served too well. But all this had not changed his inner nature to the same degree as that fateful wedding night. And at the end, when everything is done, he has left only one wish: to see Lara and his daughter. All the experiences of ideals, of horrors, and evil had not been able to destroy his desire to live, to belong, if only for a short hour. To have only one last look at Lara and his daughter is Antipov's final wish. All these years had not been able to erase that love which, as a boy, he had felt for Lara. Pasternak demonstrates with the insight of a psychoanalyst that a vivid personal experience, in Pasha's case, his experience of the wedding night, is the strongest, perhaps the only force, which can effect a metamorphosis of the inner man.

Lara's life begins a new chapter when, as a nurse, she goes to the front in search of her missing husband. Here Yury's and Lara's life lines cross for the third time. Their spiritual kinship is felt more than it is expressed, and the author with his foreboding insight into the story's progress, leaves no doubt in the reader's mind that Zhivago and Lara will meet again.

When they separate, the war has ended and the Revolution is gaining momentum. Zhivago's first poetry is being published in Moscow by his friends Gordon and Dudorov, and Yury is longing for "an honest productive life." Lara returns to Yuryatin, in the Urals, Yury to Moscow.

Hunger, vandalism, and typhus rage in Moscow. Evgraf reappears, his role in the new system seems to be one of influence.

He helps the Zhivagos in their struggle for survival, but suggests that they exchange Moscow temporarily for the country. Varykino, a lonely estate in the district of Yuryatin, becomes their home for several years during the Civil War. At first, Yury seems fully absorbed in the struggle with the elements of nature in his attempt to wrest survival from the soil. But then again his mind begins to long for books and knowledge. In Yuryatin, in the public library, he sees Lara. Their fate, an irresistible magnetism, draws them together and closes in on them. But these blissful hours of secret love, on the one hand, and deceit and disloyalty, on the other, are suddenly brought to a stop. On his way from Lara in Yuryatin, symbolically at the crossroads to Varykino, Yury is "drafted" under gunpoint to serve as medical doctor to the Forest Brotherhood, the partisans.

Yury had experienced his first taste of the discipline of the new order when he was escorted to the feared leader Strelnikov when they had first arrived in the area. Zhivago then had not known that Strelnikov was no other than Pasha Antipov who, as Pasternak says, had decided not to return to Lara before he had finished his "life's work" (cf. 413).

Masterfully, Pasternak describes in these passages the implacable realities of those cruel years, when friends became enemies, when neighbor fought against neighbor, when sons denounced their fathers, and when values and virtues changed overnight. Pasternak depicts man reduced to his lowest—deprived of all human qualities. The laws of human civilization were replaced by jungle laws: man had become a wolf to man. "Only nature," says Pasternak, "had remained true to history" (Zh-M, 388).

After years of deprivation and regimentation, Yury escapes from the young partisan leader, Liberius, who, with his machine-like conviction of a better future, had driven him almost to insanity. In the meantime Yuryatin, too, has suffered destruction and horror. Tonya, her children, and her father have left for Moscow and are subsequently deported to France. Yury returns to Lara. They have only one wish: to be alone, to live—even if it is only for a limited time—their own lives. They go to Varykino. "Again Varykino" is the most poetic of all the chapters in Doctor Zhivago. In long drawn-out conversations, Yury and Lara reflect on the meaning of life, on man's relation to man, and to God. Yury again writes poetry.

But the days of "quiet madness" are numbered. In Yuryatin the axe is being sharpened for Yury and Lara. Lara was already afraid of it when her father-in-law, old Antipov, and a former friend and neighbor of her childhood had returned to Yuryatin. Komarovsky, on his way to the Far East in the capacity of a minister for a Soviet-approved, temporary buffer state, recognizes this danger. He begs Yury, Lara, and Katya to flee with him to safety. But Yury refuses. However, Komarovsky succeeds in taking Lara and Katya with him. Knowing that Lara will not leave without him, Yury gives the appearance of following them to the train in a different sleigh. But Zhivago stays behind. "My bright sun has gone down," he laments. Long before, he had sensed that with the loss of Lara he would inevitably lose "the will to live and perhaps life itself." He is left with one wish, to write Lara's "memory into an image of infinite pain and grief." Many of the Zhivago poems reflect the mood and spirit of this pain and grief.

Varykino harbored one more vital experience for Zhivago. Antipov-Strelnikov, who was believed to have been shot, spends his last hours with Yury. Some previous misunderstandings are removed. They try to understand the upheavals of the time, and the social and political developments. But their common bond is Lara. Pasha confesses that everything he has done in his life has been done for the sake of Lara. Lara, for him too, since childhood, had been the consummation of all realities of life. One could read the restlessness of the century in her face, in her eyes. "Everything that made our time, all its tears and insults, impulses, the whole accumulation of revenge and pride was ingrained in her expression and in her carriage, in that mixture of her girlish shyness and daring posture. One could indict the century in her name, from her lips" (Zh-M, 472).

During the night Pasha Antipov shoots himself.

The last chapter, the conclusion, is the brief story of Zhivago's last years in Moscow. Pasternak refers to these years as the time during which Zhivago "went more and more to seed" (416). He publishes a few booklets on problems dear to him: on the theory of personality, his definition of health and sickness, his philosophy of life. He meets Marina who becomes his third and common-law wife, he has disappointing conversations with old but "rehabilitated" friends, and he writes endlessly. His death comes at a time when Evgraf is helping him to begin a new and orderly life, when he had promised to reunite him with Tonya and his lawful family.

The novel is full of coincidence. And so it ends with this last one: Lara has just come from Irkutsk to arrange for Katya's acceptance to a conservatory. Passing by Kamerger Street, she wants to look into the room where she once had been with Pasha, on the day before she took the shot at Komarovsky. Instead, she finds the funeral of Yury. In a last monologue with Yury, in conversation with Evgraf, who arranges the funeral and is also looking after Zhivago's papers and manuscripts, Lara tells of her years of torment with Komarovsky, and of her lost daughter, Yury's child. She helps Evgraf sort Yury's papers, but one day she does not return.

Pasternak concludes his Odyssey: "In those days, she must have been arrested in the street and no one knows where she died or vanished as a nameless number on a list which later was lost, in one of the countless mixed or women's concentration camps in the north."

The novel's "Epilogue" takes us beyond the Second World War. Here we meet Lara's and Yury's lost daughter, Tanya, the laundry girl, and she tells the story of her life. A new generation has come into being. New sacrifices have been made. And Pasternak leaves the reader with an observation that is at the same time gloomy and yet, not completely without hope: "Although the enlightenment and liberation for which everyone waited after the war had not come with victory, nevertheless, a presage of freedom was in the air throughout the postwar years, and this was their only historical meaning."

III   *Communion between Mortals is Immortal*

In his introduction to *The Last Summer,* George Reavey asks: "What would the Boris Pasternak of 1914 or 1917 have thought of the Pasternak of 1959?"[11] Perhaps we could also add to this comparison the year 1934. In this year, two major events took place in the life of Boris Pasternak. He moved to Peredelkino, an artists' colony, which remained his residence for the rest of his life, and *Povest'* (*The Last Summer, A Tale*) was published in the Soviet Union. Between *The Last Summer* and *Doctor Zhivago* (1958), Pasternak veiled himself in deep silence as far as creative prose is concerned. Did he really think so differently of his role and purpose as a writer when we compare some of his thoughts expressed in *The Last Summer* with those in *Doctor Zhivago*?

Both works are to some degree autobiographical, although there is ample evidence in *Doctor Zhivago* that Pasternak, by this time, had mastered the art of concealing personal experiences in symbols and images. Two passages from these two major prose works, the publications of which are separated by more than twenty years, demonstrate, at least to us, that Pasternak always attributed to himself, to his calling as poet and writer, a somewhat Messianic role. Often this conviction reached the unpleasant extravagance of arrogance. We find it expressed strongest in *Doctor Zhivago*. Dudorov and Gordon, he says, do not know that having average taste is worse than having no taste at all. And he continues his thoughts about them, and he grants them validity of existence only because it is given to them to walk in his own shadow and to live at the same time. Zhivago paraphrases almost literally the words of Christ spoken to his disciples in Pasternak's poem "Gethsemane": "God has granted you to live in my time...."

However, throughout the years, Pasternak's mission was and remained the concern for man. Not man as an abstract philosophical concept, but man as an individual who, in coping with everyday realities, must find a generally acceptable way of communicating, of having communion with his fellow man. Only such communion can secure everlasting renewal of life. This is what Pasternak tells us in *The Last Summer* through Seryozha, the major character, who is echoing the author's own ideas and who, like Pasternak himself, was employed as a tutor in a wealthy Moscow family. Seryozha wants to acquire wealth immediately, but not through work. The earning of wages is, as he sees it, no great victory. Yet, he has realized that there is no freedom without victory. Therefore, he looks toward Galilee where an obscure, local event had spread into the world. Seryozha wants to help the insulted and downtrodden, the women of Tverskoy-Yamskoy Street—here we have, though not clearly expressed, the prelude to the Mary Magdalene motif of *Doctor Zhivago* and the poems—and he wants to renew the world, a calling which for him assumes paramount urgency (cf. *Soch.*, II, 176).

In *Doctor Zhivago* we find the same personal thoughts of

the author. This time, however, not identified with a major character, but camouflaged by the philosophical theories of Nikolay Nikolaevich. Pasternak's philosopher, as before him Seryozha, places the beginning of the era of individualism in Galilee. From the moment of Christ's coming, there were neither peoples nor gods, it was the beginning of man as he is sung in lullabies and eternalized in portraits and pictures (cf. *Zh-M*, 44). The average man, Seryozha feels, can experience and expose his secrets in a human way. But is he himself capable? Pasternak refers to Seryozha in this connection as a good-for-nothing, a very Christ of passivity (cf. *Soch.*, II, 198).[12] A poet, according to Pasternak, is entitled to what we have called Messianic arrogance. Pasternak has not invented this attitude; it is steeped deeply in the tradition of Romanticism. The early German Romantics, especially, had hoped for union with the eternal through art; Pushkin's *Exegi Monumentum* expresses unmistakably the conviction that he, the poet, has found a way of communion with future generations as long as there shall be poets on this earth; and in the last line of *A Defence of Poetry* Shelley decrees: "Poets are the unacknowledged legislators of the world." Pasternak wrote in this tradition. He felt this prophetic destiny throughout his literary career, from his earliest poetry to *Doctor Zhivago*.

The Shakespeare poem in *Themes and Variations* (1924), still full of skepticism, expresses the claim for immortality through the sonnet: "I'm with all my nature in lightning, that is, I am nobler than any man." And Yury Zhivago? Pasternak bestows upon him the confidence that in moments of inspiration his hand, too, was guided by a higher power. How else, he wonders, would he be able to create poetry with new rhyme and with rhythm or forms and formations until now undiscovered (cf. *Zh-M*, 448). Zhivago is conscious of being blessed with the gift of greater perception than ordinary man. Poet and poetry are nearer to the divine than mortals. "Why hast Thou allowed me to come to Thee ... ?" Zhivago asks in admiration. In the last chapter of his novel, Pasternak completes this image by giving his hero a Christ-like physical appearance.

If at all *Doctor Zhivago* can have claim to being an autobiographical novel then, we think, it is precisely in its zeal for prophecy and its Messianic style. Indeed, in this sense

Doctor Zhivago is, as Michel Aucouturier calls the novel, a "symbolic autobiography."[13]

What do we mean when we say "Messianic Style"? Perhaps this question can best be answered if we once more ponder Pasternak's major task of finding a way of communion that makes mortals immortal. Almost every character of intellect, major or minor, in *Doctor Zhivago,* is concerned with finding ways and means of overcoming his Existential fear of ceasing to be, of any energy that threatens to terminate what Nietzsche called the eternal recurrence of life. At the very outset of the novel, Pasternak leaves no doubt as to what shall constitute the indisputable essence of his major characters. The ideologist of the novel, Uncle Kolya, sees it quite clearly. He is convinced that work throughout history was devoted to the systematic solution of the enigma of death and its eventual elimination. This is why people discover mathematical infinity, electromagnetic waves, and why they compose symphonies (*Zh-M*, 10). Much earlier, in *Safe Conduct* (Part III, Chapter 1), Pasternak calls natural scientists commentators on death.

Pasternak wrote poetry, novels, and letters, not just in an ordinary way, but as we called it above, in a Messianic way, which is a very liberal way and, furthermore, in the style of the Gospels—as he understood the Gospels. And Pasternak understood the Gospels as Nikolay Nikolaevich understood them. He preferred the parables which explain truth in terms of everyday reality compared to the ethical teachings and the Commandments. This concept of communication was not born with *Doctor Zhivago*. In *Safe Conduct,* Pasternak views mankind's total ontology similarly: "I understood that the history of culture is the chain of equations in images" (*SC*, 87). This must mean equations, uttered through images, that is, through parables.

Thus, Pasternak's novel should not be read as a moralistic catechism. It has, indeed, "no neat ethical categorical imperative,"[14] as Mrs. Miriam Taylor Sajković has suggested. But we agree with Professor Tschizewskij that it is a "belehrendes Werk."[15] Pasternak's novel consists of a chain of loosely connected parables, its messages are implied, not formulated or expressed in dogmas, its categorical imperative is the freedom of every individual to choose his own doom or salvation. And herein lies the greatness and reality of Pasternak's characters, that they cannot be divided into good and bad.

They all, including Komarovsky, who is perhaps the greatest villain in the novel, reveal in many instances sparks of both good and evil. And the theory that Pasternak used the evil lawyer Komarovsky only "for contrast," because, "art is reserved for the beautiful,"[16] as Ralph E. Matlaw seems to have understood Pasternak, must be challenged. This concept narrows down Pasternak's conception of reality, that central part of the novel which Matlaw recorded in his interview with Pasternak so vividly. From the same interview Matlaw concludes that Pasternak could not accept a reality of predetermined causality. Pasternak, the interviewer states, did not believe in the presupposition that every "action has a consequence." He is quoted as having said: "I wanted to get away from the idea of causality. The innovation of the book lies precisely in this conception of reality."

Pasternak's assertion, in the same report, that for him "reality lies . . . in the multiplicity of the universe, in the large number of possibilities," suggests that the poet did not intend to reserve art only for the beautiful and the good, but depicted reality with all its attributes, including ugliness and evil. Multiplicity, on the other hand, must evolve from inspiration rather than free imagination. Although Pasternak owes much to the Symbolists— his early writings admittedly were seeking "richer" expression through symbols and new imagery—in *Doctor Zhivago* imagery, perhaps, but not symbolism was of prime consideration for moulding the desired style to express that which was his greatest concern. In *Doctor Zhivago*, Pasternak's aim was simplicity.

To Renate Schweitzer he wrote that *Doctor Zhivago* will be criticized "because of the simplicity and transparency of the language."[17] He complains in the same letter that long letters can become tiresome. "Otherwise I would clearly explain to you why a book about the most important things that have demanded so much blood and madness from our century must be written with clarity and simplicity." In a nutshell, Pasternak has told us here how he would like to see his work read. The language, he says, is transparent; the most urgent things are expressed clearly, simply. According to the report by Ralph E. Matlaw,[18] Pasternak also rejected Edmund Wilson's overly zealous discoveries of symbolic meaning,[19] because they go not only beyond, but are out of harmony with the author's own aims and intentions.

Pasternak believed in a mystical inspiration and had, as Gerd Ruge reports, "a profound and unmistakable sense of divine presence."[20] He himself has explained that man does not have this experience too often. This divine presence can become apparent "in love of a work of art, or in love of one's country, or in love of a woman." Any interpretation of Pasternak's works must bear in mind his convictions out of which grew the reflections of his characters, as well as his own witness. Pasternak spoke to Gerd Ruge repeatedly of the "sense of obligation to bear witness, to provide a document of the time." But he assured him also that what he had in mind is "the witness of an artist, not a politician." In bearing witness as an artist, in presenting truth and reality as the artist sees it, the artist should have unrestricted freedom. This, Pasternak knew, was not granted. A life of constant duplicity was, therefore, inevitable. This duplicity is imposed upon Zhivago by the time in which he lives, by the inherent nature of things. Duplicity and duality are the challenging forces in the shadow of which *Doctor Zhivago*'s characters struggle with basic human concerns, such as life, death, immortality, illusions and disillusions, and with concepts such as good and evil, history, Nature or God, and man. Although we gladly agree with Edward Wasiolek that "the high points of the novel are lyrical-philosophical reflections on the meaning of history, on the significance of Christ's example, and the understanding of life after death,"[21] these high points cannot stand alone and divorced from man. Babette Deutsch has rightly stressed the cohesiveness between man, events, and concepts. After she had read *Doctor Zhivago,* she expressed her feelings thus: "There are times when the hero of the book seems to be not a person at all, but history, or freedom, or the revolution...."[22] We shall proceed to discuss some of these concerns and concepts as we see them depicted in the novel through the experience of Zhivago, Lara, Antipov, and other characters.

IV *Dualism, Duplicity, and Paradox*

Duplicity, duality, and paradox are some of the most predominant novelistic characteristics in *Doctor Zhivago*. Pasternak did not choose this vital, challenging life element for the novel's major theme, but it hovers over the characters' relationships with the divine, with nature, and with history; it influences, almost dominates, thought and action of the various protagonists and guides their behavior towards fellow men; it is an invisible force which lies in wait for the human conscience, for human hopes, and anticipations. In *Doctor Zhivago*, we find a constant change from the ideal to the real, from good to evil, from happiness to sadness, and from fancy to the most ordinary, to everyday trivialities.

Yury Zhivago is most noticeably affected by such contrapositions. From his very youth to his last days in Moscow, the controlling forces in his existence were life's everyday polarities. With his adolescent friends, Tonya Gromeko and Misha Gordon, he is trying to discover the real meaning of love, but soon realizes that their search is on a dangerous path, with its pendulum swinging between the purely spiritual side of life and a physical obsession, which is almost morbid. Just before the revolutionary years to which Pasternak refers as the days of the triumph of materialism, and when, as the novel distinctly emphasizes, the future approached like a monstrous machine, Doctor Zhivago feared that future, and at the same time loved it and was even proud of it. He was willing to sacrifice himself for it, but resigned because he was convinced that he was powerless to do anything (*Zh-M*, 187).

But not only do we find Yury's wishes, desires or his will often reversed because of his own inconsistent nature or lack of will (cf. Tonya's letter to Yury). Circumstances and events are just as much responsible for Yury's deeds being lamentable reversals of his intentions. After one of his many secret visits with Lara in Yuryatin, Yury is overcome by the weight of his guilty conscience toward Tonya. He hurries home to Varykino, filled with remorse and willingness to confess everything, to ask for forgiveness, and never to see Lara again (*Zh-M*, 312).

If Yury's spontaneous resolution would have found its application, the love triangle, Lara-Yury-Tonya would have been destroyed and with it one of the most opportune love stories in modern literature. But the partisans, historical events, prevent Yury's return to his wife. The crossroad in Yury's life is brought upon him by this external force. Whether or not he would have been able to break with Lara of his own inner strength is questionable, since he had decided in favor of one more meeting with Lara just moments prior to being "conscripted" by the

partisans' liaison officer, Kammenodvorsky. Somewhat earlier in
the novel, Yury had assured Tonya that she and her father
were the "only people" he loved, yet his real love finds expression
much later when his love for Lara becomes identical with joy
for life and with life itself.

Even in Zhivago's dreams we find the constant burden of a
contradictory, twofold world. After his dreadful ordeal with
the Forest Brotherhood, Zhivago returns to the house in Yuryatin, to Lara. Exhausted from the many weeks of walking and
disappointed that he does not find Lara at home, Yury falls
asleep. The two dreams that follow at this point of the novel
are a reflection of the dualistic and contrapuntal nature inherent
in characters and events alike. Zhivago dreams that he is aban-
doning his son, sacrificing him for a woman who was not the boy's
mother, but to whom he felt compelled, in the words of the
author, by "false honor and duty" (Zh-M, 403).

Yet, it is apparent throughout the novel that love and passion,
but never duty, were the cause for most of Doctor Zhivago's
actions. His lack of duty reaches the highest point when he
finally relinquishes Lara to Komarovsky.

More paradoxical is the second dream in which Yury sees
Lara turning away from him. In self-pity he reminds the reader
that he had sacrificed everything for her. Yet, Lara had remained
loyal in her relationship to Zhivago. It is Zhivago himself who
at the end betrays his thoughts, desires, and intentions. He
betrays his own love. It is not that Zhivago does not try to
understand such a double standard in his behavior. In endless
hours of soul-searching with Lara, with the partisan leader in
the Forest camps, and also with Strelnikov-Antipov during that
last night in Varykino, he was captivated and dazed by the
fraudulent nature of reality. When he attempted to determine
the causes for his own sclerosis of the heart, later in Moscow,
he finds them in "a common illness of our times." The causes,
he asserts, are moral, because the majority of people is required
to live a life of constant duplicity which has been introduced
by the system (Zh-M, 494).

But not only do we find contradictory dispersion in Yury
Zhivago. Most of the other characters, and in particular, Lara,
are endowed with a plurality which does not lend itself to a
traditional classification of characters, such as good and bad,
positive and superfluous, or simply protagonists and antagonists.

Lara is "both amused and irritated" when young Pasha Antipov becomes didactic. And Pasha himself tells Zhivago at their very last meeting that he went to war in order to win Lara back. Yet, he leaves the person whom he in reality needs most in life. Komarovsky both helps Lara and destroys her life, and Yury's attitude toward Lara is just as ambiguous as that of other characters. Thus, one is confronted throughout the novel with ever-present forces which are not necessarily opposed to each other, but which evoke some degree of schizophrenia in almost every character. Michel Aucouturier, in his evaluation of *Doctor Zhivago*, claims: "Evgraf reflects most distinctly the constant duplicity of *Doctor Zhivago*."[23] In Evgraf, Aucouturier feels, Pasternak consciously aimed for a pronounced confrontation between historical truth and fictional truth. In most characters, but above all in Evgraf, this dualistic nature is not only transparent, but artistically intentional. As a character in a historical novel, Evgraf is marked by time and circumstances in which he renders services and of which he is an integral part. As a fictional character, he is a mysterious force. Yury sees Evgraf's role in his own life as a secret, unknown force, which is symbolical and protective, a hidden spring of his own life. Aucouturier says that Pasternak has incarnated providence in the figure of Evgraf. This is the fictional side of Evgraf. On the historical side of the novel, all characters are deeply rooted in and firmly knotted to the tentacles of their time, yet as fictional characters they are free and have become legendary. It is in this sense that Zhivago could say, "there is no plurality in art." Through art (poetry), he was able to subdue the agonies of constant duplicity, of living a dishonest life, of endlessly confronting his own two faces. In order to live, his life and his art had to become one. In this Yury Zhivago is an unmistakable image of his creator, of Pasternak himself.

As in real life, the major characters in *Doctor Zhivago* are not only entangled in a multi-angular love affair—love affairs seem to be the result of upheavals and unwanted displacements —but they become deeply implicated in social and political concerns and crises. Graphically, one could link the interplay between the various characters with the help of several interlocking triangles.

The characteristics of this chart, the different number of lines which run to and from each of the five outer points are symbolic of the degree to which Pasternak implicates the various characters. And over the complexity of these magnetic lines linger the opposing forces of duty and irresistible human inclination.

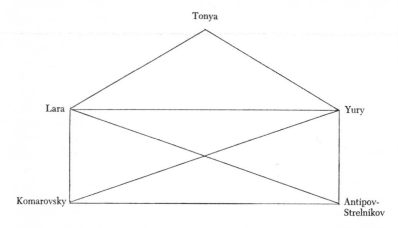

The triangular constellation of Tonya-Yury-Lara is not as intricate as it is providential, a "preordained coincidence," and willed so by the author of the novel. Mademoiselle Fleury, mystical and symbolical in each of her appearances, predicts very early in the novel that the nurse and the doctor are going to like one another and, in spite of Lara's bewilderment and Yury's anger, Mademoiselle adheres to her illusions, and soon the illusions become reality. How real and singular the affinity between Yury and Lara had been is expressed by Lara's thoughts when she is left alone at the side of the coffin to mourn Yury's death. "Oh, what a love it had been, how free, how unique.... They had loved each other not out of necessity, not because they burned with passion, as it had been falsely assumed, but because everybody around them wanted it (Zh-M, 513).

If one goes through the novel, one can follow step by step, from boyhood to death, how Yury was disconcerted when he realized the frightfully weird, yet mutual understanding between Komarovsky and Lara. He saw, how both were irresistibly drawn together, as a fly into a spider web (Zh-M, 61). While they were sharing wartime hospital experiences, the inevitable happens: Yury and Lara reveal their secret feelings to one another. Yury's explanation is the opposite of what he intended to tell her.

He wanted to part from her; instead, he unseals his longing and love for her. With this submission and Lara's response, Yury admits that he had been afraid that this might happen. The die has been cast, the fight against providence is lost.

What are the secret forces of the magnetism that dictate the relationship between these two people? What do they mean to one another, what do they take from, and give to one another? It is within the interplay of his characters that Pasternak designs man's anxieties and concerns. The mysticism that surrounds the Yury-Lara attraction only strengthens the pathos of this union. After Lara's departure from the hospital in Melyuzeevo, her image continues to haunt Yury. By injecting mysticism into human behavior, Pasternak seems to belittle man's own will towards responsibility and perhaps even justify man's digression from the law. Voices that make longings and wishes sound real and inevitable are especially strongly articulated in dreams. In Varykino, Yury dreams of a woman's voice, but when he wakes up, he cannot identify the familiar voice. "It remained a mystery." The mystery, naturally, is cleared up a few pages later in the novel. Yury goes to Yuryatin, and in the library, where he recognizes Lara, everything falls into place.

Yury's life of routine and domesticity is disturbed, and Pasternak is a master in juxtaposing the normal and orderly with the unusual and unruly. Yury's diary, written in the solitude of Varykino, is a typical example of the paradoxes and the dualities which are deeply rooted in human nature and decisive in man's behavior. Pasternak begins Yury's diary with a description of an almost idyllic setting of married life. He is at peace with himself and full of new thoughts because his hands are busy, and physical effort, says Zhivago, "brings its reward in joy and success." With his wife he reads Tolstoy, Pushkin, Stendhal, Dickens, and Kleist. Imagining that Tonya is pregnant, Yury's entries in the diary about her become a testimonial and a eulogy of motherhood, an affirmation of his great sense of belonging to Tonya. He records that the year in Varykino had brought them even closer together. Yet, shortly thereafter, they part forever. The tone of the diary, highlighted by the exclamatory lines from Tyutchev, "what a summer, what a summer! This is magic indeed," assures the reader of Zhivago's complete happiness and inner harmony. The sudden turn from Tonya to Lara, therefore, may seem puzzling. But this is typical of Pasternak's

style. All antipodes (that is, opposite poles) have in real life
only imaginary dividing lines. Since the explanations with Lara
in Melyuzeevo, Yury lived in two worlds, in two circles of
thoughts:

The one circle was made up of his thoughts of Tonya, of their
home, and their former settled life where everything, down to the
smallest detail, was touched by poetry and rich on sincerity and
innocence. Yury was fearful about this life and wished that it remain
safe and whole . . . after two years of separation, he yearned for
this life. (*Zh-M*, 102)

And then there was the other circle of his thoughts, quite
different in nature from the first. Yury observes that the new
things in this circle were unfamiliar, not hatched by what was
known, but unchosen and prescribed by reality, and coming as
suddenly as an earthquake. Nurse Antipova, too, was in these
thoughts. Yury's relationships to Tonya and to Lara have their
beginning in sources which are diametrically opposed to each
other: Tonya enters his life gradually, in a conventional and
orderly way: Lara, as Yury says, was among the new things,
"unchosen and prescribed by reality." Tonya, on the other hand,
is Yury's physical home. His worries about her are filled with
the usual questions on everyday existence. Zhivago feels guilty
because he cannot provide for his family. "Tonya, you are my
everlasting reproach, and I am guilty before you" (*Zh-M*, 350).
But Lara means more to him. "Lara, I daren't speak your name
for fear of losing my soul together with it." Together with her,
he can feel and understand humanity. And while with the Forest
Brotherhood, separated from both women, he has a vision of
Lara and he addresses her "as the whole of his life, as all of
God's earth, as all space sunlit and spread out before him"
(*Zh-M*, 353). The providential role of Lara in Yury's life is
purposely created by the author. At one point Yury admits that
her "beauty and dignity" almost frightened him.

The magnetism between these two people was mutual. Indeed,
Zhivago feels that they had become one. To his greatest antagonist, Komarovsky, whom Yury despised and Lara hated, of
whom alone he was jealous, Yury admitted that the occasions
were rare when Lara's and his anxieties were not the same.
"And what did she [Lara] mean to him?" Zhivago asks rhetorically when he did not find Lara at home after the long journey

from the Forest Brotherhood. His answer to this question is
all-embracing. To him she was Russia, incomparable in splendor,
grief, and temperament. Lara was synonymous with life.

Lara, we read, knew Yury's writings, "with my heart, with
my life's blood." And while mourning his death, she again is
overcome by a feeling of pride and relief. To her, he had been
freedom and unconcern, with him she again was able to free
herself "of the sorrows which imprisoned her." With him she
felt again "the joy of liberation."

In the analysis of their relationship, one can go one step
farther. Yury's and Lara's nearness and homogeneity were un-
surpassed, and their communion had reached a degree of
immortality as discussed above, under the heading, "Communion
between Mortals is Immortal." The circle is closed. At the
outset of the book we learn from Uncle Kolya that man's entire
life is "devoted to the solution of the enigma of death." From
Yury, Lara has learned not only the highest joy of life but
also "a preparedness for death," and it is this acceptance of
death that removes all helplessness in man's final hour.

The triangle Lara-Yury-Tonya reveals a very strong Romantic
undercurrent, and if Pasternak would have limited his novel
to this love story, his place would be among the Romantic
writers of the nineteenth century and not among the writers
of the twentieth. But Pasternak was very much aware of our
present-day realities. Pasha Antipov's impact on Lara—he was
for Lara the fulfillment of a longing for purity—his consequent
fate, and also Komarovsky's role remind us, without failure, of
the pluralistic nature of the world around and within man.
Lara tells Yury that she and Pasha were as different as they
are. And yet, she sees in Pasha the most commendable characteristics of a human being. She admits that she would return
to the home which she had shared with him at any price. And
even Komarovsky, who in the eyes of Lara was a useless non-
entity and who had turned her life into a chain of the most
unheard-of crimes, a monster of mediocrity, had some meaning
to Lara and thus to life. And during the final days in Varykino,
Lara is willing to exchange their chaotic freedom for work and
obligations. Her final departure with Komarovsky, although
she is equally deceived by Zhivago and Komarovsky, represents,
on her part, some sort of hope for a life of routine and cares
for oneself and for others. She had observed Katya's instinct

for domesticity and realized that the longing for home and for order cannot be destroyed. That Lara again had miscalculated lies in the nature of things.

After Zhivago was left alone, a double monologue began to take shape in his mind. The one was directed toward himself and was concerned with his new situation. The other was addressed to Lara. Zhivago promises to write Lara's memory "into an image of infinite pain and grief." He will trace her image as the sea that, after a fierce storm has turned it up to its foundations, leaves its traces in the sand as Lara had left her traces on him and on others.

This memorial to Lara is never written; instead, Zhivago writes booklets containing his philosophy of life, views on medicine, theory of personality, and thoughts about religion and history. And only through Tanya, the laundry girl, are some hints and guesses about Lara's final fate given to the reader. It was the author's choice to return fully to Zhivago in the final chapters of *Doctor Zhivago,* and in describing his final years and his death, he prophetically alluded to his own fate which, similar to the fate of his characters, had mostly been overshadowed by temptations and energies not congruous, but dualistic and paradoxical in nature.

V *Man*

Man was Pasternak's main concern in *Doctor Zhivago.* The author has portrayed man in his entirety. Indeed, "he brings us face to face with the complexity of our human nature."[24] Pasternak's people are not divided into good and bad. We find them drawn in the likeness of the divine, as the highest spiritual existence, and at the same time reduced to a state of absurdity. "It's only in bad books," says Lara, "that people are divided into two camps and have no contact with each other. In real life everything is intermingled" (*Zh-M,* 307). This double nature in man is reminiscent of Goethe's "geeinte Zwienatur," whether man is torn in his consciousness between God and himself or between his ego and fellow man. Throughout the novel, Pasternak attempts to define man. But no matter how diverse and comprehensive his assessment may be, the basic components of men are always of a twofold nature.

At the very outset of the novel, Nikolay Nikolaevich singles out two concepts which make up the essence of modern man, "the ideas of free personality and of life regarded as sacrifice." Lara, in a conversation with Yury, points to the insurmountable abyss within "the naked force of human psyche" which, she feels, has remained unchanged throughout human history. She regrets that the human way of life, which was being built up gradually with its guiding principle of home and order, was destroyed and ruined in the upheaval and in the attempt to reorganize the whole of society. The most philosophical and yet realistic definition of man Pasternak offers through Sima Tuntseva who, it is said, was "a bit odd—not quite right in the head," yet, as Lara saw her, she was deep and original and her views were extraordinarily similar to those of Yury. Sima defined man as consisting of God and of work (*Zh-M*, 421).

No matter in how many variables Pasternak's characters see the making of man, the major components are always of a dualistic nature. The "zwei Seelen" of Goethe's *Faust* are noticeable throughout *Doctor Zhivago*. In contemplating the purpose of his existence, Doctor Zhivago declares that every man is born a Faust in order to embrace, to experience, and to express everything. Goethe's "geeinte Zwienatur" is precisely this dualistic totality which we find so vivid in most of Pasternak's characters. In letters to Lavater, Goethe defines man as "God and Satan, Heaven and Earth, all in one"[25] and stands in silent reverence before the enigma of the human personality. Only in the character of man do we find simultaneously exaltation and despair, law and caprice, or freedom and compulsion. And it is man's aim in life, says Goethe, "to move these two worlds towards each other, to manifest their dualistic characteristics in a passing phenomenon of life, this is the highest form towards which man must educate himself."[26]

But in spite of all attempts and strife, man has remained a mystery to himself and to others. Pasternak comes to a similar conclusion in an observation on Yury, Lara, Galiullin, and the other characters, who had known each other in Moscow.

Of special concern to Pasternak was the relationship between man's personality and his nature. Yury is convinced that the inward image of man's personality is formed and shaped in childhood, in man's *Lehrjahre*, and remains constant for life. A man's character determines to a large extent his relationship to his fate. Pasternak, however, digresses from Goethe's "Everyone is master of his own fortune (luck),"[27] and believes that the true measure of man is, as Nicola Chiaromonte so fittingly formulates it, "the capacity to give himself to life, to generously obey its rhythm."[28] This is not a fatalistic attitude towards life, but rather the realization that, to a great extent, man's moral action depends on his character, and since a person's character receives its coloring in childhood, this period of life unconsciously predestines human fate.

Thus, the moral behavior of Pasternak's major characters in *Doctor Zhivago* stands in some proximity to their environmental experience. Lara's inconsistency, although full of heart, can be traced back to the fitting rooms of Madame Guishar, her mother; Pasha Antipov's single-mindedness was born in the shadow of his arrested revolutionary father and his struggle with life. Yury grew up in an academic environment, and his entire life remained for him an academic question. But by struggling for an answer to these questions, Pasternak reflects, like in a mirror, the many realities of life, seen differently by each and everyone, and yet concentrating always on life's meaning and purpose.

The beginning of man, as man is known today, says Pasternak, goes back to the time of Christ, and in a conversation between Yury and Gordon, later in the novel, we find a similar idea expressed. In a Kingdom of God, they feel, there are no nations, but there exist people (*Zh-M*, 125). It is this modern, liberated man who is full of wishes, desires, and ambitions, and who wants to be useful to mankind and to his immediate neighbor. However, he wants to be of use in his own way, as an individual, as a free person. Sima's definition of man, as consisting of God and of work, becomes more transparent.

Man feels his usefulness, his fulfillment through work. Yury expresses this sense of fulfillment the first time when he and his father-in-law, the doctor and the professor, were able to supply the family with food and other necessities in return for some services to the new regime (*Zh-M*, 215). But Yury felt greater satisfaction and fulfillment when his genius was active, when he was able to write. Pasternak makes this very clear. When Yury found the necessary leisure, in Varykino, to write, to create, he also realized the purpose of his existence. This feeling relieved him for a time of self-reproach, of dissatisfaction with himself, of the sense of his own nothingness. In his strife for life's fulfillment, Pasternak, again, was akin to the Classical

Goethe, who once wrote: "Man experiences and enjoys nothing without immediately becoming productive."[29] Pasternak's main character admits freely that hard physical work, work from dawn to dusk, can be rewarding because of its visible joy and success. But if man aims for work in imitation of the Creator, he must create his own world. Yury felt that he could do this best through writing. And while Pasternak unfolds Zhivago's daily torments and anguish—his fear that he will lose Lara, who, he knows, is his "will to live"—he is quite aware that it is Yury's greatest longing, to express his grief so that everyone should weep (*Zh-M*, 451).

It is man's eternal longing to meet the Thou, perhaps more for the sake of seeing his own image reflected, i.e., recognizing himself beyond his own limits, than to congregate with fellow man. It seems conceivable to Pasternak that whenever human experience can assume "the appearance of the transcendental" (*Zh-M*, 388), then this is always in connection with the other. Man's desire to remain eternal is unequivocal. By preserving one's personal integrity, in spite of all social enticements and pressures, and by striving continuously with one's whole personality to make the value of one's own services to others more meaningful, man's personal self can come to life in fellow man. By devoting one's best efforts for others, one transcends oneself.

Yury's greatest longing in life was oriented towards fellow man and, at the same time it was directed inwardly, towards himself. He expresses his desire to be useful as a farmer or a doctor, but at the same time he wants to create something lasting, either a scholarly work or a work of art (*Zh-M*, 293). However, he is prevented from living a creative and useful life. He cannot live such a life, not because of his privations and wanderings, but because of a continuous grinding of empty clichés about the dawn of the future, the making of a new world, or the torchbearers of mankind! All these slogans are confusing, says Pasternak. When one hears them for the first time, one thinks they are rich in fantasy and imagination, but in reality they are empty and pompous because the thought behind such fanfare is second-rate (*Zh-M*, 294). Rhetoric and empty cliché mould man into types, and Pasternak is convinced that if man becomes a type, it will be the end of him as a man. If he cannot be placed in a category, he remains what a human being ought to be. Man then is free from himself and has thus acquired a grain of immortality (*Zh-M*, 306).

Pasternak recognized in man's urge for evolution two basic energies: his concern for "his own inner consciousness,"[30] on the one hand, and, on the other hand, his outer social life. Inner consciousness is that part of man's being which is independent of and unbiased by society. It is an unconcern that relieves and ennobles man, it determines man's private and true self, his religion, and his relationship to the divine. A person's relationship to fellow man is guided by these utterly private concerns.

VI *Man in History*

On one of the first pages in *Doctor Zhivago*, Pasternak poses through his ideologist, Nikolay Vedenyapin, the often quoted question on the nature of history. The direct question "what is history" remains unanswered. However, throughout the novel, the author projects his characters into history. Professor Renato Poggioli, in his short but excellent exposé on Pasternak, has drawn attention to Pasternak's unique interpretation of history and also to his change in attitude towards it. Pasternak's early famous poetic line, "children, what century is it outside in our courtyard," suggests that the creative mind must remain aloof from and, as Poggioli puts it, "indifferent to the dimension of time, to the category of history."[31] In *Doctor Zhivago*, however, and in other later works, Pasternak, indeed, must have realized that a continuous isolation of the artist is not only impossible but also hopeless, and "that the self was bound to merge, whether willingly or unwillingly, with the historical process."[32]

Poggioli especially takes notice of Pasternak's particular search into the relationship between history and the individual, compared to Tolstoy's concern with nations in history.[33] For Pasternak, as Poggioli sees it, it has become a proven fact "that through technology, ideology, and social planning, history is now able to submit to its will the nation, the class, and the family—perhaps the world itself."[34] But the single person, the individual, the human soul, may prove to remain the strongest enemy of history, the antagonist that cannot be conquered, not even in "permanent revolutions," in wars, through any sort of repression, or with temporal enticements. In *Doctor Zhivago* it is, indeed, the voice of the "I" and not the "we" that is protesting. "At every point," writes Nicola Chiaromonte, "the novel draws its life from the will to oppose the true story of individuals to history as it is made by force and chance on the world's stage."[35] For Pasternak the concept of history is rather all-embracing. History's beginning, as he thinks that civilized man should comprehend it, can be recorded since the birth of Christ. Only since that time, Pasternak writes, has man consciously devoted his talent and his effort to the enigma of death in order to resolve it. Man cannot do this without striving for an unusual upsurge of the human spirit because the teachings of the Gospels include everything that is necessary. The Gospels, thus, are civilizing books, books for advancements, and Pasternak, indeed, uses "the Christian myth to express a secular philosophy of history."[36] Man's view of history, of life and death, and his conduct depend largely on his convictions and his faith, that is, on his religion.

In Pasternak's estimate, religion is the merger of two human energies: of man's feeling of utter dependence on the unknown, man's ability to tune in with the illogical voices of the transcendental, and of man in his ontological strife.

Pasternak's concept of God is man-centered (cf. *Zh-M*, 423-25). Through the birth of Christ, God became man and man's private life became the life story of God. Yet the story of human life is man's personal experience. The group, the state, or society at large cannot have a similar experience. Pasternak symbolizes this with the Mary Magdalene episode. Lowly and conscious of her digressions, she comes before Christ. She comes before Him not only to receive, but also to give. She offers Christ her hair, but wants relief from her debt. She knows that she has to confront Christ as an individual and in person, that no one can go instead of her. Her relationship with the divine is a private matter. She confronts Christ in the knowledge of her sins and marvels at the omniscience of His judgment. The man-God relationship, as interpreted in this passage of the book, is very personal. Sima exclaims: "What intimacy, what equality between God and life, God and the individual, God and the woman!"

How a person's concept of God can change, Pasternak describes very vividly through Yury's reflections after Tonya's mother, Anna, had died. In his childhood, after the death of his own mother, God had been the good Father, the keeper of life, to whom man owes obedience and love. As a grown-up, Yury's

personal experience, "the chronicles of his house, his family
tree," became a determining factor in his understanding of
the divine.

Now he was afraid of nothing, neither of life nor of death, everything
in the world, all things were concepts in his dictionary. He felt he
was on an equal footing with the universe and appreciated the
prayers for Anna in a different way from those for his mother in
his childhood. Then he became confused in pain, and fearfully he
prayed. Now he listened to the funeral service as if it were a
personal message to him. He attended to the words and expected
of them a clear meaning, clearly expressed, as this is expected of
any other communication. (Zh-M, 89)

Man's concept of God relates to his personal experience.
And for Pasternak, experience is at the same time the essence
of reality. In a philosophical discussion with Gordon, Yury
upholds that facts only exist if man puts into them something
of his own. "Man's individuality is his Kingdom of God."[37]
Similarly he looks upon the birth of Christ, through whom a
private human event was elevated above a whole people, above
nations.

Pasternak is critical of religious institutions just as much as
of any secular spiritual patronage. He feels that church and
state act out of the same motivation: it is mostly blind heroism.
Pasternak exemplifies this view in the "Epilogue" when the
church canonizes Christina Orletsova-Dudorova for her heroic,
but blind sacrifices behind the German lines. Blind submission
is void of inspiration and primitive. Moses and the crossing
of the Red Sea are compared to modern leaders and nations.
Moses is the magician whom multitudes followed and elements
obeyed. To Pasternak the entire picture, as audible and tre-
mendous, is in reality deafening because it carries within it
compulsion and the destruction of the individual.

Pasternak's observations remind us of Thomas Mann's *Mario
and the Magician,* of Zamyatin's *We,* and of the other modern
works on leaders and nations. In juxtaposing miracles from the
Old Testament and the New Testament, Pasternak points to
the relativity of their intent. A quiet and humble birth of a
child, an illegitimate creation against the laws of nature, a
private event—but, it becomes miraculously the beginning of
a new era in history. Stuart Hampshire's findings that "Pasternak

repeats Hegel's account of the historical role of Christianity in creating the modern man, who need no longer be either master or slave"[38] are, if held against the above passage, of great interest and merit a detailed investigation in a separate study.

As in the beginning of the book, where Christianity is proclaimed as the mystery of personality, we find towards the end, expressed by Sima, similar proclamations. She tells Lara that duty to the state, imposed in the past by leaders and nations with the help of armed force, has been abolished. Instead of peoples and nations, there is now personality and freedom (Zh-M, 423).

In these discussions, the characters of the novel try to recognize and understand the presence through the experience rendered by the past. Pasternak's concept of history is built on the foundation of this recognition. In Doctor Zhivago, we cannot find a coherent and well contoured definition of the author's concept of history. A few excerpts, however, chosen from throughout the book, may bring us closer to a historical image against which Doctor Zhivago was written. Here are a few examples: History is interpreted as the awareness that man does not live in isolation and that human lives flow into one another, or of their flowing into one another as the Kingdom of God. Nikolay Nikolaevich, Pasternak's most philosophical character, sees history "as another universe" which man has built with the help of time and memory in answer to the challenge of death. But to the same Nikolay Nikolaevich, the fighting at the barricades is history. In excitement he calls for Yury: "You've got to see it. This is history" (Zh-M, 193).

And to Yury history is not only what was, but it is also looking forward. He is shaken and overwhelmed by the November uprising, but he also thinks of its significance for the future. To live in history means to be civilized, elevated, orderly; it means to guard the individual way of human life in spite of urgency for the recognition of the whole of society; it means to be loyal to the greatness of the past and to the wisdom of the future.

Man can also quarrel with history. Pasha Antipov is seen as having fallen prey to such a discord. Pasternak analyzes the motivations for Antipov's departure from the norm with the help of Lara. Pasha and she, Lara recalls, had become "idiotically pompous with each other." The symptoms of such pomposity are showy, artificial, and forced relations. Yet behind all this, if one can generalize, the author sees foment, adolescent vanity, and stupid ambition (Zh-M, 415). Strelnikov admits this to Yury, with whom he spends the last hours of his life. Regretfully he recalls: "But for us life was a campaign." This campaign had left Strelnikov with nothing but an insurmountable burden of guilt. The campaigners had become guilty because in their struggle for social and political changes they had derogated the individual and with it the sanctity of the human soul. They had seen history consisting only of cultures and epochs, and blindly excluded man, whose human spirit is developed in stages of work and over generations. Cultures and epochs are only the result of such stages in the development of man. In the words of Sima, Egypt, Greece, and the teachings of the Old Testament prophets presented three such stages. Christianity, the most recent stage, has not been replaced and still inspires further development (Zh-M, 421).

Pasternak sees the urge for evolution superior to revolution. He explains the course of history in terms and images taken from nature. Constantly moving energies are responsible for the continuous sustenance of history and nature, and man in history and nature. Pasternak was fascinated by the speed with which, for example, the transformation of a forest moves, in spring. Nonetheless, he realized that just as this movement of incessant transformation of the forest in spring appears motionless to the observer, so history and the developing life of society change invisibly (Zh-M, 465). It must have been Pasternak's firm conviction, especially towards the end of his life, that history cannot be made, and that men who attempt to make history through revolutions are always one-track-minded fanatics, geniuses of narrow-mindedness. "History evolves purposefully, regardless of man,"[39] writes Janet Oldham in comparing *Doctor Zhivago* and *Babbitt*. This somewhat fatalistic interpretation of man's role in history is based on the assumption that man's consciousness of history is in essence his fate. But man is not completely helpless in structuring his consciousness of history. He can bias it through his own creativeness.

Disappointing to Yury was not the fact that history was being changed on the operating table, but that the spirit of narrowness which leads to upheavals is worshipped for decades and centuries thereafter as holy. Even earlier in the novel, when

Pasternak depicts Yury as being in sympathy with the Revolution and as a believer in the likelihood of its ultimate greatness, he endows his hero with skepticism and doubts toward revolutionary characters who, Yury already then felt, were extremists in everything, who reminded him of nineteenth-century Nihilists and of Dostoevsky's characters. Above all, Yury was dismayed with the arrogance of revolutionaries as typified by the anarchist Klintsov-Pogorevshikh. He believed it is our natural history which brings forth the evolution of man. From it man has learned the urge for endless creativity and, finally, the desire to evolve into a higher existence.

VII *Illusions and Disillusions*

When the publication of Pasternak's *Doctor Zhivago* was rejected in the Soviet Union, the editors of *Novy mir* quibbled particularly about the novel's attitude towards the Revolution and towards Socialism as a way of life. And yet, one cannot say that the ideas expressed on these subjects, in the novel, are of singular and preconceived opinion. The novel's major characters, Yury, Lara, and at times even the philosopher Nikolay Nikolaevich, were not always harsh critics of the Revolution. At the beginning of the novel they are in sympathy with the fermenting spirit of the time. True, they were never as actively involved in it as, for example, Antipov was, but they were convinced that it was a Revolution "in the name of humanity." Only with this in mind, could Lara have been in sympathy with bullets in the streets. The boys involved in the shooting, Lara was convinced, were good, decent boys. Important, however, for the entire development of the novel's controversial tone towards political and social changes is Lara's afterthought: "They are good and that is why they are shooting" (*Zh-M*, 51).

The youthful Yury especially admires the courage and genius of the Revolutionary idea. In an almost dreamlike fancy, he daydreams of the fearlessness of the revolt, "this miracle of history" (*Zh-M*, 199). Yury calls the Revolution a "splendid surgery," in which the old monster of injustice is sentenced to death. And earlier, in Melyuzeevo, with Lara, he compares the Revolution to a breath of air that had been held too long. In a revolution, everyone is revived, reborn, changed, and transformed. Pasternak pictures the young Zhivago as a believer in future political and social Utopia. Socialism is seen as an all-embracing sea of life in which everyone's own personal revolution is aiming at a life as it is transformed through art and enriched through the creative capacity of genius.

In spite of all the agreeable references to the political events and realities, the larger part of the novel is, as it appears, intentionally critical of and often hostile to the time in which Pasternak lived. Why, then, this change to disillusionment from the initial state of enthusiasm and hope? A short survey of some of the ideological reflections throughout the novel may shed some light on this question.

Most ideological questions are in one way or other discussed in connection with Yury Zhivago's personal experiences. From a theoretical point of view, he feels that Marxism has led astray the honest struggle for truth and justice. When Samdevyatov, although without great enthusiasm, defines Marxism as "a positive science, a doctrine of reality, a philosophy of historical design" (Zh-M, 267), Yury denounces Marxism as unbalanced, self-centered, and void of facts. But worst of all is the realization that those in power reject truth in their attempt to promulgate the myth of their infallibility. It is the political mysticism and passion, also of the later Soviet intelligentsia (cf. Zh-M, 494), which, as Gustav Herling has pointed out, ultimately leads to self-accusations and self-destruction, and this was repulsive to Zhivago, as well as to Pasternak.[40]

During the course of the novel, Pasternak inflated his hero's dislike for political developments to the degree of complete alienation. Initially believing in a likelihood of the Revolution's ultimate greatness, Zhivago gradually comes to the conclusion that the Revolution was a mistake. Like any other disappointment, this, too, had several sources. Firstly, Zhivago's ideals of and loyalty to the Revolution were prejudiced by his middle-class background (Zh-M, 162). The upheavals were seen as a transitional necessity which would enlighten the people and then put everything again in its proper place. However, a second source for the gradual deterioration of Yury's compassion for the Revolution was of external nature, evidently marked by events, people, and by experience. And it is through Pasternak's mastery in telling us about human fate that we are able to follow Yury Zhivago's gradual alienation from his early considerations and ideals.

At a time when Yury still trusted the Revolution, he intuitively predicted that the "sea of blood" will bypass no one (Zh-M, 185). But Yury's greatest treasure, in spite of the consequent titanic happenings, is his conviction that man must preserve his respect for fellow man. "May God grant us not to lose each other and not to lose our souls" (Zh-M, 184), is Zhivago's greatest wish. The entire chapter, "Moscow Bivouac," and also later parts of the novel dramatize the nakedness of existence during the Revolutionary years and show how people lost their humanity and with it reverence for life. Pasternak's description is not at all one-sided. He has not condemned the Reds and praised the Whites. In both political factions, Pasternak's hero found good and evil. What was so distasteful to Zhivago were the revolutionaries who were armed with means of intimidation and with revolvers, and who dealt with their opponents "without pity and with Mephistophelean smiles" (Zh-M, 199). It is because of this that we find in the novel accusations that members of revolutionary committees, armed with rules and principles, "aren't human," "are made of stone."

Revolutionaries, we read, were dehumanized men (Zh-M, 327), yet, the author also refers to them as the foundation of ferment in Russia (Zh-M, 347). Revolutionary temperament is described as severely extreme, ranging from the warmheartedness of the half-Buryat Svirid to the heartless and machinelike partisans at the execution scene, where vodka-distillers and conspirators against the Revolution alike were "sacrificed" without hearing the word "forgive," without a second thought about the singularity and sanctity of life. Not only had the doomed men endured degradations, but their sufferings had removed all human likeness from their faces. With this description, the author foreshadows the path the new order would take.

But not only the Revolution, the Reds, or the peasant forces are described as "forces of evil," always "up to something," the Whites too—or for that matter any brute force—are presented in the novel with all their cruelties and evil deeds. A dying man who has just escaped from a White general's investigating and punitive squads tells of senseless atrocities, of how people were boiled alive or how strips of skin were cut out of them (Zh-M, 379).

Vladimir Markov is not completely right when he observes that the "revolution has no use for men of talent if they also

happen to have integrity."[41] Zhivago, the doctor and poet, could
be and was much more daring towards Revolutionary leaders
than the average conscript. This is amply demonstrated in
Zhivago's relationship to Liberius, whose name ironically suggests liberty and freedom, yet who in reality was a man of iron
will and little tolerance. The shooting of Vdovichenko, who
rivaled the influence of Liberius, is another prelude to the
realities of later days.

Babette Deutsch has pointed out that the novel purposely
underlines that life cannot be improved "by purely mechanical
means,"[42] and that, as Tonya's father saw it, the Revolution
had exchanged one oppression for others. But Deutsch did not
fail to observe that in spite of this recognition the doctor wanted
"to live by his confessed 'illusion.' . . ."[43] Yury Zhivago's involvement, or lack of involvement, in the political struggle is poetically
expressed in an old Russian folk song. Zhivago is compared
to a lop-eared hare with a timorous heart who is frightened of
the wild beast's tracks (the Revolution), of the wicked enemy,
and the wicked raven (who could be Komarovsky).

As the novel progresses, Zhivago's disappointment in the new
order grows. The unending, uncompromising nature of the
regime becomes monotonous, the single-mindedness and uncompromising language which he had admired so much in his youth,
were now lifeless, meaningless, and gave him the feeling of
being enslaved. He also realizes that the original purity of ideas
never goes behind the minds of those who conceived the ideas.

Zhivago loses faith in the new regime because the Revolution
was taking more and more the appearance of permanency. He
deplores the fact that nothing definite has been achieved through
revolution. Change and turmoil continue. Zhivago is also disappointed with the endless slogans on the preparation of life.
"Man is born to live, not to prepare for life." All the emphasis
on sacrifices for a better future, the new ideals and ideas are,
in the words of Zhivago, "nothing but garnishing words in praise
of the revolution and the existing régime" (*Zh-M*, 417). Zhivago
is discontent with the regime because he feels it has betrayed
the ideals of the Revolution, or, as Stuart Hampshire puts it,
"the Soviet state is indeed condemned as a degeneration from
the revolution, which was the moment of liberty and of the
assertion of the forces of life."[44]

The philosophical reasons for Yury's gradual rejection of the

Revolution, as well as the Soviet regime, are best revealed in some of the love scenes between Yury and Lara, and also in the endless nightly discussions between Yury and Liberius. Quite early in the novel, and at the beginning of the Revolution, Yury laments the destruction of all that he held dear and, therefore, the foundations of a person's life. Strelnikov, who is struggling for a new life, fails in his attempt, not only because of his political disasters, but because he has separated himself in an unnatural manner from a way of life that was his own. As Pasternak saw it, life is constant. And if Zhivago openly admits to Liberius that he is not at all sure that social improvement, as it is understood since the October Revolution, really justifies the sea of blood, he is absolutely convinced that life itself cannot be reshaped. "Reshaping life! Only people who never really lived, who never felt its breath, its heartbeat can speak of such things" (*Zh-M*, 347).

Zhivago's ultimate disappointment in the new era, thus, has two major sources. It is deeply rooted in his conviction that life itself is the principle of self-renewal and, therefore, beyond and not in need of any political theories or forceful surgery. Furthermore, Zhivago has long recognized that wars, revolutions, or any other brute force bring fear and despair in man's existence, they remove from man faith and hope, and reduce him to a level unworthy of man. Consequently, the Revolution too, is, as Markov concludes, "rejection of the life principle itself."[45] When man becomes a wolf to man, when a whole human way of life is destroyed and dehumanized, then not only the individual is threatened by destruction, but mankind as the whole.

Aside from such philosophical considerations, both Zhivago and Lara had realized that not all who joined the Revolutionary forces were revolutionaries out of principles and civic sentiments. Pasha Antipov, for example, admits freely to Zhivago that the source for all his deeds and digressions can be found in his personal experience. In Pasha's case, this experience was Lara. For him Lara had become the symbol of life's realities. Not that he denied the existence of valid reasons for the Revolution. Everything that made the time of the prerevolutionary years, the tears, insults, hope, revenge, and pride—all this, says Pasha, one could read in Lara's face. The entire century was consummated in the expression of her eyes.

At the end of his life, when Pasha painfully admits that all

144 BORIS PASTERNAK

his calculations had come to nothing, the irony of human fate is simply this: firstly, the girl for the sake of whom he had studied and absorbed a great mass of knowledge, for whom he went to war and into the Revolution in order to avenge all her sufferings—this girl continues to suffer and in part, because of him, because of the man who was in the eyes of Lara "the highest example of a human being" (*Zh-M*, 475). Secondly, that Strelnikov who was constantly preparing for life, who during the six years of inhuman self-restraint had committed himself not to return home unless freedom was wholly won, is left with one wish, to see his family. Thirdly, that in order to improve the human lot, pitiless remedies were invented "in the name of pity."

So-called sacrifices in the name of higher justice were, as Lara relates it, mostly motivated by personal revenge, or were simply sellouts and denunciations in the hope for special favors from the new authorities, or, in Strelnikov's case, by the mystical urge of the Party to free itself of "those nonparty officers who got too near the top and know too much" (*Zh-M*, 407). Lara, for example, fears most of all her father-in-law, old Antipov, who had been transferred to the town's Revolutionary tribunal. Lara describes him and Tiverzin as people who are more frightening than wolves. In a conversation with Yury, after the latter had returned to Yuryatin from the Forest Brotherhood, she singles out a recurring pattern in the new regime's bid for absolute control. Two stages are especially apparent. In the first stage, the spirit of criticism and the fight against prejudices dominates. But then come the false sympathizers, the informers with intrigues and hatred.

It was this second stage that was so distasteful to both Lara and Zhivago and, no doubt, to Pasternak himself. Through his female philosopher, through Sima, who, Zhivago was convinced, had borrowed all of her ideas from Uncle Kolya's books, Pasternak underscores in his evaluation of the Revolutionary period two currents of which the second ultimately will destroy the intent and the achievements of the first. Sima explains that the Revolutionary era is a wonderful era in terms of social betterments. But she cannot believe in the new interpretation of life or in a philosophy of happiness that excludes the present (*Zh-M*, 423).

History cannot be reversed. In this conviction lies Doctor

Zhivago's optimism. It is the same optimism with which Pasternak
has endowed the aging Gordon and Dudorov, in the "Epilogue"
to the novel. The two friends realize—perhaps in 1948 or 1953—
that the enlightenment and liberation which had been expected
at the end of the war had not come. "Yet there was some presage
of freedom in the air throughout the postwar years, and it was
their only historical meaning" (Zh-M, 530).

Visitors to Pasternak soon discovered that in spite of all the
deprivations he had experienced, he was not an embittered
man. "He is an optimist, deeply religious, who believes in life
and in the superiority of life to any theory or dogma,"[46] wrote
Gerd Ruge in his report of March, 1958.

VIII *Free Personality*

At the very outset of the novel, it is said that modern man
is inconceivable without two major components, the idea of
free personality and that of life regarded as sacrifice. Pasternak
must have viewed both elements as integral parts of modern
man. The many references to them, throughout the novel, suggest the author's theory of free personality, as well as his concept
of life.

Gerd Ruge reports that he had found in Pasternak "one of
the freest human beings I have ever known, using the word
not to denote external freedom but as the attribute of someone
sovereign, confident, open, and true."[47] Nicola Chiaromonte, on
the other hand, speaks of Pasternak as a Russian writer who
"has resumed his freedom of speech"[48] in order to freely testify
to all the sufferings Russia and her people have endured since
the turn of the century. Chiaromonte, like most critics of *Doctor
Zhivago*, especially has in mind freedom from political bondage.
But Pasternak's theory of a free personality embraces more than
political freedom; it is just as concerned with being free from
the dictates of capital, free from religious prejudices and the
imperatives of one's own character, or it ponders the desire
for happiness either through unconcern or through a *Lebensplan*.
Furthermore, in his search for human freedom, Pasternak does
not exclude the possibility of absolute freedom which neither he
nor any of his characters can define, but which prophetically
speaks from many pages throughout the novel.

Pasternak's concern for political freedom can occupy the

reader's entire ear if he fails to discriminate between the time in which the actions of the novel took place and the author's human concerns which are timeless and projected into the novel with the help of people and the flow of events. To be sure, the destruction of man's inner freedom is, as Pasternak saw it, equal to death. Doctor Zhivago's life was in this sense a constant struggle to overcome death, and he succeeded, because he was "free of time."[49] This freedom is especially apparent in his poetry.[50]

With the help of poetry, Zhivago establishes his inner freedom in spite of the crushing powers of history. His most apparent struggle is that against political dogma, because political and social upheavals involve, as Pasternak saw it, less the inner life of an individual than his physical existence. Pasternak was not opposed to political changes, but in his prolonged silence he refused, as Uncle Kolya in the novel, to cling to a prescribed political dogma. And as Pasternak had hoped that the Revolution would bring freedom to the individual, so his "professor and philosopher of the revolutionary movement" hoped to show to the world a clear path to better the world. However, Pasternak makes it quite clear in these early pages that Nikolay Nikolaevich was an exception. His mind moved with freedom, he welcomed the unfamiliar, yet he had nothing in common with other Revolutionary thinkers but their terminology. To be a Tolstoyan and at the same time a Revolutionary idealist, this was the youthful Zhivago's dream and, no doubt, Pasternak's.

As in reality so in the novel, there is a difference between theory and practice. Pasternak's Zhivago soon finds himself in the midst of historical circumstances which shatter his earlier ideals and burden him with a feeling of being unfree. As a result, Zhivago's life, as Pasternak demonstrates, is one way of asserting the right of an individual to protect his inner freedom in spite of being "caught up in the mills of history."[51]

It may be true that "the freedom that Doctor Zhivago and his kind seek is irreconcilable with any social and political system."[52] But Zhivago's freedom is personal and never imposed either upon a group or a system. Zhivago loses faith and feels unfree in the new system when he realizes that it, as previous systems, attempts to hold down the beast who sleeps in man "by threats." Yury himself had been caught in a mortal struggle against young cadets with whom he felt morally and spiritually akin, yet he had to submit "to the order of events" and shoot at the children. Yury admits to Liberius, the partisan leader, that he (Liberius) and his type are Russia's liberators without whom "she would be lost, marred by poverty and ignorance" (Zh-M, 348), yet he does not accept their aims and dislikes them. And Zhivago explains to Liberius his rejection this way: he does not like empty clichés, he's willing to say A but not B, he wants to preserve his freedom to choose; in short, he wants privacy, and without fear he announces: "You can take a horse to the water, but you cannot make it drink."

Revolutionaries themselves, Zhivago tells Lara, have lost their freedom. They are horrifying because they have taken the law into their own hands, because they have turned into machines that have gone out of control (Zh-M, 306). In Doctor Zhivago, Pasternak demonstrates that people with "oversensitive generosity" towards forcefully implemented political changes run the risk of being enslaved forever, and that single-mindedness in matters of political power consequently blinds the torch-bearers. In either fear for their own future or in a fit of self-righteousness, they rave of things which in reality do not exist. It might be said that the novel is directed against men and systems who know nothing of what Henry Gifford calls "freedom from the despotism of the phrase."[53] A person is only free, and these are Zhivago's thoughts, if and when everyone's life exists in its own right, and not as an illustration in support of the higher policy (Zh-M, 466). To enslave an individual is, as Pasternak saw it, an act which is out of tune with human nature and reality, and N. Lossky calls the removal of freedom from the individual a "severe crime."[54]

Forceful changes in the political and social structures of a society are, in Pasternak's opinion, destructive to the individual and result in a setback to the advancement of civilized man. The Revolution had suspended the laws of human civilization. The human spirit had died, yet, to be a free man means, as Nikolay Nikolaevich had explained in one of his philosophical discussions, to advance. Advancement, however, is impossible without a renewal of spirit, and in order to advance, man must be spiritually equipped. This, Zhivago's uncle argues, can be found in the Gospels.

In discussing Doctor Zhivago, Edmund Wilson has pointed out that Pasternak, like Christ, shifted in his concern for the

148 BORIS PASTERNAK

free personality "the normal emphasis from the society, from the nation, from the people in the sense of 'populus Romanus,' to the individual soul."[55] For Pasternak the idea of a truly free personality has its beginning with Christ. Nicola Chiaromonte believes that Christ meant to Pasternak "absolute faith in man's innerness and freedom."[56] Man and time, says Nikolay Niko- laevich, could break free only after the birth of Christ. Such observations, and Miriam Taylor-Sajković is right, "rest upon the ultimate foundation—the religious view of life."[57] And Sima, in a conversation with Lara, interprets the symbolism of the birth of Christ as a human act free of necessity, free of com- pulsion, and henceforth, the basis of life for each and everyone. "Pasternak's third article of faith is human freedom, the freedom of the individual,"[58] writes Noline Kanta Gupta. However, Gupta warns that freedom of the individual can be "a double-edged sword." If wisely used, it will stimulate progress and advance- ment; but, if freedom of the individual means whims and caprices, it will be destructive and a barrier "in the forward march."

The doctrine of personality and freedom had replaced the urge of necessity as exercised by societies and nations before Christ. Moses, ancient Egypt, and Rome had been, as Sima saw it, possessed by such urge, and "Pasternak who has seen and experienced so much after Dostoevskij, does not share the concept of national messianism."[59] D. F. Grigorieff sees in Zhivago a representative of those individuals who passively resist the process of being cataloged in favor of groups and societies, regardless of whether their doctrines captivated the individual soul by religious or political persuasion. In preserving his inner freedom, Zhivago, indeed, has become symbolic of "a divine liberator of the world soul suffering in the captivity of sin."[60]

Religion and politics, however, were not the only forces that helped shape Pasternak's theory of a freed personality. Human nature and human character are fundamental in the development towards a free personality and for living a civilized life. And to be civilized, to Pasternak, means to live an orderly life. Robert L. Jackson has drawn attention to "the question of the apocalyptic and the nihilistic as elements in the Russian nature."[61] Both elements have their roots in the emotional sphere of man and, therefore, can be stumbling blocks in man's capability of free choice. Human nature, thus, can be two-faced. It can be a force for freedom and productive idleness or, if not constantly cultivated and advanced, an indolent sanctuary for those who relinquish independent thought and, in tasteless public self-criticism, try to improve the mental image of themselves. Such was the case with Misha Gordon, says Pasternak. However, his attempts spelled jocular behavior when he had aimed for happiness.

Genuine happiness can only be experienced by people who know "the worst,"[62] who are "happily drunk with the general flow of life" because they succeeded in remaining, at least inwardly, indifferent to the jungle detail and the compulsions of everyday life. Lara experiences such happiness as joy of liberation when she is taking leave of Yury and when she is able to escape into freedom with Yury's help, out of the sorrows which have confined her.

To be free, an individual must enjoy privacy and treat his life as Pushkin and Chekhov treated their lives and their work. Man must be careful not to become captivated by his own prejudices, but above all, a free personality must have love for his neighbor which, according to Pasternak, is the supreme sum of living energy. However, even Zhivago, and also Lara, are often doubtful of their inner freedom. They wonder whether their insecurity in Yuryatin is fate, or whether they are free to plan and direct their lives. And earlier, Zhivago expresses skepticism with regard to the freedom that human nature might have. It is so mysterious, so contradictory. Even though Lara assures Zhivago that she despises Komarovsky, Yury doubts that she can know herself as well as that. Yury senses something in Lara that keeps her bound to Komarovsky more surely than to any man whom she would love of her own free will and without compulsion (Zh-M, 411).

Robert Payne has suggested that Pasternak developed Yury Zhivago into "a man who thirsts for freedom—not the small freedoms of everyday life, but the absolute freedoms which are almost beyond the power of man to conceive."[63] What is this inconceivable absolute freedom? Can it really be obtained? And how did it enter Pasternak's novel? Robert Payne has attempted to answer the last question. He believes that Pasternak, as before him Dostoevsky and Tolstoy, was influenced by the philosophical writings of the nineteenth-century historian, Nikolay Fyodorovich Fyodorov. Fyodorov had defined freedom

as the "absolute power over nature."[64] Man must become master
over the forces in nature which are directed against him and
which jeopardize his freedom. Absolute freedom will only be
obtained when man will have firm control over death, that is,
destroy death itself. Fyodorov's philosophy, if indeed it had
such influence on Pasternak, must have suggested to the author
of *Doctor Zhivago* the theme of resurrection. Already Payne
has observed how this theme is "constantly reiterated and described under many aspects."[65] It is presented through various
images of rebirth in nature, through the author's discussions on
art, and, above all, through the unburdened love between Yury
and Lara, and the birth of Tanya, the illegitimate daughter.

Absolute freedom through resurrection, this is the recurrent
theme in *Doctor Zhivago*. However, Pasternak, as his source
Fyodorov and others, could only allude to this freedom. And that
what we have viewed in an earlier chapter as arrogance, or
even Messianic arrogance, comes closest to Pasternak's concept
of absolute freedom. In this connection, it may be of interest to
point out that Zhivago's arrogance is never expressed through
action or behavior, rather it always remains thought; and it is the
capability and the right "to think with freedom" that distinguishes
a free personality from men who, like Gordon and Dudorov, had
learned to idealize their bondage (Zh-M, 494), or from those
leaders who enslave.

Pasternak, however, is well aware that, in spite of man's reach-
ing out for the highest form of freedom, this is not obtainable.
He does not even grant it to his most spiritual character, Zhivago.
Happiness, joy, and unconcern, which above were discussed as
expressions of inner freedom, are not granted to him without
an undercurrent of doubt, suspicion, or even physical pain.
Nevertheless, the novel ends on a hopeful note. The final paragraphs have prophetic meaning, in a real Russian tradition.
The lie, Pasternak is convinced, cannot triumph forever, and the
free personality will finally rank above all social, political, or
religious achievements.

IX *The Meaning of Life*

Life itself is the all-embracing theme in *Doctor Zhivago*.
Throughout the novel, reference is made to life's biophysical
composition, its spiritual sources, to life's needs and demands,

and to its meaning for man in his knowledge of ultimate death. In connection with Zhivago's prophetic pondering over the misfortunes of the future and his own powerlessness over it, Pasternak defines the component elements of life as "air and water, need for joy, birth, sky." By not distinguishing between the physical and spiritual aspects of life, Pasternak stresses the wholeness of life, as understood by Zhivago and, no doubt, by Pasternak himself. The interplay between nature and human life is not only a Romantic mien in Pasternak's writing, but a final acceptance of, and saying *yes* to, all the forces that bring to man joy, beauty, and hope for self-renewal, as well as a demand for sacrifice, and then, leave him to suffering and final death. However, Pasternak's major character realizes only at the end of the novel, and this after a disconcerted odyssey of experience, that to him and to Lara the breath of life lay in the harmonious adjustment of the whole.

Pasternak did not see life as a harmonious melody. Especially the spiritual side of life, as he saw it, develops in a most complicated and complex way, often "as a constant counterpoint"[66] to, or even outside of, immediate reality. Pasternak's references to life are not a neatly packaged gospel, but rather, in a confusing way, they raise new questions instead of finding solutions to a few derailed old principles. Nevertheless, the author leads the various characters masterfully through a labyrinth of personal experience, each and every one with his own outlook towards life. And he advises the reader enigmatically that all of life is symbolic, because all of it has meaning. With this axiom in mind, Pasternak purposely creates a rather mosaic-like interpretation of life. Every major character sees life in his own way, a fact that contributes so vividly to the novel's progression.

Treachery and ambiguity, for the young Lara, constitute life. At least this was her experience of life as exercised in her mother's sewing salon and even more so in her relationship with Komarovsky, for whom life is, above everything else, entertainment. But Lara lacks this treachery. She longs for an "inward music" which she later finds in communion with nature and with Yury Zhivago. Nature, Pasternak writes, "was dearer to her than her parents, better than a lover, wiser than a book" (Zh-M, 76). And in nature Lara once more finds the essence and purpose of life. If she could not discover its wild enchantment or call each thing by its right name, at least her progeny, created out of her own exuberant love of life, could do so in her place (*Zh-M*, 76). The above passage anticipates the Lara-theme, later in the novel, in her relationship with Zhivago.

Young Zhivago, similarly to Lara, finds life analogous to nature, to forest that "contained everything in the world." But Zhivago is more philosophical than Lara. Through the death of his parents, especially through that of his mother, he had learned early that life is personal and meaningful only through another person. For Yury, Lara became this other person and by answering the question, what did she mean to him, he defines his concept of life. And again, to make this concept comprehensible, Pasternak draws his images from nature and from Russia itself.

Lara represents to Zhivago a spring evening, voices of playing children, Russia, or life itself. And since Yury could not communicate with life, he took Lara as its representative, its expression (*Zh-M*, 402).

In spite of Yury's total commitment to Lara as the living incarnation of life's sacred source and in spite of Lara's observation that she and Yury "both understand and feel in the same way," she insists that "in our philosophy of life, it's better that we remain opponents" (*Zh-M*, 309). Pasternak obviously attempts to demonstrate in this passage that a person's philosophy of life can be prejudiced by his social environment, but, at the same time, there is an independent force in man's nature that seeks out its equal. The principle of Goethe's *Wahlverwandtschaft* is not alien to Pasternak.

How different from this understanding is Antipov-Strelnikov's meaning of life! Antipov has become Strelnikov because the world for him is a vast arena where rules are rigidly observed in the competition for perfection. Pasternak further argues that although, or perhaps because, Antipov has acquired great moral purity and sense of justice, he becomes disappointed with the world that surrounds him. For Antipov, his own values and norms constitute life as it ought to be. And his ambition, to become the indisputable judge "between life and the dark forces which distort it," to "be life's champion and avenger," is, as Pasternak sees it, an ambition that grows beyond the realms of a single individual, and it, therefore, leads Antipov down the path of self-destruction.

Pasternak's vision of life is that of constant renewal. Vladimir Markov has linked this aspect of Pasternak's view on life with

Albert Schweitzer's reverence for life.[67] There is no doubt, Pasternak treasured this reverence. But beyond that, he felt that there are active two opposing forces in life, namely, the force of creation and the force of destruction. Although life at its best constitutes a rhythmic whole, life means also "growing, advancing, progressing,"[68] as Gupta has pointed out. And during this "inevitable urge of evolution," Gupta concludes, "together with creation comes destruction." Destruction, man knows, is the agent of death and to live in consciousness of its inevitability makes life, Gupta writes, "a Calvary" and "a cross." Man fades just as much under the pressures of his own inner conflicts as, Gupta juxtaposes, "the collective urge grinds the individual down."[69] But man can learn to accept destruction as nature accepts it. However, he then must also learn from nature the process of self-renewal.

Pasternak, in his novel, gives us hints how life can undergo such renewal. His Yury Zhivago experiences new hopes and new life especially after his first ordeal on the front and through physical work in Varykino. In both cases, it is either a coming home to the family or to oneself that constitutes renewal of life. And at one point Zhivago wonders whether there is anything in the world worth more than a peaceful family life and work (Zh-M, 173). Max Hayward interprets this position as an attempt to rehabilitate the nineteenth-century "obyvatel attitude which ends in an apotheosis."[70] It is precisely in this homecoming, in the desire for an orderly—bourgeois—life where Pasternak's "deep sense of responsibility before Russian life"[71] rests.

With regard to the essence of life and its meaning, Strelnikov and Zhivago tug on opposite ends of the rope. Strelnikov acts out of the conviction that the Revolution was a judgment of an entire way of life and, being successful, would change not only principles and rules, but life itself. Zhivago knew that this was impossible.[72] This viewpoint is supported by Edward Wasiolek who declares that "real life . . . is vastly different from the mind's pretension to control reality."[73] And in doing so, he echoes Zhivago's thinking as expressed in a discussion with Liberius. Life cannot be reshaped because it is infinitely beyond man's theories about it. It is with this in mind that Edmund Wilson suggests "that the sea represents for Pasternak the principle of life itself,"[74] whereas Babette Deutsch speaks of a life progressing "unsteadily and brokenly."[75]

Pasternak concludes the first poem of Doctor Zhivago, "Hamlet," with this Russian proverb: "To live your life is not as simple as to cross a field." "It was in this mood," writes Max Hayward, "that *Doctor Zhivago* was conceived."[76] And, indeed, none of Pasternak's characters, including the happy-go-lucky Komarovsky, is exempted from the malignities inherent in life. In creating his characters, this realization must have been for the author a very important factor. In depicting Pasha Antipov, Zhivago, and especially Lara, Pasternak's probing into the secrets of each of these characters is psychoanalytical.

A case study is Lara, for she acts simultaneously as patient and doctor. After Zhivago has returned from the Forest Brotherhood, she tells him her life's story. She dislikes people like Samdevyatov, characters who are resourceful, self-confident, but also impertinent and endowed with male complacency. Such people, Lara feels, are very practical, but without feeling, and are useless, self-satisfied egoists. They remind her of Komarovsky. "It's thanks to him that I've become what I am," she grieves, and completes her life story with this self-analysis: "There's something broken in me ... in a criminal way and much too early I was made a woman, I was made to discover and see it from the very worst side ... through the eyes of a self-assured elderly roué" (*Zh-M*, 409). Lara is convinced that life hasn't revealed its beauty to people like Samdevyatov and Komarovsky. She is also somewhat fearful for herself and her ability to perceive, because she is convinced that in order to see beauty a person must have a childlike vision and his imagination must be intact. "And it is precisely this of which I have been deprived" (*Zh-M*, 410).

This is how Lara saw herself in retrospect. Much earlier in life, on the German front, when the war seemed lost and the Revolution had changed the moral climate, when established rules were discarded and nobody knew what to think, Lara expresses the desire to entrust herself to something absolute—to life, truth, or beauty. Here, Lara already reveals her spiritual kinship with Yury. Even a spiritually free person, and he perhaps more so than anyone else, must have faith in something, and Pasternak must have felt that truth, beauty, hope, or love are absolute ideals because they are unique for each and everyone. "To give up hope for an ideal is to give up life,"[77] writes Robert C. Mottley, Jr., in discussing the late phase of Pasternak's work.

Hope is life's motor. Evgraf has formulated it in the most positive way. It is not only advice but, perhaps, just as much criticism of Yury and Lara. Evgraf tells Lara: "Whatever the
circumstances, you must never despair. To hope and to act,
these are our duties in misfortune. To despair in idleness is to
fall into oblivion and to neglect our duty" (*Zh-M*, 510). However,
Pasternak immediately offsets this reprimand with Lara's conviction that everything was preordained for herself and for Yury
since that winter night when Yury had seen the candle burning
in her room. The poem "Winter Night" has these prophetic
lines: "And like an angel, the heat of temptation/ Raised two
wings in the form of a cross."

The way of the cross was predestined, as Pasternak wanted
to show, by Lara's and Yury's own making, which was their
fate. Furthermore, Yury Zhivago was by nature and by calling
an artist. He struggled as the nineteenth-century Romanticists
struggled to overcome the discord between art and life. The
author himself had found this unity through his work, and in
Doctor Zhivago he affirms, as Henry Gifford has suggested, "that
poetry and life, art and history, mean most in their interplay.
To separate 'the man who suffers' from 'the mind which creates'
was never his purpose."[78] An artist's life can only become meaningful if he can build on absolutes such as beauty, truth, faith,
and love. With regard to beauty, Pasternak has bestowed upon
Zhivago the belief that "art always serves beauty, and beauty
is the joy of acquiring form, and form is the organic key to
life..." (*Zh-M*, 466).

To live means also to have faith in humanity. Such faith
saves, especially suffering man, from inner disintegration. The
complexity of life prevents that full understanding; and "full
seeing of life can be obtained through reasoning alone. The
heart must open itself, and that's when love enters into everything that gives a spiritual meaning to the passing of time."[79]

Pasternak himself has described love as the supreme form of
living energy, but Janet Oldham mutates this concept into a
somewhat lighter vein and defines love as "the supreme virtue"[80]
within the total life stream. In *Doctor Zhivago*, we have ample
proof that for Pasternak love was indeed the most powerful
force in man's existence. The sound of love, deep in the Siberian
forest, turns Yury's mind again to Lara. He calls her his beauty
and his love, and he vows to find her. And after they are re-

united in Varykino, their love seems to become identical with life itself. It is only in the knowledge of such love that Yury can say to Lara that she stands at the end of his life, she who arose at its beginning and who sowed the seeds in him which have spread throughout his whole existence. Zhivago is convinced that it is only through Lara that he can understand everything else in the world (Zh-M, 437).

Lara reciprocates in Biblical terminology: "You are my strength, my refuge, and my confirmation." For Lara, Yury has assumed the role of the divine. A love dialogue is a declaration of faith in each other and, beyond that, a testimonial of their consciousness. Yury is convinced that his real life began and shall end with Lara. He assigns to Lara the Goethean vision of eternal femininity which fills him for the rest of his life with longing and sorrow.

Pasternak depicts this mystical process as a longing for supreme love. Why love, that supreme human virtue, must be accompanied by sorrow is paradoxical. But Pasternak alludes to the Christ story, in which torment and suffering are charged with energy of love. And it must be even more painful to be a woman, to be the energy and the source of this love, writes Pasternak (Zh-M, 437).

It has been said that if only man could read the history of fellow man, he would find enough sorrows in it to erase all hostility towards him. Perhaps, if this is true, man would feel pity for his fellow man, but would he obtain, as Zhivago desired, the means of understanding everything? Pasternak's inference raises just as many questions as it gives answers. Does the above really mean that only in common sorrows is full understanding possible? Does man not also come closer to fellow man in common happiness? Pasternak never leaves the reader with a neatly thought-out answer to a question or problem. Although Lara admits that what she and Yury have together is a supreme harmony, without limits or degrees and everything of equal value, joyful and spiritual, Lara questions the workability and wisdom of such an attitude. When extreme spiritualism and worldliness clash, Lara feels, logic must stand above love, otherwise it can become "a destructive element hostile to the home" (Zh-M, 445). And in this Pasternak sees and underscores the fundamental difference between man and woman. Lara had never lost her longing for home and order. If man would be given wings, he would fly above the clouds (*Zh-M*, 446), but life on earth would go on, and a woman, Lara explains, must stay close to the ground and shelter the young.

For Pasternak, the process of life-renewal is both a spiritual one and an act of nature to which man must learn to attune himself. Only if man feels that he belongs to the whole of the universe, will he experience the full joy of life. However, man will be able to remove all helplessness in life only if he lives with a knowledge of death, and Pasternak granted, as we read toward the end of the Conclusion, to Zhivago and to Lara the gift to understand the riddle of life, as well as the riddle of death.

X *Death and Immortality*

Stuart Hampshire, in his short but very well formulated exposé on *Doctor Zhivago*, believes that Pasternak was convinced that death is no waste "whenever a man achieves some heightened sense of his own part in the process of life...."[81] Only if the sources of life's renewal have been discovered, man can say, as Yury consoles the dying Anna: "There is no death." But Yury explains before he makes this proclamation. Death is over because of man's knowledge of the resurrection, a resurrection through the survival of consciousness. Pasternak unrolls the mystery of consciousness through the image of a beam of light directed outwards for the benefit of others and as a guideline for man himself. And in some way, as one is able to recognize oneself always in some external, active manifestation, man's identity after death shall live on either in the work of a person's hands, in the family, or in other people. In the poem "The Wedding Party" death is once more seen as sacrifice and gift: "And life itself is only an instant,/ Only the dissolving/ Of our selves in all others/ As though in gift to them."

Pasternak's Zhivago has not only negated death, but opened the gate to immortality. He tells Anna that she is herself only in others and that she always will remain in others. With this simple declaration, Pasternak's Zhivago is showing why death, that is, going to Mother Earth, is equal to being reborn; why only living a myth makes life livable; and that only through kenosis in life and in death can man lay claim to immortality.[82] Zhivago's short discussion with the sick mother of Tonya includes all other answers: that not being able to love is equal to death without

hope and that "death is merely the daily confrontation of un-
imaginative people and dull regimentation of thought,"—"a
dénouement of the vapidity on earth."[83] All these answers, as
Grigorieff rightly states, reduce "personal eternity to the memory of the dead by the living."[84] But to say that "in trying to
explain eternal life logically both writers [Dostoevsky and Pas-
ternak] fail,"[85] is a complete reversal of Goethe's "He who
aspires unweariedly. . . ." Dostoevsky and Pasternak may have
failed in finding a definitive answer to life eternal, but their
search was human. It should also be noticed that later on in the
novel and in the poems "In Holy Week," "August," "Mary Magdalene," and "Gethsemane," Pasternak expar ded his thought on
immortality and "a clear belief in the Christian sense of eternal
life"[86] becomes more and more transparent. Pasternak attempts
to show that death loses its singularity for people who have
"come to terms with it," as in the case with Yury, with Lara,
and also with Evgraf. Pasternak's parallelism between the
kingdom of plants and the kingdom of death (Zh-M, 505) expresses a Romantic understanding of the mysteries of transformation and the mystical interplay between man and nature.

XI Epitome

In a letter to Renate Schweitzer, Pasternak recognized, even
before Doctor Zhivago was published, that his work would invite
a chain of controversy. "The appearance of this book will bring
not only joy, but it will also evoke attacks."[87] His predictions
have come true. The book has been praised because of its objective approach to reality and at the same time accused of lacking
instinct for and understanding of the same reality. It has been
called "Geschichte des Lebendigen,"[88] a continuation of "the
chronicle of mankind," or "Roman-Khronika,"[89] "a historical novel
of manners,"[90] and "Geschichtsphilosophische Betrachtungen."[91]
Others have referred to Doctor Zhivago as a "political and social
novel,"[92] "a novel about the purity and nobility of the human
soul,"[93] or as a "composite portrait."[94]

Doctor Zhivago has also been reproachfully reprimanded as
"the heavy ornamentation"[95] of Pasternak's autobiography, understood as an account of personal experience expressed through
"the unity of personal reminiscence and of poetical perception,"[96]
and placed on a level of greater universality by defining it as "a
testimony of thought and experience."[97]

Gerd Ruge records the author's own definition simply and convincingly. "*Doctor Zhivago*," the author is supposed to have said, "was not an autobiographical book, but it moved in a milieu that he knew well, the world of his friends, professors, writers, actors, artists."[98] *Doctor Zhivago*, indeed is "deeply anthropocentric."[99] It is a work of art "in defence of the dignity of the small man";[100] and yet, it is not only concerned with individual man, it also conveys, as Vladimir Markov has recognized, symbolically "the history of Russian conscience."[101] Therefore, the novel is historical and psychological at the same time. The novel has also been read as "a love story, told with a truly Russian purity and seriousness,"[102] as "realistic symbolism,"[103] a term borrowed from Vyacheslav Ivanov, and at the same time "full of literary allusions and references."[104]

The most outspoken disapproval of *Doctor Zhivago* is voiced with regard to the novel's artistic structure, to novelistic norms and architecture. For Edgar H. Lehrman the novel is "too diffuse, obscure, and disorganized to be considered a great novel."[105] Edward Wasiolek thinks "the characters are weak, the plot line is slender and at times lost in the clutter of almost accidental detail...."[106] This criticism is countered by Miriam Taylor Sajković's suggestion that the novel fuses various approaches of "artistic methodology."[107] The novel stresses in addition to other methods the "polyphonic or 'many-voiced' structural development," and the "hundreds of separate lyric notations"[108] of which Henry Gifford speaks, are in reality nothing else but "parables taken from daily life." Pasternak highly admired this persuasive method of communicating as used by Christ, and the artistic style in *Doctor Zhivago* is an imitation of that Biblical style. Not only "the union of Yury and Lara is a parable,"[109] but the entire novel is a panorama of parabolic expression, as well as of personal and universal experience. Pasternak has concerned himself deeply with the meaning of that experience which had been placed upon his generation. He did not bring forth practical and permanent solutions, but he has raised many questions in the Nietzschean way.

Doctor Zhivago is a *Künstlerroman*, "the story of an artistic vocation."[110] Proof of this are Doctor Zhivago's poems, without which the affirmative intent of the novel is lost. In spite of all the suffering and deprivation, Lara and Yury, as well as their creator, have highest reverence for life, because life is meaningful. *Doctor Zhivago* is a most realistic human story, because it glorifies the whole of life. Glorifying, however, does not mean to make poetry and sing songs in praise of only the beauty of life. It means more than this: it dictates to man an unconditional confidence in life, a trust that is deeply rooted in the realization that life itself is eternal.

CHAPTER 6

The Short Stories

BETWEEN the years of 1915 and 1929, Pasternak wrote five short stories. None of these stories was immediately published. *Il Tratto di Apelle* (1915), *The Childhood of Luvers* (1917), and *Aerial Ways* (1924) reached the public reader in 1933, in an edition of collected works under the name *Vosdushnye Puti*. Prior to this, individual printings had been scattered in various journals and periodicals. *The Letters from Tula* (1918) appeared first in 1922, in an almanac, whereas excerpts of the last short story, *The Last Summer*, also known under *Povest'* (*Tale*), was published in *Literaturnaya gazeta*, Nr. 13, of the year 1929.

I *Il Tratto di Apelle*

Il Tratto di Apelle (The Sign of Apelles) is perhaps the most complex of Pasternak's five short stories. It was written in the Urals at a time when the author translated from the works of Heinrich von Kleist and there can be no doubt that Kleist's style and artistic mannerisms left their traces in Pasternak's own creativity. The beginnings of *Die Marquise von O...* and Pasternak's first short story read, indeed, as if they had been kneaded from the same clay and by the same maestro.[1] Perhaps what is even more striking is the affinity in purpose of Pasternak's story if compared with Kleist's *Das Marionettentheater*. In neither of the two stories is story-telling the end in itself, but rather it is a vehicle with the help of which certain literary, psychological, and philosophical theories are effected.

The story begins in Pisa. Heinrich Heine returns from Westphalia on the same day on which the Italian poet Relinquimine arrives from Ferrara. However, they do not meet in Pisa. Relinquimine leaves with the lackey a bloodstained visiting card and promises a visit for the next day and at the same hour. Heine immediately associates the name of the visitor with the anony-

161

mous person from whom, a few days earlier, he had received a defiant letter. The letter speaks of generation-bound and inherited roots of poetry, and demands from Heine proof of identity in the style of Apelles. This claim of the unknown goes beyond the frontiers of the permissible, concludes the author, and he expresses this with the motif of a story in which the identity of the artistic self is the major theme. In addition to a poet's "search of his signature,"[2] the story expresses also a consummation of jealousy and revenge. It reminds us of Pushkin's *Mozart and Salieri* and it reaches out, to be sure in an imaginary way, into the artistic relationship that existed between Mayakovsky and Pasternak himself.

The aphorism which introduces us to the story does not suggest so much the thematic motto of the story as it provides the basis for a purely artistic atmosphere. The aphorism reads,

It is said that when the Greek painter Apelles did not find his rival, Zeuxis, at home, he drew a line on the wall. By this line Zeuxis guessed who the visitor had been during his absence. Zeuxis did not fail to repay. At a time when he was certain that Apelles was not at home, he left his sign, which assumed allegorical meaning in the world of art. (*Soch.*, II, 53)

Pasternak attempts to extend this artistic atmosphere to the realities of life. The way Heine accepts the challenge and the manner in which he breaks into the ethical life of his challenger, by blackmailing and consequently seducing the latter's wife, is a unique demonstration of how an artist is tempted to fashion personal life similar to that of a work of art. Pasternak does this with Heine's life, postulates Michel Aucouturier, "while subjugating life to the laws of inspiration, improvisation, and of pure yet purposeless creation."[3]

"We spend our entire lives on the stage," Heine tells the beautiful Signora Camilla when she at first seems confused by the dramatic speed of the German poet's advances. In order to speed up the tempo of the story, the author replaces action and reaction with stage directions. The response to Heine's "I am awakening, I am awake—I am on my knees before you, my love," is not narrated but acted. Pasternak inserts stage directions: "Camilla leaped." Nevertheless, words like "the stage" or "play-acting" are only used symbolically. The voice of art in the story, estheticism, is an inner magnetism, a force which, as Heine admits to Camilla, "rouses all his fibres within him, and to which he must yield, as one yields to the crowd." Heine also says it differently. When, in his artistic rage, he explains that he has to express with a single line, with the line of Apelles, "all my being, all that is essential," when he attempts to concentrate upon himself too much light because of his desire for a life as on the stage, of continuous "bridges and crossroads," he suddenly realizes that Camilla "already has acquired the line, the unique one, like life itself" (*Soch.*, II, 64). Signora Camilla is drawn to, what Aucouturier has called, "the played estheticism of the line of Apelles,"[4] but her ethical constraint calls for moderation. She reminds Heine that she is no longer a young girl and that she must have control over herself. However, the author himself does not allow her to withdraw into a state of mind where conventional ethical norms would neutralize the magnetism of a played estheticism of life. Her knowledge of her own beauty—as Pasternak expresses it, "beautiful to the extent of being unrecognizable"—excites in Heine a longing of such irresistible want that Signora Camilla cannot withstand the magnetism and, instead of offering resistance, she is overwhelmed by the poet's kisses. Her outstretched body submits to the embraces. "I will be a boat for such kisses, only carry, carry her, carry me."

At the time when Pasternak was writing *Il Tratto di Apelle,* his desire for the exploration of new frontiers, or even, to pass "the frontiers of the permissible," was too strong; the moralist, although already present in Pasternak at that time, had to take the back seat. Life was still too much tempted by art and poetry, and poetry is fantasy, this Pasternak tells us through Heine.

When Signora Camilla, torn between her moral conscience and the ecstasy of bliss, thinks that she saw a man throwing crumbled leaves and shadows through the window, she explains to Heine how much she wanted to turn her face there in order to catch it on the cheeks. But then, again, "there was no one. . . ." Heine interrupts her: "This is poetry, Camilla."

Life is art and art is fantasy, this complexity Pasternak had recognized in the estheticism of the Futurists. He recognized it in the Romantic manner to which Mayakovsky had fallen prey, yet he had also recognized that, if life is being totally subjugated to art, life may have its exalted moments, but these smiles are removed from reality as are "the smiles of school boys who are laying siege to Troy in the courtyard." Pasternak's artistic and playful absurdities are quite apparent and perhaps deliberate. In them we find a certain degree of toleration and even humanity because of the humor that Pasternak injected into the story. *Il Tratto di Apelle* is for Pasternak the beginning of a long struggle in search of an acceptable synthesis, an harmonic unity, between life and art, a task which the author had to leave to some degree unfulfilled to the very end of his life.

II   *The Letters from Tula*

This story is written in form of letters to the beloved. The poet is in a nostalgic mood. He finds the departure from his love senseless, the new surroundings in Tula are unfamiliar, the people are strangers, and there is no one with whom the poet can share his experience. Yet the poet observes, reacts, and even passes judgment. What a headache it is to be born a poet! What torture imagination is! (*Soch.*, II, 76). Even "to write is only to torture oneself," but the young poet cannot stop writing. Compared to *Il Tratto di Apelle,* these letters are totally void of humor.

In the restaurant of the railroad station in Tula, the poet observes a group of actors from Moscow who are part of the cast of the planned film called "The Time of Troubles." The title could refer to a historical period in Russia, between the years 1598-1613, but should rather be translated as "Disturbed Times" which expresses without concealment the actual concern of the hero of this story. The poet himself is the hero, and he is shocked by the vulgarity and outrageousness of the actors' behavior. It saddens him that all this can happen a few miles away from Yasnaya Polyana, the place where Tolstoy lived and wrote. Pasternak's account sounds quite familiar: "They act like geniuses, recite, and are tossing mottos at one another." The author also criticizes their table manners: "The worst appearance of Bohemianism."

The poet had previously expressed his concern about the nature of poetry, but he now asks himself what his own function might be, what society should stand for, and whether or not an understanding between the two is at all possible. "I am sick," writes the poet. "This is an exhibition of the ideals of the age." But he also immediately recognizes that he himself cannot stand idly aside. The steam or smoke raised by the actors, he realizes, is common to most people; words, such as "genius, poet, boredom, verses, lack of talent, *petit bourgeois,* tragedy, woman, I and she," are a part of his own vocabulary. It is as if he were seeing himself in a mirror. "How terrible to see one's own image in strangers." A too permissible way of life, the author feels, also removes the feeling of shame. Yet man needs the fire of shame in order to warm his soul. While looking into the mirror of self-analysis, the poet feels that for the first time since his childhood he is being consumed by fire.

Pasternak turns away from his time, from Futurism, Symbolism, and other isms. Tolstoy is reclaimed as the antithesis to glamorous and blatant modernism. The ethical values of the Russian nineteenth century, thinks Aucouturier, "are in the process to gain the upper hand over modern estheticism."[5]

Robert Payne has stated without further explanation that "nearly all of *Doctor Zhivago* is contained in embryo in this short, closely written sketch."[6] Such an assertion may gain more in perspicuity if we take a close look at the poet's relationship to the old man in the story. The poet records in his letter that he has seen him before—the man from the neighborhood—which here perhaps means a kin in spirit and mind. "He has seen him once, more than once, in the course of a single day, at different times, at different places." The poet names in particular the station Astapovo where Tolstoy had died ten years before Pasternak wrote these letters and he associates the lonely night with Tolstoy. But it also appears that at times the poet, the old man, and Tolstoy grow into one. The poet speaks of Tula as a "territory of conscience." Again and again the poet stresses that while the old man was writing, "night was over the whole length of the moist Russian conscience," and that although "nothing changed within the whole spectrum of conscience," stripes of light fell on the floor, beneath the benches (the basis of life) and fought one another" (177). The fighting stripes of light are, as we see it, symbolic of those who inherited Tolstoy's poetic and spiritual testament. The poet, the man, whose thoughts and actions are purposely fused, "thought of his own art, of how to find the right way." And then came the realization that the right way could only come to him when he ceased listening to himself. Only concern for others can fill man's soul with complete physical silence.

Tolstoy had become an example for Pasternak. His manner of

writing and his philosophy of life are in imitation of this great predecessor. Tolstoy's early life was that of the Bohemians in the station's restaurant. On the other hand, the mature Tolstoy was for Pasternak a revelation of a synthesis between the actor and the poet. The physical silence for which the young poet longed so much is Tolstoy's revealed reality, and Pasternak recreates this image only toward the end of his life, namely through Hamlet and through Yury Zhivago. In this sense, *The Letters from Tula* is the most characteristic story that Pasternak ever wrote.

III   *The Childhood of Luvers*

Comparing the two stories discussed above with *The Childhood of Luvers*, Miss Angela Livingstone writes: "While they [*Il Tratto di Apelle* and *The Letters from Tula*] are concerned with different aspects of the artist's sense of inescapably acting out a role, of posing, and having to regard naturalness as a special sort of task, *The Childhood of Luvers* depicts a life lived wholly naturally and unselfconsciously."[7] And even this story, as clear and finished as it may be linguistically and structurally, does not have a real plot, but is the direct and chronological stream of consciousness of a young girl who struggles alone and in loneliness to cross the barriers which besiege her in the process of growing up, of struggling through the various stages of puberty.

When the story begins, Zhenya (Evgenia) Luvers is perhaps three years old. She has an older brother, Seryozha, with whom she shares some of her experiences, but their understanding of one another barely scratches the surface. Zhenya's father, fully absorbed in the directorship of some mine works, remains to his children, especially when he is irritable, a complete stranger. Madame Luvers is beautiful and mild, but removed from the world of her children. A good-tempered English nanny is replaced by a consumptive and capricious French governess who, as Zhenya remembers her, "resembled a fly" and who was loved by no one. Finally, the education of the children—and the story is a type of *Bildungsroman*—is put into the hands of the house teacher, Dikikh. The story is also populated with many other persons, friends of Zhenya, of her parents and her brother, neighbors, soldiers, a doctor and servants of the household. But they all are presented to the reader only through the flow of consciousness and the memory of Zhenya.

The various events or crossroads in Zhenya's life are in themselves no exception to the ordinary. What is characteristic in them is a systematic progression of how they affect the maturing consciousness of a young person. They also reveal the mystery of how the act of perceiving reality mutates from the particular to the general and in direct proportion with the experience that a person acquires.

The first frightening encounter that Zhenya has with the unknown are the lights of Motovilikha, an industrial complex across the river, which Zhenya sees one night while she is awake and which she had never seen at night. This phenomenon from the unknown becomes a nightmare to the girl; it causes tears because it has no name. When her father reproachfully explains that it is Motovilikha, Zhenya's agony seems to vanish. And the author reflects: "This was all that was needed, to find out the name of the unknowable . . . for during this night a name still had a complete and reassuring significance for the child" (*Soch.*, II, 84). But, observes the author, that morning she began to ask questions, she ceased to be a child. For the first time in her life she realized that an appearance, a phenomenon holds things concealed and does not reveal itself to everyone alike. And Zhenya too, began to conceal whatever was to her "most essential, necessary, and disturbing."

At thirteen and thereafter, Zhenya perceives reality differently, and her method of perception is gradually modified. Zhenya experiences as before; she still asks questions, but she also supplies her own interpretation to the perceived. The name of a thing or of an event is no longer the total sum of that for which it stands. Pasternak inserts at this point of the story a lesson of educational psychology which ultimately turns into a plea against all prejudices of which, the author feels, psychology is "the most dazzling and amusing of them all." Pasternak recognizes the misunderstanding between parents and children. He sees the reasons for generation gaps in prejudices—among which he also lists "christianism," because, he says, he cannot call it Christianity—all generalizations, and also the conventional use of words. Pasternak postulates, "for there is rarely one, even among grown-ups, who understands what it is that forms, creates, and binds him together. Life enlightens only very few with an insight of what it is going to do with them" (*Soch.*, II, 86). Man can consider himself in the grace of fate if once in a while a ray of light shows him the way.

And so are all the episodes—everything Zhenya Luvers experiences—rays of energy which shape and form her life to the extent to which reality is being perceived and assimilated by a consciousness into which have penetrated "ideas of punishment, retribution, reward, and justice."

Zhenya's perception also undergoes a constant reorientation when the family moves from Perm to Ekaterinburg, when, for the first time, she sees the Ural Mountains, the insignificant road sign of the imaginary divide between Europe and Asia, when she is in company with the cheerful Belgians or the noisy friends of her brother, when she compares her mother to a peasant woman and when her mother assumes, at least in Zhenya's consciousness, a full and familiar face only through this comparison.

The second part of the story, the longest chapter, Pasternak placed under the title "The Stranger." The stranger is a man whom Zhenya often seees in the company of Dikikh, her teacher. This chapter, too, is filled with events of consciousness, but three episodes seem to influence Zhenya's state of mind in particular: first, a moment of tears when Zhenya suddenly feels that she is very much like her mother, and Pasternak explains that it was the feeling of a woman who perceived or saw from within herself her outward charm; secondly, the night when Zhenya's mother had her stillborn child; and finally, the death of Tsvetkov, the lame man, the stranger whom Zhenya had known in a mysteriously spiritual way. These three experiences seem to have changed the maturing girl, at least this is what the house teacher thought.

Of special interest, however, is how Zhenya juxtaposes the physician and the young teacher, and their confidence in the ability of her qualified, yet legitimate, perception of reality. When the tutor tells Zhenya about Tsvetkov, he speaks almost without words, and through his silence he shows his humanity. It is this humanity which cannot always express its most urgent inner thoughts, but only through which bridges of understanding can be built.

However, Pasternak does not end his story with a final harmonious understanding between Zhenya and the teacher. On the contrary, as soon as Dikikh attempts to utter a few words, among which we hear the word "theater," Zhenya is more upset than ever before. With the word "theater," Pasternak established some link with the first two stories. If we recall the poet's unsympathetic image of the actors, of how they played life, and how they distorted it by doing so, we may suspect that Zhenya imagines herself in the role of such an actor. Pasternak tells us that "Zhenya cried because she considered herself guilty in everything." In reality, she had done nothing. All her meetings with the stranger are imaginary, are a product of her consciousness. And how does the world outside of this consciousness judge sensitivity? Pasternak gives us the answer in relating to us the tutor's thoughts: "Obviously the dead man must have produced a very deep and indelible impression upon this little woman. Sentiments of this sort have a name."

However, Pasternak does not stop his story by just stating this impression; he analyzes for us the entire case, not with the help of psychology, which he rejects, but by perceiving life in its totality, by accounting for that which is continuously created in us and which ultimately determines man's relationship to fellow man.

With regard to Dikikh, Pasternak writes:

He was mistaken. The sentiment of which he thought played no part in the situation. At the same time, he was not mistaken. The sentiment which lay concealed in all this could not be erased. It went deeper than he supposed . . . it lay outside the girl's conduct because it was existentially important and significant, and its significance lay in the fact that it was the first time *another* person entered her life, the third person, entirely indifferent to her, without a name or even a coincidental name, inspiring neither hatred nor love, but the *one whom the commandments bear in mind* when they speak Thou shalt not murder, Thou shalt not steal, etc. They also say: "You who are particular and alive must not commit against the confused and general that which you do not want to do to you." Dikikh was mistaken when he thought there was a name for sentiments of this kind. There is no name. (*Soch.*, II, 135)

As much as Pasternak might have been steeped in the freedoms of artistic estheticism, his concept of man, his *Humanitätsideal*, was always based on moral principles which are not only Biblical, but also practical, because they prevent the human race from self-destruction. *The Childhood of Luvers,* today a classic, has been compared, especially in its style, to a number of works of Western poets. Perhaps it is most closely related to Rilke's *Malte Laurids Brigge.* In spite of this affinity, there is no evidence of direct influence. Pasternak's work is highly original. According

to D. S. Mirsky, he is the only contemporary Russian prose
writer who has kept in mind "that neglected and tabooed thing—
the human soul."[8] In *The Childhood of Luvers*, Mirsky recognizes "a work of profound importance, and inspiration to a new
and yet unborn school of prose in the far distant future." Perhaps
this prediction has not yet come true, but this story of a young
girl's reaction to a world that surrounds her, a story of feminine
puberty, is the first in which Pasternak tried out his talent for
creating great female characters. As a story, understood in the
traditional sense of narrated reality, *The Childhood of Luvers*
is the most perfect and even conclusive of Pasternak's short
stories, and this in spite of its fragmentary nature.

IV   *Aerial Ways*

Professor Roman Jakobson has called *Aerial Ways* the most
dramatic of Pasternak's short stories.[9] Its plot consists of several
lucid events which, as the story progresses, become more and
more interrelated and, as their complexity grows, so grows the
tragic fate of its characters.

At the outset of the story, we are confronted with two parallel
evolving events: A little boy has left his perambulator and
crawled away toward a conduit, and then is lost while the
nurse is sleeping under a mulberry tree. At the same time, the
parents of the child are on their way to the harbor to meet a
midshipman who—Pasternak characterizes him in a few words—
"once loved her and was a friend of her husband." Pasternak
intensifies his narrative scheme by injecting anticipation into the
waiting couple: "The husband was burning with impatience
as quickly as possible to initiate his friend into the meaning of
fatherhood. . . . Comparing her to her husband, it dragged her,
like an anchor in water . . . ," and the author heightens the
suspense by simply stating: "Their motives were not the same"
(*Soch.*, II, 138).

The parents and midshipman are shocked when they hear the
news of their lost son. An unsuccessful search is undertaken and
when all hope of finding the child has been abandoned, the
mother whispers, half in despair, to Polivanov, the midshipman:
"We can't stand it any longer. Save us. Find him. He is your
son." Then they part.

More than fifteen years go by. A woman is trying to see Polivanov, now a high official in a local Soviet government. The woman is Lyolya. She has come to ask clemency for a boy who is on the list to be executed because he was caught fighting for the wrong cause. But Polivanov, the functionary, cannot save his own son. His duty and loyalty to a cause had closed the doors to all other perceptions.

Pasternak does not tell us how the boy had been found in the first place, and we do not hear much of the crimes that death alone could vindicate. What, however, is very striking in the story, is the artistic projection of various levels of reality. Psycho-disturbances are rivalled by mysterious occurrences in nature; and horror and pain throughout the story, mixed with allusions and references to political and social circumstances, mirror a time filled with despair and anguish. The style of the story resembles that of a modern symphony, nonmelodic because of the complexity with which numerous independent melodic circles interweave into one opaque and multi-lineal opus. Parallelisms between nature, events, and characters are full of paradoxes and ambivalence. Here is an example:

Night had ended. But dawn was still far away. The earth was covered with shapes like haystacks, stupefied by silence. The shapes were resting. The distances between them increased toward the daybreak, and as if for the sake of better resting, they scattered and moved into the distance. . . . It happened that some of these shapes turned out to be a tree, a cloud, or something recognizable. But most of them were obscure accumulations, without a name. . . . They were rocked from the past into the future, from the future into the past like sand in an hourglass repeatedly turned over. (*Soch*, II, 140)

Everything in this passage is alive and personified. The author draws no sharp lines between time, events, phenomena of nature, or the movements of man. Past and future have ceased to exist, because memory and anticipation are absorbed by the intensity of the present. The author observes the behavior of people in confusion. He sees in man simultaneously "harmony and violence." But Pasternak also infers that man cannot suffer endlessly. The cup of suffering, as the cup of joy, can have its fill, and this is man's second fall.

In this story, we follow step by step how the wounds of the parents' soul grow more and more painful. And Pasternak notices that as long as they were searching in order to find, as long as there was hope, they remained like others, but as hope vanished, the parents became unrecognizable; they ceased to understand the meaning of life.

In none of the other stories can we find the author's direct confrontation with Communism and dictatorship. Not that he is highly critical of a system that in 1920 had scarcely left its cradle. He mentions "rectilinear thoughts of a Liebknecht, a Lenin," which came to the people every day like a train, through aerial ways. But he also senses a growing inhumanity: "This was the sky of the Third International." The author is reproachful of an attitude that displays assumed indifference, that allows the usual to assume the appearance of the unusual and extraordinary, and he exemplifies this attitude through the soldier-guardsman's "stupid obstinacy" towards Lyolya while she is close to despair. The soldier has an attitude, says Pasternak, "as though he had from his very childhood breathed no other air than that of dictatorship." Polivanov, the midshipman, shows parallels to the beloved Spectorsky (in the poem *Spectorsky*) whose face had also been changed by the Revolution. Yet there is a great difference between the two. While the woman has been fully conditioned to the new order and is not only willing to accept sacrifices, but demands them, Polivanov is confronted with a human conflict of the most personal concern. Like Lieutenant Schmidt, Polivanov, too, considers his duty to a common cause as his highest ideal. But Polivanov goes far beyond this call. He sacrifices the life of his own son, yet the conflict within him remains unresolved. In placing an ideological cause above pity, a theory of truth above life itself, and the collective above the individual, Polivanov has transgressed the line which divided the year 1905 from the year 1917.

Various critics see *Aerial Ways* as a *Doctor Zhivago* in a nutshell. However, elements of Pasternak's great novel can be found in almost all of the short stories, and certainly in *The Childhood of Luvers* and in *The Last Summer*. But Pasternak must have felt some preference for *Aerial Ways* and therefore used its title for his collected works of short stories.

V   *The Last Summer*

Aerial Ways, published in 1933, also included Pasternak's last short story, *The Last Summer* (*Povest'*). Excerpts of it had been

printed earlier in papers and periodicals, and *Novy mir* had
published it in full. The author introduces his work with a
reminder: "For the past ten years the scattered fragments of this
tale have kept coming into my mind, and in the early days of
the Revolution some portions of it found their way into print."[10]
He also warns the reader that "there will be no difference of
opinion between my novel in verse, *Spectorsky,* which I wrote at
a later date, and this prose offering: the life in both of them
is the same" (19).

Nevertheless, in 1929, Pasternak pronounced *The Last Summer*
an independent work and, in No. 4-5 of *Na literaturnom postu,*
relates a short story to *Spectorsky,* the novel-in-verse, as follows:

That part of the fable which is furnished by war years and the
Revolution I have given to the prose work because verses have not
the power . . . to characterize and to formulate. With this in mind,
I sat down to write the story, which is going to be a direct continuation of everything that has been published in *Spectorsky* up to
this time.[11]

The two works, in spite of this proximity, have very little in
common, at least in terms of plot. We do, however, encounter
several allusions to related episodes and most of the characters
we find in both works play their assigned roles according to the
will of their creator. But in *The Last Summer* we also have
passages that are analogous to sections in *Doctor Zhivago*—a
work which appeared thirty years later—and some affinity to
The Childhood of Luvers.

The Last Summer is autobiographical, and a frame-story of
rather complex architecture. The outer frame relates, in a few
pages, Seryozha's visit to his sister Natasha. It is the year 1916,
and the place is the small salt town, Usolie, near the Ural Mountains. Natasha, who is married to the factory official Pasha
Kalyazin, is alone at home. The children are in school while
she is preparing for evening guests. After a short exchange of
family news, Seryozha withdraws to the bedroom. He is tired.
Half asleep and half awake, as if in a trance, Seryozha's thoughts
go back to the summer of 1914, to "that last summer when life
still appeared to pay heed to individuals, and when it was easier
and more natural to love than to hate" (90). These recollections,
or reflections, constitute the greater part of the story within the
outer frame. But Seryozha is a poet, and in his sleepless sleep he

perceives an idea for a play. The plot of this play, an allegory, is the inner story of the frame story and gives in its interplay of reflections an air of a *Künstlernovelle* to the entire work.

The issues of this art novella are just as complex as its structure. First there is the young poet Seryozha for whom artistic creativity becomes destiny. His memory is the source of his art, and the author tells us how memories, purposely interwoven into the flow of the story, became the driving force in search for form of expression. Spontaneous creativity, which Pasternak calls writing of "initial outburst," is only concerned with the most general idea which remains unformulated and devoid of vital detail. But such writing, says the author, is natural because "the idea is born out of the circumstances of experience" (75). *The Last Summer* is exactly such a natural way of writing. Everything in the story is based on experience, which does not mean that the author lived every inch of it—physically—but that he experienced it through his thoughts and ideas, through perception and reflection.

The suffering woman and the poet's will to alleviate this suffering, by his confessed affinity to her and through his art, is the central theme of the story. While serving as tutor to the son of the rich Fresteln family, the poet Seryozha, gets deeply involved with Anna Arild, a virtuous young widow from Denmark and, supposedly, social companion to the lady of the house. But her actual duties fall below her original contract, and she is, therefore, deeply hurt. Seryozha has pity on her, and after several meetings and episodes he asks her to become his wife.

At the same time, Seryozha is deeply disturbed by the suffering of the prostitute Sashka whom he visits during nights while her husband is drunk and snoring immediately next to what Pasternak calls the "professional bed." The two cases, taken separately, are of no particular interest because they are not unique. What is of interest, however, are the different aspects of reality as perceived and reflected by the poet. Problematic is also the duplicity which is suggested in the Anna/Seryozha and Seryozha/Sashka relationship. It is basically a philosophical struggle between the two confronting energies, the principles of ethics and those of esthetics, which the author attempts to synthesize in this work as well as in the poetry of *Second Birth*.

In the beginning of the story, in the frame, it is implied, at least through the eyes of Natasha, "that her brother's story [his love life] had in it the elements of free love" (32), and when, in the inner story, her brother offers his friendship to Anna, Anna reminds him of her Nordic and religious background, and tells him that she would not tolerate license. And even later in the story, when Seryozha finds Mrs. Arild sick in her room, and when his feelings for her explode into unrestrained thoughts coupled with a surprise marriage proposal, Anna remains herself, and this in spite of her quiet love for him. Anna represents the principle of ethics. She naturally cannot accept his proposal because she is convinced of its emptiness. "Doesn't an unfulfilled promise or a neglected duty leave its mark?" (67) she asks reproachfully. But what bewilders her more is that a responsible person should be able to commit himself out of the weakness of the moment. She tells Seryozha that there are things larger than being concerned for the self, and she wonders whether there is something like that inside of him. For Anna, it is frightening if a person can go beyond accepted human norms, and her self-control is part of her background. Anna's realism is an inherited realism of the mind. Pasternak writes: "That was all inherited. It explained her calm mastery of it all" (89). In spite of her unhappiness, the author explains metaphorically, "she had not severed her connection with the outside world and had a window in her room" (75).

Then there is the other relationship: Seryozha's nights with Sashka. It appears that the poet implies that she, too, is being visited out of pity. Nevertheless, the author betrays in Sashka the stronger force, the irresistible energy of beauty and innocence. Seryozha is certain that he has loved no one as much as Sashka. Pasternak emphasizes that Sashka was a woman "who, by all the thrust of her hoarse beauty, levelled everything she touched" (50). One of the nocturnal women even tells the young poet "that he was in some way like them" (49). Pasternak speaks of this likeness in his autobiography: "Two expressions have long reached a common triviality: a genius and a beautiful woman. And how much they have in common!"[12]

If we now juxtapose these two relationships, we find that the force inherent in the principle of blind beauty seems stronger than that represented through Anna. Seryozha is surprised "by the fact that in Anna's hour, he could still be interested in something which had no connection with Anna" (71). This was not the case in his relationship with Sashka. But Pasternak does

not argue this thesis. He demonstrates it by introducing to the
novella a parable-like inner story in which the "nocturnal sky"
and "examples of complete and arrowlike submissions to the
earth" are proclaimed, in music and in verse, as the morality of
tomorrow (78). All this is prophesied by a certain Mr. Y, perhaps
the poet himself, who, like Faust, is willing to sign away his life
in exchange for wealth. And it is now Mr. Y, as before it was
Seryozha, who is willing to give himself and all his profits to
suffering women everywhere. He has to sacrifice himself because
he is convinced that it is the poet alone who has the capacity
to embrace life as a whole. Pasternak enlarges these thoughts. He
explains: "But how strangely this man appears to experience all
this. It is as if someone kept showing him the earth . . . and he
interpreted living beauty as a limiting distinction between existence and non-existence" (78).

For Mr. Y, for Seryozha, and for Pasternak, it appears that
the ethical and the esthetical forces of life can find their synthesis
only in "living beauty," which is synonymous with Goethe's or
Blok's eternal femininity or with Soloviev's world soul which
triumphs only because of its feminine universality. Whereas
Lemokh, the rather mysterious character in *The Last Summer*
and in *Spectorsky* is the antithesis of living beauty and of feminine universality, which, as it appears, is the only challenging
energy to creativity and, therefore, to life itself. Lemokh, says
Pasternak at the very end of the story, is "the personification of
the masculine spirit of fact, the most modest and the most terrible of spirits" (92).

In the last analysis, this work, as various other short stories, as
Spectorsky, as *Doctor Zhivago*, and as *The Blind Beauty*—a play
that could not be completed because of the author's death—is
above all concerned with the poet himself. Mr. Y is concerned, as
Yury Zhivago is, and later Agasanov in *The Blind Beauty*, that
"he has no current value" (79), that he is "a very Christ of
passivity" (88). Yet Pasternak, like his heroes, also knows that
in the debate between the artist and the man of action—both
agents of two orders of reality, of poetry which is timeless, and
of history which exists only in time—the poet or the artist, in
all their apparent weakness, are representative of the higher level
of reality. Their level of reality is higher because it is eternal, and
through its very passivity it may procure, to use the words of
Max Hayward, "grace to human activity or even redeem it."[13]

The Last Summer will remain for years to come one of the most modern stories, both in form and in content. It ignores events and the detail of things and yet comments on history through revealing moods and images, it reminds us of an abstract painting, meaningless and challenging at the same time, and, as described earlier, of a symphony with fantasy and infinite allusions. This is characteristic of all of Pasternak's prose. Vague associations, visions, metamorphic powers that animate objects and nature, unexpected paradoxes and ambiguities, mixture of facts and poetry, interaction of past and future, and dangerous elements in his characters—all are characteristics of a prose which attempts to say what could not be said in poetry. It is a prose which tries to express the unspeakable: torment, joy, wildest desires of the flesh and deepest meditations of the eternal soul, most private and sacred contemplations about man's relationship to the divine and, on the other hand, efforts towards generalizations and the formulation of philosophical theories. Pasternak's prose, written out of "almost intolerable necessity,"[14] in a well-marked poetic epoch, unlocks new approaches and new vistas for poets and writers of generations to come.

CHAPTER 7

The Translator

PASTERNAK'S translations occupy a substantial part of his
literary works. One of his earliest attempts in this art is
the translation of Heinrich von Kleist's comedy, *The Broken Jug*,
published in Maxim Gorky's periodical, *The Contemporary*, in
1917. Later, throughout the years, but especially during the
1930's, Pasternak translated many other German and English
authors and also from the works of several poet friends from
Georgia. Hans Sachs, Goethe, Schiller, and Kleist were his favorites from German literature, but he also translated Georg
Herwegh, the Stuttgart-born, early nineteenth century promoter
of Republicanism, and some of the writings of Johannes R.
Becher, whom Pasternak had singled out with praise in his 1936
address to the Writer's Plenum in Minsk, and whom he knew
personally. From the English language, Pasternak translated
Keats and Shelley, Sir Walter Raleigh, Ben Jonson, and Swinburne. His Shakespeare translations, especially, are well known.

Pasternak was an excellent linguist. He was especially fluent
in German, and he read and spoke French and English freely.
But he also translated from languages with which he was unfamiliar. In 1948, he published translations from the Hungarian
poet Sándor Petöfi, thereby familiarizing Russian readers with
Hungarian poetry, as he had a decade earlier brought to their
attention Georgian poetry. Pasternak did not know Georgian.
He translated from that language because he had listened to the
poetry of his Georgian friends. Paolo Yashvili, Titsian Tabidze,
and others had invited him to the Causasus.

In *An Essay in Autobiography*, Pasternak compares Yashvili's
poetry to that of the post-Symbolist period. In Yashvili's poetry,
he recognizes affinities with the prose writings of Bely, Hamsun,
and Proust. "This verse," writes Pasternak, "is built on the
precise and carefully established evidence of the senses" (*Essay*,
112). In his poetry, he sensed "untouched resources of the spirit,"

and thought of Yashvili as one of the best storytellers. The Tabidzes remained Pasternak's lifelong friends. At one point in his autobiography, Pasternak remarks: "If we kept alive [this was in the early 1930's], it was thanks to our Caucasian friends" (*Essay*, 112). Tabidze died in 1937. The many letters to Tabidze's widow, Nina, and to other Georgian poets are moving testimonies not only of an inspiring friendship, but also of a unique and mutual challenge for continuous and untiring creativity.

Pasternak had his own views on certain rules which a translator must observe. He was often accused of claiming too much freedom for the translator. On October 12, 1933, he willingly admitted to Titsian Tabidze: "All translations—good and bad—are to a certain extent a violation of the original text."[1] But Pasternak understood the task of a translator creatively and not technologically. In the letter of September 9, 1945, to S. I. Chikovani, he insists:

One has to make Russian poetry of it [poetry of Baratashvili] as I made it of Shakespeare, Shevchenko, Verlaine, and others. . . . One must, if possible, give something light, fresh, and unconventional. Many will think it debatable, they will say it is too free a translation of Baratashvili, but that does not frighten me.

In spite of his enthusiasm for Georgian poetry, Pasternak felt that he was unqualified to translate from this language. He had to depend fully on interlinear translations provided by his Georgian friends. Unless the poetry was read to him in the original, rhythm and melody could hardly be captured. After many disappointments, he finally made the decision never again to translate from languages unfamiliar to him. On June 14, 1952, he writes to S. I. and M. N. Chikovani: "It is obvious that I must never again translate from interlinear translations but only from languages I know."

Russia has a rich tradition in the art of translating. From the time of Zhukovsky to this day, translated literary works have received high recognition among poets and writers. Pushkin, Lermontov, and many other poets before Pasternak felt it quite honorable to recreate an existing work of art. Pasternak was in good company when he published his Russian *Hamlet, Romeo and Juliet, Macbeth,* and four other Shakespeare tragedies, when his Russian *Maria Stuart* became one of the most performed tragedies in Soviet theaters, and when the immortal *Faust* of Goethe appeared on Russian bookshelves.

In quantity, Pasternak's translations may very well exceed his original writing, and the question of whether or not a talented poet wasted his creative gifts too freely is not new. But for Pasternak, the labor of translating from great Western classics was not only a safe way of providing sustenance and physical survival, it was even more a foundation in the crisis of spiritual existence and a medium of communicating with a past, which was forbidden, and with a present that was silenced and, therefore, mute. In a letter of May 28, 1959, to Boris Zaytsev, Pasternak confesses:

I have sent *Faust* to your daughter. However, my work of this nature is connected with compassion and pain. Not once have they allowed me to preface my own works. And it might very well be that I translated Goethe and Schiller only with this in mind. During my work there was revealed always something unique and unexpected and how (!) it longed for being communicated, concisely and vividly! But for . . . "intellectual work" we have other specialists, it is our job to find the proper rhyme.[2]

In spite of such restrictions, Pasternak left a few remarks on translation in general and on his translations fom English in particular. He set for himself the aim of providing for theaters and readers easily comprehensible renderings. The translator should shy away from using a vocabulary that is uncommon in ordinary speech, Pasternak suggests in a short discourse on general aims in translating.

Translating also means interpreting and, therefore, it is not astonishing that the translator and author turned critic, at least at times. He agrees with the view that *Hamlet* is "a tragedy of will."[3] But lack of will was no subject of concern during Shakespeare's time, says Pasternak. How then must one understand the above interpretation? Pasternak explains that it is up to the spectator to judge how great Hamlet's sacrifice really is, how binding his duty to do the will of him who sent him. Therefore, *Hamlet* is a drama of duty and self-sacrifice, and the hero of the tragedy cannot be accused of lacking character.

In *Romeo and Juliet*, Pasternak underlines the uncompromising nature of the powers of unspoiled youthful love and of hatred and the lie which are kept alive, and of empty pride and other hurly-burly from which the human ego seems unable to free itself.

With regard to *Othello,* he rejects racism as a theme in this tragedy. He recognizes in Othello just as much a historical person as in any white character. But in spite of the central theme, which is concentrated in the forces of passion and genius, and takes less than one-fifth of the drama—in their explication the spectators laughed and wept also over that what they found in the other four-fifths, because all of it was close to life. Pasternak has left notes of such insight on all of his Shakespeare translations.

In discussing *Macbeth,* the last in his list, he places Shakespeare and Dostoevsky in immediate proximity. Neither in Macbeth nor in Raskolnikov can he recognize the born criminal, but sees their downfall both in the faulty adjustment of the mind and in a faultily warped mind. In Lady Macbeth, he sees nothing out of the ordinary, no great will power or coldbloodedness. To Pasternak, she is an average woman who overestimated her strength and invited ruin not because of a corroding conscience, but because she succumbed to a heart full of loneliness and fatigue.

To sum up, all of Pasternak's translations, whether from writers of the past or from his contemporaries, are colored with his own emotions. He speaks in his own idiom, in a language "as spoken today,"[4] and in this lies his originality and his merit.

Epilogue

IN spite of the turbulent times during which Pasternak wrote, both his poetry and prose are a distinct renunciation of a life of hubbub and ferment, of pomp and ceremony. Instead, his art is marked by solitude, humility, and deep silence; it is the tranquil teaching of quietude; it expresses—to use the author's own words about Titsian Tabidze's work—"The feeling of loyalty to life, to the history of his country, and to nature."[1] Such unity of experience is rare in the history of literature and unique in present-day Russian thought.

Pastenak's works reveal an almost pantheistic conception of the universe. Man and nature constitute a perfect unity, and Pasternak was convinced that as long as science is unable to solve the enigma of nature, as long as there are no satisfactory answers about the aims and the purpose of man's existence, man will be only a coincidental ray of light, extinguished at will by the impenetrable darkness of an indifferent night. By injecting optimism into this inherent impotence of man, Pasternak may have penetrated deeper into the basic truth of life than any other writer.

Boris Pasternak created his art out of experience and at the same time intuitively. The spirit of prophecy, attributed by Berdyaev[2] to Tyutchev, has again entered Russian literature. One of Pasternak's central concerns, especially beginning with *Second Birth*, is the theme of individualism as compared to collectivism. The justification of the Russian Messianic idea, of culture, takes second place to the theme of the meaning of life and to the suffering of man. Russian Communism, which Berdyaev has described as "a distortion of the Russian Messianic idea,"[3] had for Pasternak some attraction because of its attempt to improve man's physical existence, because of its social truth. But Pasternak rejected the Messianic defense of collectivism, for he believed he recognized in it a systematic process of dehumanization which is Nihilistic in nature and, if carried out, leads to the destruction of life itself. Although a poet is usually considered great when

182

through his poetry the particular becomes general and universal, Pasternak's writings must also be read with the knowledge of the time in which he lived and the events that surrounded him. He is a master in describing situations and creating spiritual biography. In the latter, he is singular in present-day Russian literature.

The attempt to assess, at this time, Pasternak's influences is premature. In Russia itself, access to his works remains restricted, although we know from Evtushenko[4] that many young poets read their unpublished poems to Pasternak and would have liked to emulate his art and quiet courage. An effective influence on non-Russian writers will remain frustrated by language barriers. Pasternak's poetry and prose reveal great mastery of language, and language, "the home and dwelling of beauty and meaning," was the foundation of esthetics. However, his images of ideals are accessible to all men of good will, and in this lies his greatness and his success.

Notes and References

Chapter One

1. Renate Schweitzer, *Freundschaft mit Boris Pasternak: Brief-wechsel* (Munich, 1963) and David Magarshack (trans. from the Russian with Introduction and Notes), *Letters to Georgian Friends* (London, 1968).
2. Quoted from Gerd Ruge, *Pasternak: A Pictorial Biography* (London, 1959), p. 87.
3. Robert Conquest, *Courage of Genius* (London, 1961), p. 137.
4. *Ibid.*, pp. 173-81.
5. Gerd Ruge, *Pasternak: A Pictorial Biography*, p. 123.

Chapter Two

1. Henceforth identified immediately after quotation as *Essay*. My own translations refer to the Pasternak edition by G. P. Struve and B. A. Philippov (Ann Arbor: The University of Michigan Press, 1961). *Sochineniia* (*Works*) identified immediately after the translation as *Soch*.
2. Quoted from: Stefan Schimanski (ed.), *Boris Pasternak: Safe Conduct* (London, 1945). Henceforth (but only with regard to *Safe Conduct*) referred to as *SC*.
3. Boris Pasternak, *Doctor Zhivago*, trans. by Max Hayward and Manya Harari (London, 1958), pp. 47, 53. Henceforth identified as *Zh*.
4. I. N. Bushman, "Pasternak i Rilke," *Sbornik statei* (Munich, 1962), p. 233.
5. *Ibid.*, p. 238.

Chapter Three

1. William E. Harkins, *Dictionary of Russian Literature* (Paterson, New Jersey, 1959), p. 378.
2. *Ibid.*, p. 1.
3. Boris Eichenbaum, *Aufsätze zur Theorie und Geschichte der Literatur* (Frankfurt a/M., 1965), p. 7.
4. René Wellek and Austin Warren, *Theory of Literature* (New York, 1949), p. 10.
5. Eichenbaum, p. 40.
6. *Ibid.*, p. 11.

7. Harkins, p. 127.

8. George Reavey, Introduction to *The Last Summer* (New York, 1959), p. xviii.

9. My own translation from *The Black Goblet*. (J.W.D.)

10. Manya Harari recognized the same attitude of Pasternak, in 1958: "The artist's right to stand outside politics—his own right, to exist as a non-Marxist in a Marxist society—just as he would claim his right to stand outside any political struggle were he living in the West," *Twentieth Century*, CLIV (1958), 526.

11. George Reavey, *The Poetry of Boris Pasternak* (New York, 1959), p. 256. Hereafter identified as Reavey.

12. *Ibid.*, p. 255.

13. Victor Erlich, "The Concept of the Poet in Pasternak," *The Slavonic and East European Review*, XXXVII (1959), 330. Hereafter identified as Erlich.

14. Nils Åke Nilsson, "Pasternak: We are the Guests of Existence," *Reporter*, XIX (1958), 34.

15. Eugene M. Kayden, *Poems by Boris Pasternak* (Yellow Springs, Ohio, 1964), pp. xx, xxii.

16. *Ibid.*, xxi.

17. "Gorkii and Soviet Writers," in *Literaturnoe nasledstvo*, LXX (1963), 300.

18. Max Hayward, "Pasternak's 'Doctor Zhivago,' " *Encounter*, X (1958), 48.

19. Translated from: *Boris Pasternak: Stikhotvoreniia i poemy.* Introduced by A. D. Siniavskii; edited by L. A. Ozerov (Moscow-Leningrad, 1965), p. 14. Hereafter identified as either Siniavskii or Ozerov.

20. *Ibid.*, p. 25.

21. Ruge, "A Visit to Pasternak," *Encounter*, X (1958), 23.

22. *Ibid.*

23. Kayden, p. xviii.

24. *Ibid.*

25. Lydia Pasternak-Slater, *Pasternak, Fifty Poems* (London, 1963), p. 13.

26. Schweitzer, pp. 87-88.

27. *Ibid.*, p. 94.

28. *Doctor Zhivago*, University of Michigan Russian Edition (Ann Arbor, 1958), p. 451.

29. Translated from: Gleb P. Struve, "Slovo o poezii," *Sbornik statei* (Munich, 1962), p. 9.

Chapter Four

1. Bushman, p. 209.

2. Schimanski, p. 115.

3. *Ibid.*, p. 112.

4. Siniavskii, p. 59.

5. *Ibid.*, p. 39.

6. D. L. Plank, *Pasternak's Lyric: A Study of Sound and Imagery* (The Hague-Paris, 1966), p. 15.

7. Helen Muchnic, "Toward an Analysis of Boris Pasternak," *The Slavic and East European Journal*, XV (1957), 103.

8. Erlich, p. 325.

9. Ozerov, p. 625.

10. Erlich, p. 229.

11. N. Anatoleva, *Poeziia* (Frankfurt/Main, 1960), p. 20.

12. Siniavskii, p. 21.

13. Kayden, p. xx.

14. *Ibid.*, p. xix.

15. Kornei Chukovskii, Introduction: *Boris Pasternak—Stikhi* (Moscow, 1966), p. 15.

16. Lydia Pasternak-Slater, *Pasternak—Fifty Poems*, p. 13.

17. *Ibid.*

18. Plank, p. 63.

19. *Ibid.*

20. Siniavskii, p. 36.

21. Erlich, p. 331.

22. Reference is made to Roman Jakobson's article "Randbemerkungen zur Prosa des Dichters Pasternak," *Slavische Rundschau*, VII (1935), 357-74.

23. Fedor Stepun, "Der 'Fall' Pasternak," *Neue Rundschau*, LXX (1959), 152.

24. V. Veydle (V. Waidle), "Boris Pasternak i modernism," *Soch.*, I, p. xli.

25. Most translations of this poem are taken from the edition of George Reavey.

26. Michel Aucouturier, *Boris Pasternak* (Reinbeck/Hamburg, 1965), p. 85.

27. Ozerov, p. 655.

28. *Ibid.*

29. Gleb Struve, "Boris Pasternak about Himself and his Readers," *Slavic Review*, XXIII (1964), 127.

30. *Ibid.*

31. *Ibid.*

32. Members of a secret organization, "Narodnaya volya" (People's Will), which in the latter part of the last century used terror in order to make themselves heard.

33. Aucouturier, p. 90.

34. Veydle, p. xlii.

35. *Soch.*, II, 293.

36. Reavey, 255.

37. Josephine Pasternak, "Patior," *The London Magazine* (1964), pp. 42-57.

38. *Ibid.*, p. 47.

39. Reavey, p. 93.

40. Victor Erlich, *The Double Image* (Baltimore, 1964), p. 152.

41. Henry Kamen (trans.), *Boris Pasternak: In the Interlude—Poems, 1945-1960* (London, 1962), p. 79.

42. Quoted from the "Notes" by George Katkov, *Boris Pasternak: In the Interlude—Poems, 1945-1960* (London, 1962), p. 137.

43. Angela Livingstone, "Pasternak's Last Poetry," *Meanjin Quarterly,* XXII (1963), 388.

44. *Ibid.*

45. *Ibid.*, p. 390.

46. *Ibid.*, p. 391.

47. *Ibid.*, p. 394.

48. *Ibid.*, p. 395.

49. Kayden, p. 312.

50. Robert Payne, *The Three Worlds of Boris Pasternak* (London, 1961), p. 171.

51. Reavey, p. 97.

52. *Ibid.*

53. Donald Davie (trans. with Commentary), *The Poems of Doctor Zhivago* (New York, 1965).

54. Katkov, in his "Notes" to *In the Interlude—Poems* (117), states: "They [Doctor Zhivago's poems] have, however, an even closer relation to the life of Pasternak himself and to his spiritual development."

55. Rosette C. Lamont, "As a Gift . . . Zhivago, the Poet," *PMLA,* LXXV (1960), 621-33; Dimitri Obolensky, "The Poems of Doctor Zhivago," *Slavonic and East Europeon Review,* XL (1961), 123-35; F. D. Reeve, "Doctor Zhivago: From Prose to Verse," *The Kenyon Review,* XXII (1960), 123-36; Ludolf Möller, "Die Gedichte des Doktor Schiwago," *Neue Sammlung,* III (1962), 1-16.

56. Lamont, p. 621.

57. Reeve, p. 131.

58. Lamont, p. 621.

59. *Ibid.*, p. 622.

60. Reeve, p. 123.

61. Obolensky, p. 123.

62. Heine's poems, too, grew out of his sorrows. Cf. similar observations on Pasternak by Countess Jaqueline de Proyart in her introduction to the first volume of the Michigan Pasternak edition.

63. Davie, p. 68.

64. Lamont, p. 623.

65. Obolensky, p. 125.

66. Reeve, p. 131. It is also possible that the author alludes to Rilke, whom he first met near Kursk.

67. Davie, p. 75.

68. *Ibid.*, p. 78.

69. Lamont, p. 631.

70. Davie, p. 129.

71. Lamont, p. 630.

72. *Ibid.*, p. 629.

73. Möller, p. 6.

74. *Novy Zhurnal*, No. 80 (1965), p. 76.

75. Lamont, p. 632.

76. Obolensky, p. 134.

77. Lamont, p. 629.

78. *Ibid.*, p. 631.

79. Reavey, pp. 75-100.

80. Lydia Pasternak-Slater, *Pasternak: Fifty Poems*, p. 11.

81. Chukovskii, p. 7.

82. Joseph Barnes, "Pasternak's Poems," *Swanee Review*, LXV (1960), 336.

83. V. Veydle, p. xxxviii.

84. Siniavskii, p. 15.

Chapter Five

1. All page references to the novel are inserted parenthetically in the text. Cf. also footnote 3, Chapter Two.

2. Lydia Pasternak-Slater, *Pasternak: Fifty Poems*, p. 11.

3. *Ibid.*, p. 17.

4. In "Pasternak's *Doctor Zhivago*: My Greatest Wish a Quiet Life," *Encounter*, X, 5 (1958), 41, Max Hayward writes "that the idea of *Doctor Zhivago* was hatched" at the beginning of the Second World War "when in the midst of physical privation and fear some natural freedom and moral courage could be recovered."

5. Lydia Slater, ed., *Boris Pasternak: The Last Summer* (London, 1960), p. 7.

6. Reavey, *The Poetry of Boris Pasternak*, pp. 57, 58. See also Reavey, *Pasternak: The Last Summer* (New York, 1959), pp. 125-27.

7. Ruge, "A Visit to Pasternak," 23.

8. Schweitzer, p. 24.

9. *Ibid.*, p. 43.

10. Edgar H. Lehrman, "A Minority Opinion on *Doctor Zhivago*," *Emory University Quarterly*, XVI (1961), 77-84.

11. Reavey, *Pasternak: The Last Summer*, p. ix.

12. Cf. *Ibid.*, p. 111.

13. Aucouturier, p. 120.

14. Miriam Taylor Sajković, "Notes on Boris Pasternak's *Doctor Zhivago*," *SEEJ* (New Series), IV, XVIII (1960), 319.

15. Dmitrij Tschizewskij, "Nobelpreis für Literatur," *Ruperto-Carlo Mitteilungen der Vereinigung der Freunde der Studentenschaft der Universität Heidelberg*, XI (1959), 12-19.

16. Ralph E. Matlaw, "A Visit with Pasternak," *Nation*, CLXXXIX (1959), 135.

17. Schweitzer, p. 47.

18. Matlaw, p. 134.

19. See: Edmund Wilson, "Legend and Symbol in *Doctor Zhivago*," *Encounter*, XII (1959), 5-16.

20. Ruge, "A Visit to Pasternak," 24.

21. Edward Wasiolek, "Courage but not Excellence," *Chicago Review*, XIII (1959), 81.

22. Babette Deutsch, "Talent for Life in a new Novel," *Harpers*, CCXVII (1958), 76.

23. Aucouturier, p. 132.

24. Taylor Sajković, p. 319.

25. Letters to Lavater of April 9 and May 7, 1781.

26. *Goethes Sämtliche Werke* (Jubiläums-Ausgabe), (Stuttgart und Berlin, 1902), XX, p. 209.

27. *Ibid.*, XVII, p. 78.

28. Nicola Chiaromonte, "Pasternak's Message," *Partisan Review*, XXV (1958), 132.

29. *Goethes Werke* (Weimarer edition), (Weimar, 1896), XLVII, p. 323.

30. Nolini Kanta Gupta, "Boris Pasternak, an Indian Viewpoint," *The Russian Review*, XIX (1960), 250.

31. Renato Poggioli, *The Poets of Russia* (Cambridge: Massachusetts, 1960), p. 335.

32. *Ibid.*, p. 335.

33. Vladimir Markov, "Notes on Pasternak's Doctor Zhivago," *The Russian Review*, XVIII, 1 (1959), 17. Markov recognizes "Tolstoy's philosophy of history" in *Doctor Zhivago*, which needs to be qualified.

34. Poggioli, p. 335.

35. Chiaromonte, p. 130.

36. Deutsch, p. 73.

37. Dmitry Felix Grigorieff, "Pasternak and Dostoevskij," *SEEJ*, XVII, III (1959), 337.

38. Stuart Hampshire, "Doctor Zhivago—As from a Lost Culture," *Encounter*, XI, 5 (1958), 5.

39. Janet Oldham, "Doctor Zhivago and Babbitt," *English Journal*, XLVII (1960), 243.

40. Gustav Herling, "Boris Pasternaks Sieg," *Merkur,* Jg. 12 (1958), 476-78.

41. Markov, p. 17.

42. Deutsch, p. 75.

43. *Ibid.,* p. 76.

44. Hampshire, p. 5.

45. Markov, p. 17.

46. Ruge, "A Visit to Pasternak," 24.

47. *Ibid.,* p. 22.

48. Chiaromonte, p. 127.

49. Douglas Grant, "Zhivago and the Law," *The Tamarack Review,* X (1959), 98.

50. Hampshire defines Pasternak's writings as "naive art, in Schiller's special sense of the word," pp. 3-4.

51. Grant, p. 98.

52. Cf. Richard Howard Power's reference to Mojmir Soukup's defense of a system that responds "with equal intolerance . . . to the disturbing element in its midst." *The Antioch Review,* XIX (1959), 231.

53. Henry Gifford, *The Novel in Russia: From Pushkin to Pasternak* (New York, 1964), p. 191.

54. N. Lossky, "*Voyna i mir* L. Tolstogo i *Doktor Zhivago* B. Pasternaka," *Novy Zhurnal,* No. 61 (1960), 294.

55. Edmund Wilson, "Doctor Life and His Guardian Angel," *The New Yorker* (November 15, 1958), 206.

56. Chiaromonte, p. 133.

57. Taylor Sajković, p. 321.

58. Gupta, p. 250.

59. Grigorieff, p. 336.

60. *Ibid.,* p. 336.

61. Robert L. Jackson, "*Doktor Zhivago* and The Living Tradition," *SEEJ,* IV, XVIII (1960), 104.

62. Hampshire reasons that Western writers "not knowing the worst" are "incapable of any tested, unqualified statement. It is not surprising, therefore, that they turn to satire or sentimental mannerism . . . ," pp. 3-4.

63. Payne, p. 140.

64. *Ibid.*

65., *Ibid.*

66. Chiaromonte, p. 129.

67. Markov, p. 16.

68. Gupta, p. 249.

69. *Ibid.,* p. 251.

70. Hayward, p. 42.

71. Jackson, p. 103.

192

BORIS PASTERNAK

72. The Russian letter in *Novy mir,* however, accuses Pasternak's *Zhivago* of being "least concerned about mankind and most concerned about himself." Quoted from: Edgar H. Lehrman, "A Minority Opinion on Doctor Zhivago," *Emory University Quarterly,* XVI (1961), 77-84.
73. Wasiolek, p. 80.
74. Wilson, "Legend and Symbol in *Doctor Zhivago*," p. 10.
75. Deutsch, p. 72.
76. Hayward, p. 41.
77. Robert C. Mottley, Jr., "Boris Pasternak: The Late Phase," *Shenandoah*, XIII (1962), 47.
78. Gifford, p. 187.
79. Mottley, p. 47.
80. Oldham, p. 243.
81. Hampshire, p. 5.
82. Cf. Mary and Paul Rowland, "The Mission of Yury and Evgraf Zhivago," *The University of Texas Studies in Literature and Language*, V, No. 2 (1963), 202, 204, and 215.
83. Mottley, p. 47.
84. Grigorieff, p. 340.
85. *Ibid.*
86. Taylor Sajković, p. 323.
87. Schweitzer, p. 47.
88. Hans Winter, "Boris Pasternak: 'Doktor Schiwago,'" *Wort in der Zeit*, V, i (Vienna, 1959), p. 9.
89. Mark Slonim, "Otkrytoe pismo sovetskim pisatelyam," *Delo Pasternaka* (Munich, 1958), p. 68.
90. Edmund Stephen Urbansky, "Revolutionary Novels of Gironella and Pasternak," *Hispania*, XLIII (1960), 191.
91. Alexander Gerschenkron, "Notes on *Doctor Zhivago*," *Modern Philology*, LVIII, No. 3 (1961), 198.
92. George Gibian, *Interval of Freedom* (Minneapolis, 1960), p. 149.
93. Markov, p. 14.
94. Payne, p. 141.
95. Markov, p. 15.
96. Hayward, p. 43.
97. Hampshire, p. 4.
98. Ruge, "A Visit to Pasternak," 23.
99. Grigorieff, p. 337.
100. Hayward, p. 42.
101. Markov, p. 16.
102. Chiaromonte, p. 129.
103. Taylor Sajković, p. 319.
104. Markov, p. 22.

105. Lehrman, p. 84.
106. Wasiolek, p. 81.
107. Taylor Sajković, p. 319.
108. Gifford, p. 189.
109. Mary and Paul Rowland, "Larissa Feodorovna: From another World," *The Kenyon Review*, XXII, No. 3 (1960), 499.
110. Davie, p. 5.

Chapter Six

1. Payne, p. 72.
2. *Ibid.*, p. 71.
3. Aucouturier, p. 42.
4. *Ibid.*, p. 43.
5. *Ibid.*, p. 45.
6. Payne, p. 83.
7. Angela Livingstone, "The Childhood of Luvers," *Southern Review*, I (1963), 74.
8. Quoted from William Rose and J. Isaaks, *Contemporary Movements in European Literature* (London, 1928), p. 167.
9. Jakobson, p. 371.
10. Boris Pasternak, *The Last Summer,* trans. by George Reavey and with an introduction by Lydia Slater (Penguin Books [first printing], 1959), p. 19. All further references to this work will be cited from this edition, with page number immediately following the quotation.
11. Ozerov, p. 671.
12. Quoted in translated form from the Introduction to *The Last Summer,* p. 12.
13. Boris Pasternak, *The Blind Beauty,* Introduction by Max Hayward (New York, 1969), p. 11.
14. Payne, p. 68.

Chapter Seven

1. David Magarshack (ed. and trans.), *Letters to Georgian Friends* (London, 1968).
2. Translated from: Boris Zaytsev, "Put'," *Sbornik statei* (Munich, 1962), p. 17.
3. See references to Shakespeare, *Soch.*, III, pp. 183-211.
4. Vladimir Markov, "An Unnoticed Aspect of Pasternak's Translations," *The American Slavic and East-European Review*, XX, No. 3 (1961), 504.

Epilogue

1. *Letters to Georgian Friends,* p. 164.

2. Nicolas Berdyaev, *The Russian Idea* (London, 1947), p. 84.

3. *Ibid*, p. 250.

4. Evgeny Evtushenko, *A Precocious Autobiography* (New York, 1963), pp. 103-7.

Selected Bibliography

PRIMARY SOURCES

1. Collections with Introduction and/or Notes.

Boris Pasternak: Sochineniia, eds. Gleb P. Struve and Boris A. Filippov. 3 vols. Ann Arbor: The University of Michigan Press, 1961. The three volumes include the following: (1) All poetry between 1912-1932. Valuable introductory essays by Jacqueline de Proyart and V. Veydle. (2) Prose works other than *Doctor Zhivago* and autobiographical writings. (3) All poetry between 1936-1959, poetry for children, some early poetry not included in Vol. I, and essays and speeches. Vols. I-III have an excellent apparatus and are indispensable for scholarly use.

Stikhotvoreniia i Poemy, Introduction by A. D. Siniavskii and notes by L. A. Ozerov. Moskva-Leningrad: Sovetskii Pisatel', 1965. Includes all poetry cycles with some omission of individual poems. Most informative introduction and very useful apparatus.

Poeziia, eds. N. Anatolieva, N. Tarasova, and G. Shishkin. Frankfurt/Main: Possev, 1960. Selected poems from various cycles. Introduction and chronology.

Safe Conduct, An Early Autobiography and other Works, trans. Alex Brown, Five Lyric Poems trans. Lydia Pasternak-Slater. London: Elek Books, 1959. In content similar to Schimanski's book. Poetry section has a short foreword by Lydia Pasternak-Slater.

Prose and Poems, ed. Stefan Schimanski with Introduction by J. M. Cohen. London: Ernest Benn Limited, 1959. The translations by Beatrice Scott, Robert Payne, and J. M. Cohen are commendable. Short, useful introduction. Very few poems.

In the Interlude: Poems, 1945-1960, trans. Henry Kamen, Foreword by Sir Maurice Bowra, Notes by George Katkov. London: Oxford University Press, 1962. Very good translations. The Notes are informative and interpretative.

Poems, trans. with Introduction and Notes by Eugene M. Kayden. Yellow Springs, Ohio: The Antioch Press, 1964. Among the best translations. Informative Foreword and useful Notes.

Poems, trans. Lydia Pasternak-Slater, Foreword by Hugh MacDiarmid. London: Poets' and Painters' Press, 1958. Fifteen poems. Mostly from the later cycles.

195

REAVEY; GEORGE. *The Poetry of Boris Pasternak.* New York: G. P. Putnam's Sons, 1959. Includes poetry between 1917-1959 with Introduction on author's life, chapter on Pasternak as translator, and addresses. Bibliography. Paperback edition is without bibliography and chapter on translator, but includes short discourse on poetry.

Fifty Poems, trans. and Introduction by Lydia Pasternak-Slater. London: George Allen & Unwin Ltd., 1963. The best available translations. Rhythm and melody closest to the original. Most useful interpretative introduction.

2. Individual Works.

Doctor Zhivago. Ann Arbor: The University of Michigan Press, 1958. One of two available editions in Russian.

Doctor Zhivago, trans. Max Hayward and Manya Harari. London: Collins and Harvill Press, 1958; New York: Pantheon, 1958. Poetry of Doctor Zhivago trans. by Bernard G. Guerney.

SCHWEITZER, RENATE. *Freundschaft mit Boris Pasternak.* Munich-Vienna-Basel: Verlag Kurt Desch, 1963. Letters are written in German with much information on Pasternak's theories of art and on his personal life.

Letters to Georgian Friends, trans. and Introduction by David Magarshack. London: Secker & Warburg, 1968. With general introduction, bibliographical notes, and index.

The Blind Beauty, trans. Max Hayward and Manya Harari, Foreword by Max Hayward. New York: Harcourt, Brace & World, Inc., 1969.

The Poems of Doctor Zhivago, trans. and Commentary by Donald Davie. New York: Barnes & Noble, 1965. Most exhaustive study on this poetry cycle. Poems in English and Russian.

When the Skies Clear (Kogda razguliaetsia), trans. Michael Harari. London: Collins and Harvill Press, 1960. Russian and English parallel texts. Short "Translator's Notes."

I Remember (English trans. *An Essay in Autobiography*), trans. with Preface and Notes by David Magarshack. New York: Pantheon and Collins, 1959. Includes Pasternak's essay, "On Translating Shakespeare," trans. Manya Harari.

An Essay in Autobiography (American trans. *I Remember*), trans. Manya Harari and with Introduction by Edward Crankshaw. London: Collins and Harvill Press, 1959.

The Last Summer, trans. and Introduction by George Reavey. New York: Avon Book Division, 1959. Includes *A District Behind the Front* and short interpretative introductions to both.

The Last Summer, trans. George Reavey with Introduction by Lydia
Slater. Harmondsworth, Middlesex: Penguin Books, 1960. Short,
but very informative introduction.

SECONDARY SOURCES

1. Books on Pasternak.

AUCOUTURIER, MICHEL. *Boris Pasternak: In Selbstzeugnissen und
Bilddokumenten.* Reinbeck bei Hamburg: Rowohlt, 1965. Trans-
lated from French. Comprehensive study of life and works.
CONQUEST, ROBERT. *Courage of Genius.* London: Collins and Harvill
Press, 1961. Includes entire "Pasternak Affair": Letters, reports,
Nobel Prize, and controversy around *Doctor Zhivago.*
Delo Pasternaka. Munich: Izdatelstvo Tsentralnovo Ob'edineniia
Politicheskikh Emigrantov iz SSSR, 1958. Polemical in nature,
with only few references to actual works.
PAYNE, ROBERT. *The Three Worlds of Boris Pasternak.* London: Robert
Hale Limited, 1961. Overall study of life and works, but very
little interpretation of poetry.
PLANK, DALE L. *Pasternak's Lyric: A Study of Sound and Imagery.*
The Hague-Paris: Mouton & Co., 1966. Special study of poetic
use of language in Pasternak's poetry between 1916-1932.
RUGE, GERD. *Pasternak: A Pictorial Biography.* London: Thames and
Hudson, 1959. Delightful reading with useful chronology and
index of names.
*Sbornik Statey, Posvyashchennykh Tvorchestvu Borisa Leonidovicha
Pasternaka.* Munich: Institute for the Study of the USSR, 1962.
Collection of articles of which some should be translated into
English.
TROITSKY, N. A. *Boris Leonidovich Pasternak 1890-1960: A Bibli-
ography of the works of Pasternak and literature about him
printed in Russia.* Ithaca, New York: Committee on Soviet
Studies, Cornell University, 1969. Includes Pasternak's works
(prose, poetry, translations, letters, etc.), as well as works about
Pasternak; all in Russian, published anywhere in the world. Very
useful reference book.

2. Contributions in Books.

ALEXANDROVA, VERA. *A History of Soviet Literature,* trans. Mirra
Ginsburg. Garden City, New York: Doubleday & Company,
Inc., 1963. Chapter on Pasternak, pp. 150-61.
BOWRA, C. M. *The Creative Experiment.* London: Macmillan & Co.
Ltd., 1949. Discusses Pasternak's early period (1917-1923) in

context with prevailing literary movements and in relationship
to other writers.

ERLICH, VICTOR. *The Double Image*. Baltimore: The Johns Hopkins
Press, 1964. One chapter on Pasternak, based on his article:
"The Concept of the Poet in Pasternak."

POGGIOLI, RENATO. *The Poets of Russia, 1890-1930*. Cambridge,
Massachusetts: Harvard University Press, 1960. Section on
Pasternak (pp. 321-42). Excellent observations on poetry and
prose.

3. General Articles on the Author and *Doctor Zhivago*.

Books Abroad, XLIV (Spring, 1970), 196-243, A Symposium in
Memory of Boris Pasternak (1890-1960). Ten short articles by
well-known Pasternak scholars. Among them Vladimir Weidle
(V. Veydle), Michel Aucouturier, Gleb Struve, and others. Of
special interest are hitherto unpublished letters to Professor
Ivar Ivask.

CHIAROMONTE, NICOLA. "Pasternak's Message," *Partisan Review*,
XXV (1958), 127-34.

DEUTSCH, BABETTE. " 'Talent for Life' in a new Russian novel,"
Harper's Magazine, CCXVII (September, 1958), 71-76.

DYCK, J. W. "Doktor Zivago: A Quest for Self-Realization," *The Slavic
and East European Journal*, VI, No. 2 (1962), 117-23.

GERSCHENKRON, ALEXANDER. "Notes on Doctor Zhivago," *Modern
Philology*, LVIII, No. 3 (February, 1961), 194-200.

GRIGORIEFF, DMITRY FELIX. "Pasternak and Dostoevskij," *The Slavic
and East European Journal*, New Series III, XVII (1959), 335-42.

HAMPSHIRE, STUART. " 'Doctor Zhivago.' As from a Lost Culture,"
Encounter, XI, No. 5 (November, 1958), 3-5.

HARARI, MANYA. "Pasternak," *Twentieth Century*, CLXIV (December, 1958), 524-28.

HAYWARD, MAX. "Pasternak's 'Dr. Zhivago.' 'My greatest wish, a
quiet life,' " *Encounter*, X, No. 5 (May, 1958), 38-48.

MARKOV, VLADIMIR. "Notes on Pasternak's 'Doctor Zhivago,' " *The
Russian Review*, XVIII, No. 1 (January, 1959), 14-22.

MUCHNIC, HELEN. "Toward an Analysis of Boris Pasternak," *The
Slavic and East European Journal*, XV, No. 2 (Summer, 1957),
101-5.

STEPUN, FEDOR. "Boris Leonidowitsch Pasternak. Der 'Fall' Pasternak,"
Neue Rundschau, LXX (1959), 145-61.

STRUVE, GLEB. "Boris Pasternak about Himself and His Readers,"
Slavic Review, XXIII, No. 1 (March, 1964), 125-28.

TSCHIZEWSKIJ, DMITRIJ. "Nobelpreis für Literatur," *Ruperto-Carlo
Mitteilungen der Vereinigung der Freunde der Studentenschaft
der Universität Heidelberg*, XI (1959), 12-19.

VEYDLE, V. "O Rannei Prose Pasternaka" (On Pasternak's Early Prose), *Novy zhurnal*, Nos. 63-64 (1961), 144-50.

WASIOLEK, EDWARD. "Courage but not Excellence," *Chicago Review*, XIII, i (1959), 77-83.

4. Studies of Aspects in Pasternak.

CHUKOVSKII, KORNEI. Introduction to *Stikhi*. Moscow: Khudozhestvennaia literatura, 1966, pp. 5-26. Firsthand information on background of Pasternak's poetry.

ERLICH, VICTOR. "The Concept of the Poet in Pasternak," *The Slavonic and East European Review*, XXXVII, No. 89 (June, 1959), 325-35. Views *Doctor Zhivago* as poetic biography.

GUPTA, NOLINI KANTA. "Boris Pasternak. An Indian Viewpoint," *The Russian Review*, XXIX, No. 3 (July, 1960), 248-53. Shows how Yury Zhivago accepts dualities in life, creation, and destruction as single pulsation. Recognizes author's "three articles of faith."

JACKSON, ROBERT L. "Doktor Zhivago and the Living Tradition," *The Slavic and East European Journal*, New Series IV (1960), 103-18. Interprets *Doctor Zhivago* as "a deep sense of responsibility before Russian life."

JAKOBSON, ROMAN. "Randbemerkungen zur Prosa des Dichters Pasternaks," *Slavische Rundschau*, VII (1935), 357-74. Recognizes in Pasternak's early poetic language characteristics of metonym rather than metaphor.

LAMONT, ROSETTE C. " 'As a gift...' Zhivago, the Poet," *PMLA*, LXXV, v (December, 1960), 621-33.

LEHRMAN, EDGAR H. "A Minority Opinion on Doctor Zhivago," *Emory University Quarterly*, XVI (1961), 77-84. Views *Doctor Zhivago* as failure in style and architecture.

LIVINGSTONE, ANGELA. "Pasternak's Last Poetry," *Meanjin Quarterly*, XXII, No. 4 (1963), 388-96. Very good study of *When the Skies Clear*.

————. "The Childhood of Luvers, An Early Story of Pasternak's," *Southern Review*, I (1963), 74-84. Points to the aspect of "excellent naturalness" in the process of learning and understanding.

MATLAW, RALPH E. "A Visit with Pasternak," *Nation*, CLXXXIX (1959), 134-35. Valuable because of firsthand information.

NILSSON, NILS ÅKE. "Pasternak: 'We are the Guests of Existence,'" *The Reporter*, XIX (November 27, 1958), 34-35. Valuable firsthand information.

OBOLENSKY, DIMITRI. "The Poems of Doctor Zhivago," *Slavonic and East European Review*, XC, No. 94 (December, 1961), 123-35. Study of concepts and themes in the poems.

PASTERNAK, JOSEPHINE. "Patior," *The London Magazine* (September, 1964), 42-57. Very useful firsthand information.

PROYART, JACQUELINE DE. *Pasternak.* Paris: Editions Gallimard, 1964. Translations of poetry and prose into French, and many of Pasternak's letters to author.

REEVE, F. D. "Doctor Zhivago: From Prose to Verse," *The Kenyon Review*, XXII, No. 1 (Winter, 1960), 123-36. Poems of Doctor Zhivago are seen as commentators "on the rest of the novel."

ROWLAND, MARY AND PAUL. "The Mission of Yury and Evgraf Zhivago," *The University of Texas Studies in Literature and Language*, V, No. 2 (Summer, 1963), 199-218. Russia as major theme in novel.

RUGE, GERD. "A Visit to Pasternak," *Encounter*, X, No. 3 (March, 1958), 22-25.

SAJKOVIC, MIRIAM TAYLOR. "Notes on Boris Pasternak's *Doktor Zhivago*," *Slavic and East European Journal*, New Series IV, XVIII (1960), 319-30. Good discussion of relationship between life, immortality, and death.

WILSON, EDMUND. "Legend and Symbol in 'Doctor Zhivago,'" *Encounter*, XII, No. 6 (June, 1959), 5-16.

5. Other Sources.

BERDYAEV, NICOLAS. *The Russian Idea.* London: Geofrey Bles, The Century Press, 1947.

EICHENBAUM, BORIS. *Aufsätze zur Theorie und Geschichte der Literatur.* Frankfurt/Main: Suhrkamp, 1965. Very good discussion on theory of Formalism. Contributions on Lermontov, Gogol's *Overcoat*, Pushkin's poetics, and others.

ERLICH, VICTOR. *Russian Formalism.* 'S-Gravenhage: Mouton & Co., 1955. Also discusses other literary movements which surrounded Formalism.

SLONIM, MARC. *Soviet Russian Literature 1917-1967.* New York: Oxford University Press, 1967.

WELLEK, RENÉ, AND WARREN, AUSTIN. *Theory of Literature.* New York: Harcourt, Brace and World, Inc., 1949.

YEVTUSHENKO, YEVGENY. *A Precocious Autobiography.* New York: E. P. Dutton & Co., Inc., 1963.

Index

Acmeism (Acmeist), a movement in Russian poetry, 1912, 36

Acouturier, M. (critic), 71, 76, 120, 125, 162, 163, 165, 187, 190, 193

Afinogenov, A. N. (Soviet playwright, 1904-41), 107

Akhmatova, A. A. (poet, 1888-), 36, 56

Alexander III (Czar, 1881-94), 22

Anatoleva, N., 62, 187

Anisimov, Y., 26

Arsenal Street, 22

Art, *see* Poetics in Autobiography

Aseev, N. N. (Futurist poet, 1889-), 53, 56

Astapova, 27, 165

Athens, 21

Babbitt (novel), 138, 190

Balmont, K. D. (poet, 1867-1943), 35

Baratashvili (poet), 179

Baratynskaya, Y. I., 23

Barnes, Joseph (critic), 104, 189

Baudelaire, C. (poet, 1821-67), 27

Bauman (student), 74

Becher, J. R. (writer, 1891-), 178

Bely, A. (leading symbolist writer, 1880-1934), 23, 26, 27, 35, 40, 54, 178

Beauty, 53, 83, 84, 85, 89, 90, 100, 128, 154, 155, 163, 175, 176

Berdyaev, N. A. (religious philosopher, 1874-1948), 182, 194

Blok, A. A. (symbolist poet, 1880-1921), 23, 26, 35, 39, 43, 44, 56, 89, 176

Bobrov, S. S. (poet and literary theoretist, 1767-1810), 26

Brandukov, A. A., 22

Bryusov, V. Y. (symbolist poet, 1873-1924), 35

Buch der Bilder, Das (cycle of poetry, Rilke), 31

Bushman, I. N. (critic), 28, 29, 30, 58, 185, 186

Byron (English poet, 1788-1824), 67

Centrifuge (literary circle), 37

Chekhov, A. P. (dramatist, 1860-1904), 44, 52, 107, 149

Chiaromonte, N. (critic), 132, 135, 145, 148, 190, 191, 192

Chikovani, S. I. and M. N., 179

Chopin, 89

Christ, 94, 99, 101, 102, 103, 108, 109, 110, 111, 118, 119, 122, 132, 135, 136, 147, 148, 156, 159, 176

Christianity, 35, 135, 137, 138, 158, 167

Chukovsky, K. (critic), 66, 104, 187, 189

Classic(al), Classicism, 35, 42, 45, 104, 132

Cohen, H. (philosopher), 32, 34

Cohen, J. M. (trans.), 82

Collectivism, 47, 108, 172, 182

Conquest, R. (critic), 185

Critique of Practical Reason (Kant), 32

Davie, D. (trans. and critic), 93, 97, 98, 100, 188, 189, 193

Death, 53, 67, 78, 79, 87, 88, 94, 95, 100, 101, 107, 116, 120, 122, 129-30, 135, 136, 137, 139, 146, 150, 151, 152, 153, 157, 158, 168, 176

Decembrists, 86

Dementev, N., 85

de Proyart, J. (critic), 101, 188

Desdemona, 67

Deutsch, B. (critic), 122, 142, 153, 190, 191, 192

Dickens, C. (writer, 1812-70), 127

201

Diotima, 81
Dostoevsky, F. M. (writer, 1821-81), 44, 52, 139, 148, 149, 158, 181, 190
Dualism, 79, 94, 95, 97, 103, 122-30
Duplicity, 52, 83, 111, 122-30, 131, 174
Durylin, S. (writer), 26
Dyck, J. W. (author of this book), 29, 61, 63, 75, 81, 86, 97
Ehrenburg, I. G. (writer, 1891-   ), 18
Eichenbaum, B. (critic), 36, 37, 185
Einstein, A. (physicist), 23
Ellis, 26
Erlich, V. (critic), 43, 44, 62, 89, 186, 187, 188
Esenin, S. A. (poet, 1895-1925), 26, 39, 43, 51
Eternal Femininity, 79, 83, 88, 89, 90, 98, 99, 100, 101, 102, 112, 156, 176

Faust (Goethe), 75, 88, 100, 107, 112, 131, 176, 180
Feltrinelli (publisher), 19
Fine Arts, 23
Formalist(s), 36, 37, 40, 113
Frau von Stein, 99
Freedom, 45, 63, 64, 74, 83, 87, 89, 90, 91, 95, 100, 102, 109, 117-29, 137, 142-50, 169, 189
Futurism, 23, 37, 38, 64, 104, 165
Futurist(s), 37, 38, 39, 40, 46, 47, 51, 64, 163
Fyodorov, N. F., 149, 150

Gapon (priest), 74
Gerschenkron, A. (critic), 192
Ghirlandaio, 79
Gifford, H. (critic), 147, 155, 159, 191, 192, 193
Goethe, J. W. (poet and writer, 1749-1832), 27, 45, 75, 80, 85, 99, 100, 130, 131, 132, 133, 152, 156, 158, 176, 178, 180, 190
Gogol, N. V. (writer, 1809-52), 52
Gorki, M. (writer, 1868-1936), 23, 26, 45, 178, 186
Gorodetsky, S. M. (poet, 1884-   ), 36

Grant, Douglas, 191
Grigorieff, D. F. (critic), 148, 158, 190, 191, 192
Grzhimali, I. V., 22
Gumilyov, N. S. (poet, 1886-1921), 36
Gupta, N. K. (critic), 148, 153, 190, 191
Guriev, A. (writer), 26

Hamlet, 63, 101, 154, 166, 179, 180
Hamsun, K., 23, 178
Hampshire, S. (critic), 136, 142, 157, 190, 191, 192
Harari, M. (trans., critic), 55, 185, 186
Harkins, W. E. (critic), 36, 185, 186
Hartmann, N. (philosopher), 32
Hauptmann, G. (dramatist, 1862-1946), 23
Hayward, M. (trans., critic), 46, 153, 154, 176, 185, 186, 189, 191, 192, 193
Hegel, G. W. F. (philosopher, 1770-1831), 31, 32, 137
Heine, Heinrich (1797-1856), 96, 161-63, 188
Herling, G. (critic), 140, 191
Herwegh, G. (poet, 1817-75), 178
History, 26, 59, 62, 63, 69, 77, 86, 92, 102, 108, 115, 120, 121, 123, 124, 125, 130, 131, 134-39, 145, 146, 155, 156, 159, 177, 182

Immortality, 40, 43, 62, 63, 81, 82, 88, 94, 95, 100, 101, 102, 103, 108, 109, 113, 117-22, 129, 134, 150, 157-58, 180
Impressionist(s), 37, 38
Individualism, 108, 119, 172-73, 182
International Writers' Congress, 57, 84
Isaaks, J. (critic), 193
Ivanov, V. I. (symbolist poet, 1866-1949), 35, 159
Ivinskaya, O. (friend of Pasternak), 91, 108

Jackson, R. L. (critic), 148, 170, 191

Jakobson, R. (critic), 37, 170, 187, 193
Joan of Arc, 73
Jonson, B. (dramatist, 1573-1637), 179

Kant, E. (philosopher, 1724-1804), 42, 104
Kamen, H. (critic), 17, 188
Katkov, G. (critic), 90, 188
Kayden, E. M. (critic), 45, 52, 65, 67, 68, 69, 80, 92, 186, 187, 188
Keats, J. (poet, 1796-1821), 178
Khlebnikov, V. V. (founder of Russian Futurism, 1885-1922), 37, 40
Kleist, H. von (writer and dramatist, 1777-1811), 45, 127, 161, 178
Kozhebatkin, A. I. (Serdarda member), 26
Krasin, B. B. (Serdarda member), 26
Kreutzer Sonata, The, 110

Lamont, R. C. (critic), 93, 97, 100, 101, 102, 103, 188, 189
Lavater, J. K. (writer, 1741-1801), 131, 190
LEF (Left Front [Futurist group]), 37, 47
Lehrman, E. H. (critic), 159, 189, 192
Leibniz, G. W. F. (historian, philosopher, scientist, diplomat, 1646-1716), 32
Lenau, N. (poet and writer, 1802-50), 68
Lenin, V. I. (1870-1924), 70, 71, 172
Lermontov, M. Y. (poet and writer, 1814-41), 44, 65, 67, 179
Liebknecht, K. (radical social democrat), 172
Life, 23, 24, 34, 41, 47, 48, 50, 53, 55, 57, 59, 65, 66, 67, 68, 69, 77, 79, 81, 82, 83, 90, 93, 94, 98, 100, 104, 106, 108, 109, 111-16, 122, 124, 128-33, 136, 141-43, 150-57, 160, 172, 182
Literature, 25-28, 182
Literaturnaya Gazeta, 161

Livingston, A. (critic), 91-92, 166, 188, 193
Lossky, N. (critic), 147, 191
Love, 25, 42, 48, 50, 58, 64, 67, 76, 79-83, 94, 97-104, 109, 111, 115, 122-26, 129, 135, 143, 149-51, 154-57, 162, 164, 169, 173, 175

Macbeth, 63, 179, 181
Magarshack, D. (critic), 185, 193
Makovsky, S. (critic), 26
Man, 69, 77, 104, 111, 112, 113, 114, 115, 118, 119, 122, 127, 130-39, 141-45, 148, 149, 151, 153, 156, 159, 171, 176, 182
Mann, T. (writer, 1875-1955), 136
Mandelstam, O. E. (poet, 1892-1942?), 36
Marburg (city; poem), 25, 31-34, 42-43, 58, 60, 62, 64
Markov, V. (critic), 141, 143, 152, 159, 190, 191, 192, 193
Marxism, 140, 186
Mary Stuart, 90, 179
Materialism, 123
Matlaw, R. E. (critic), 121, 190
Mayakovsky, V. V. (Futurist poet, 1893-1930), 23, 26, 37, 39, 43, 44, 50, 51, 56, 58, 61, 78, 162, 163
Messianic, 37, 44, 75, 118, 119, 120, 148, 150, 182
Metner, E. (Musaget member), 26
Mir Zur Freude, 29
Mirsky, D. S. (Lit. Historian), 170
Möller, L. (critic), 93, 101, 188, 189
Moses, 136, 148
Mottley, R. C. (critic), 154, 192
Mozart, W. A. (1756-91), 56, 162
Muchnic, H. (critic), 61, 187
Musaget (literary circle), 17, 26
Music, 22-27, 34, 35, 47, 54, 56, 82, 93, 109, 151
Mysticism, 24, 35, 44, 127, 140, 158

Na Literaturnom Postu, 73, 173
Napoleon (1769-1821), 86
Nature, 42, 53, 60, 68, 69, 80-85, 89, 94-97, 101, 104, 108, 109,

115, 119, 122, 123, 125, 128, 130, 136, 138, 147-53, 157, 171, 177, 182

Nekrassov, N. A. (poet and writer, 1821-78), 55

NEP (New Economic Policy), 77

Nicolay II (Czar, 1868-1918), 22

Nietzsche, F. W. (philosopher, 1844-1900), 47, 120, 159

Nilender (Musaget member), 26

Nilsson, N. A. (critic), 186

Nobel Prize, 17, 19, 190

Novators (literary group), 38, 39

Novy Mir (periodical), 18, 139, 173

Obolensky, D. (critic), 93, 94, 97, 102, 188, 189

Odessa, 21, 22

Odyssey, 21, 93, 113, 117, 151

Oldham, J. (critic), 138, 155, 190, 192

Ophelia, 67

Opoyaz (Lit. School for the study of poetic language), 37

Othello, 181

Ossian (3rd century Celtic hero), 55

Ozerov, L. A. (critic), 186, 187, 193

Paradox, 94, 95, 122-30, 171

Parny, 55

Pasternak, Boris (1890-1960)

WORKS OF:

Above the Barriers, 58, 61-64

Aerial Ways, 161, 170-72

Black Goblet, The, 37-38, 186

Blind Beauty, The, 176, 193

Childhood of Luvers, 106, 161, 166-70, 172-73

Chopin, 41

Doctor Zhivago, 17, 18, 19, 27, 28, 32, 42, 43, 44, 46, 47, 48, 51, 52, 53, 55, 56, 57, 58, 59, 66, 70, 71, 75, 78, 82, 83, 86, 88, 92, 106, 165, 172, 173, 176; Communion Between Mortals is Immortal, 117-22; Death and Immortality, 157-58; Dualism, Duplicity, and Paradox, 122-30; Epitome, 158-60; Free Personality,

145-50; Illusions and Disillusions, 139-45; Man, 130-34; Man in History, 134-39; The Meaning of Life, 150-57; Personae, Plot, Problems, 108-17

Epic Poem, 70-78, 103

Essay in Autobiography, 22-29, 31-32, 38, 40, 43, 46, 49-56, 59, 61, 108, 178-79

High Malady, The, 59, 70-73

Il Tratto di Apello, 33, 161-64, 166

Kruchonykh, 37

Last Summer, The, 31, 75, 83, 107, 117-18, 161, 172-77, 186

Letters from Tula, 161, 164-66

Letters to Georgian Friends, 17, 185, 193

Lieutenant Schmidt, 59, 74-75, 106, 172

My Sister, Life, 37, 58, 62, 64-70

Nachal'naya Pora, 58

On Early Trains, 59, 83-87

On Modesty and Boldness, 41

Poetry of Dr. Zhivago, 29, 59, 92-105

Safe Conduct, 23-28, 30-34, 38-43, 46, 49-52, 56, 58, 61, 78, 120, 185

Second Birth, 59, 77-83, 89, 103-4, 174, 182

Several Positions, 42, 46

Spacious Earth, 59, 83, 87-88

Spectorsky, 59, 75-77, 172-73, 176

Symbolism and Immortality, 27, 40

Themes and Variations, 58-59, 64-70, 77, 119

Twin in the Clouds (When the Skies Clear), 30, 53, 55, 58-61, 88-92, 104

Vast Earth,

Year 1905, The, 45, 72-74

Pasternak, Evgenia (author's first wife), 79

————, Josephine (author's sister), 84, 188

———— Slater, Lydia (author's sister, translator, critic, and author), 21, 33, 45, 54, 60, 66, 87, 90, 92, 106-7, 186-87, 189, 193

Index

————, Leonid Ossipovich (poet's father), 21-23

————— Kaufman, Rosa (poet's mother), 21-22

————— Neuhaus, Zinaida (poet's second wife), 59, 79

Payne, R. (critic), 92, 149, 150, 165, 188, 191, 192, 193

Peredelkino, 31, 84, 85

Perovskaya, Sophie (radical), 31, 73

Peter the Great (Czar, 1672-1725), 63, 73, 74, 86

Petöfi, S. (Hungarian poet), 178

Petrovsky (Musaget member), 26

Philipp, Moritz, 27

Philippov, B. A., 185

Plank, D. L. (critic), 60, 66, 187

Plato (philosopher, 427-347 B.C.), 37

Plurality, 73, 124, 125, 129

Poe, E. A. (poet, 1809-1849), 67

Poetics in Autobiography: Aim and Function, 51-53; Artist, The, 40-45; Concept of Art, 45-49; Poetic Climate, The, 35-39; Sources, 49-51; Style, 53-57

Poggioli, R. (critic), 134, 190

Potyomkin (battleship), 74

Power, Richard Howard (critic), 191

Prince Lvov, 21

Proust, M. (writer, 1871-1822), 88, 178

Pushkin, A. S. (poet and writer, 1799-1837), 42, 44, 55, 65, 78, 89, 92, 119, 127, 149, 162, 179

Raleigh, Sir W. (writer and explorer, 1552-1618), 178

Rachinsky (Musaget member), 26

Raevsky, S. (Musaget member), 26

Realism, 65, 70, 92

Reavey, G. (critic), 46, 72, 86, 88, 92, 103, 107, 117, 186, 189, 193

Reeve, F. D. (critic), 93, 94, 98, 188, 189

Renaissance, 79

Religion, 88, 93-96, 101, 103, 130, 134-36, 145, 148

Revolution, 18, 26, 58-59, 65-77, 86, 111, 114, 122, 134, 138-47, 153-54, 172-73

Rilke, R. M. (poet and writer, 1875-1926), 23, 25, 28-31, 50, 56, 74, 79, 104, 169, 185, 189

Romantic(al), Romanticism, 26, 39, 42-43, 51, 55, 61, 100, 119, 129, 151, 155, 158, 163

Romeo and Juliet, 49, 179, 180

Rose, W. (critic), 193

Rowland, Mary and Paul (critics), 192, 193

Rubinstein, Anton (composer), 22

Ruge, G. (critic and journalist), 107, 122, 145, 159, 185, 186, 189-92

Sachs, H. (poet, 1494-1576), 178

Sacred and Profane Love, 48, 94, 102

Sadovskoy, B. (Musaget member), 26

Samarin, D. (friend of P.), 31

Schiller, F. v. (dramatist, poet, 1759-1805), 178, 180, 191

Schimanski, S. (critic), 185, 186

Schweitzer, A. (theologian, musician, doctor, 1875-1965), 153

Schweitzer, R. (poet and friend of P.), 17, 35, 55-56, 90, 107, 108, 121, 158, 185, 186, 189, 190, 192, 196

Scriabin, A. (composer and friend of the Pasternaks, 1872-1915), 23-25, 47, 51, 73

Serdarda (literary circle), 26, 50, 58

Sergey Alexandrovitch, Grand Duke, 74

Shakespeare, W. (1564-1616), 45, 119, 178-81, 193

Shevchenko, T. (Ukrainian poet, 1814-61), 179

Shelley, P. B. (poet, 1792-1822), 119, 178

Shenrok (Musaget member), 26

Shklovsky, V. B. (critic and lit. theoretician, 1893-   ), 37

Sinyavsky, A. D. (writer, critic), 46, 51, 59, 65, 104, 186, 187, 189

Slonim, M. (critic), 192

Socialism, 46, 78, 80, 139, 140

Socialist Realism, 84

Soloviev, V. (philosopher), 176

Sonette an Orpheus, Die, 29
Soukup, Mojmir (critic), 191
Soviet Writers' Association, 19, 84
St. George, 87, 100
Stalin, J. V., 78, 107
Stendhal (writer, 1783-1842), 127
Stepun, F. (critic), 26, 70, 187
Struve, Gleb (critic), 75, 185, 186, 187
Stundenbuch, Das, 30
Sturm und Drang, 43
Superman, 25
Surkov, A. A. (poet, 1899-   ), 19
Swinburne, A. C. (poet and writer, 1837-1909), 61, 178
Symbolism, 27, 36, 40, 41, 47, 49, 62, 81, 94, 100, 109, 110, 113, 115, 118, 120, 125, 126, 135, 148, 151, 159, 162, 165
Symbolist(s), 27, 35, 37, 39, 52, 59, 60, 64, 112, 121, 178

Tabidze, Nina, 179
Tabidze, Titsian (Georgian poet and friend of Pasternak), 178, 179, 182
Taylor-Sajković, M. (critic), 120, 148, 159, 190, 191, 192, 193
Thaw, The, 18, 91
Titian (artist), 48
Tolstoy, L. N. (novelist, 1828-1910), 22, 23, 27, 44, 52, 107, 127, 134, 146, 149, 164-66, 190, 191
Tretyakov, V. K. (1703-69), 21
Tristan, 49
Trotsky, Leo, 78
Trubetskoy, E. (critic), 23
Tschizewskij, D. (critic), 120, 190
Tsvetaeva, M. I. (poet, 1892-1941), 53, 56, 74, 86
Turgenev, I. S. (writer, 1818-83), 89

Tynyanov, Y. (scholar and poet, 1894-1943), 37
Tyutchev, F. I. (poet, 1803-73), 34, 127, 182

Urbansky, E. S. (critic), 192

Verhaeren, E. (poet and dramatist, 1855-1916), 23
Verlaine, P. (poet, 1844-96), 179
Veronese, P. C. (artist-painter, 1528-88), 48
Veydle, V. (critic), 70, 104, 187, 189
Vrubel, M. (painter, 1856-1910), 23

Wagner, R. (1813-83), 26, 27
Warren, A. (critic), 36, 185
Wasiolek, E. (critic), 122, 153, 159, 190, 192, 193
We (Zamyatin), 136
Wellek, R. (critic), 36, 185
Weltschmerz, 100
Wilson, E. (critic), 121, 147, 153, 190, 191
Winter, Hans (critic), 192
Writers' Plenum in Minsk, 32, 41, 42, 43, 83, 178

Yashvili, P. (Georgian poet), 59, 79, 85, 178, 179
Yevtushenko, E. (poet, 1933-   ), 183, 194

Zamyatin, Y. I. (writer, 1884-1937), 136
Zaytsev, B. (critic), 180
Zhukovsky, V. A. (poet and translator, 1783-1852), 179
Znamya (periodical), 17, 59
Zweckliteratur, 39

85062